Making Sense of Piaget

Making Sense of Piaget
The Philosophical Roots

Christine Atkinson

ROUTLEDGE & KEGAN PAUL
London, Boston, Melbourne and Henley

First published in 1983
by Routledge & Kegan Paul plc
39 Store Street, London WC1E 7DD,
9 Park Street, Boston, Mass. 02108, USA,
464 St Kilda Road, Melbourne, Victoria 3004, Australia,
and Broadway House, Newtown Road,
Henley-on-Thames, Oxon RG9 1EN, England
Printed in Great Britain by
Thetford Press, Thetford, Norfolk

Library of Congress Cataloging in Publication Data

Atkinson, Christine
    Making sense of Piaget

Bibliography p.
Includes index.
1. Cognition. 2. Cognition in children. 3. Knowledge,
theory of. 4. Piaget, Jean, 1896-   . I. Title.
BF311.A74   1983   155.4'13'0924   83-10907
ISBN 0-7100-9580-5

TO ADRIAN

Contents

Preface

This book is intended to introduce students of child development to the underlying philosophical orientation of Piaget's theory. Without some grasp of this the theory cannot properly be understood. The book does not presuppose a previous knowledge of philosophy but aims to introduce the central issues in simple terms which will help the reader to see what is at issue.

If I have succeeded to any extent in these aims the credit is due to my husband, Adrian Atkinson, who is a severe critic of any kind of jargon or academic pretension. His gift for cutting through the peripheral details to the central issues was invaluable in keeping me on the central path. His overwhelmingly positive support and encouragement ensured that the book was finally completed.

The final draft of the book was written while I was on sabbatical leave at the University of California, San Diego. I have to thank my colleagues at the University of Aston, Graham Shute and Alan Foster, for making that possible by taking over my teaching duties for the year. In San Diego, I benefited from the environment of the UCSD philosophy department, in particular from discussion with Dr Avrum Stroll and his graduate students.

My gratitude must also go to Dr David Meister who by his pertinent questions forced me to clarify my own aims in writing the book and helped to structure the argument more systematically.

My debt to Professor David Hamlyn will be clear to anyone familiar with his work. He gave me the initial stimulus to follow through my earlier work on Piaget and has continued to be a source of help and encouragement.

Many of the themes in this book have been tried out on several generations of students at Aston. I have benefited from their comments and criticism and thank them for their forebearance.

I owe a longstanding debt of gratitude to my friend, Michael Partridge of the University of Aberdeen. It was he who taught me always to look beneath the surface of things to the philosophical issues and perplexities underneath. I hope that his influence shows throughout the book.

Finally, I thank my children, Ana and Charlie. They have shown great patience throughout the days of writing and their manifest complexity and individuality have reaffirmed my belief that understanding children is more difficult and more exciting than even Piaget supposed.

Introduction

Piaget has been publishing work on child development since 1920. In all that time he has never abandoned his original theoretical framework for the understanding of human development. This framework insists that intelligence is essentially a biological phenomenon; its development is best understood as the development of a sophisticated and highly successful adaptation device. This device enables human beings to organise and structure their experience according to concepts and ideas which eventually form the complex system of objective human knowledge.

Piaget is considered by Anglo-American psychologists and educationalists to be an empirical psychologist. His theory is seen as an empirical theory making testable predictions about how children learn. Most of the critical comment on Piaget's theory has been made by psychologists who have tried to replicate Piaget's experiments or who have made similar observations and done similar experiments. (Overviews of replications of Piaget's experiments can be found in Modgil and Modgil, 1976, vol.I.) As with most empirical theories, this has led to some revision and refinement of the original claims. But in the main, the central principles of the theory have withstood these tests even though many of the details have been altered.

However, there is a different but equally legitimate and fruitful way to approach Piaget's work. Although Piaget has not objected to the label of 'psychologist', he has always called himself a 'genetic epistemologist'. By this he means that his main concern is to explicate and account for the nature of human knowledge. Epistemology, in this sense, has traditionally been thought of as the territory of the philosopher rather than the psychologist. Psychologists can legitimately interest themselves in individual differences between learners and even attempt to develop a general learning theory. But the nature of knowledge, general questions about its source, origin and justification have always been considered the subject matter of philosophy.

This is more than a quibble about the boundaries of two jealously guarded disciplines. Psychology claims to be an empirical science. Psychologists make careful observations, perform experiments and claim to discover things (from empirical data) about the real world of people. Philosophers, on the other hand, do not have any special observation techniques; they do not perform experiments and they do not claim to discover hitherto unsuspected facts about the real world. They claim only to bring out logical and conceptual connections between ideas and beliefs by a priori analysis of those ideas and beliefs.

Piaget, surprisingly, is claiming that his apparently empirical discoveries based on apparently empirical data can illuminate questions about the nature of knowledge. These questions have traditionally been considered to be philosophical questions which can be illuminated, if at all, only through a priori philosophical analysis.

Piaget's theory can legitimately be considered in two ways. First of all it can be considered as an empirical theory. From this viewpoint we can ask: Are Piaget's experiments repeatable? Are his results reliable? Secondly, Piaget himself makes claims about the relevance of his theory to philosophical questions about the nature of knowledge. In view of these claims we can ask: Is Piaget's theory acceptable as a philosophical view about the nature and origin of human knowledge?

At first sight this question might not seem to hold much interest for the empirical psychologist intent to refute or confirm Piaget's theory by empirical means. But this question must be relevant. Philosophy is about coherent thinking and any theory which makes philosophical claims that are unacceptable is making claims that are in some way incoherent. Incoherence is unacceptable, as even the most hard-headed of empiricists must agree, at the heart of any theory.

In Piaget's work, the theory is what connects all the
detailed observations together and justifies the interpretation of the empirical data. This would, of course, be
true of any scientific theory. If the theory itself is
unacceptable either because it can be shown empirically
that it does not fit the facts or because it can be shown
a priori to be incoherent, then the observations become no
more than a string of unconnected facts and the interpretation of the data is no longer justified. If the theory
were shown to be incoherent the empirical tests would no
longer be relevant to either establishing or refuting it.
The observed facts themselves might still stand. Whether
they did or not would depend on the degree of interpretation that was required for their description. But testing
the reliability of the facts would no longer be a relevant
test of the theory itself.

In this book, Piaget's theory will be considered from the
point of view of its coherence and philosophical adequacy,
not from the point of view of its empirical testability.
The scrutiny of a theory for coherence, conceptual clarity
and philosophical adequacy is logically prior to its testing for empirical reliability. This is so because the
description of the empirical facts relies to a greater or
lesser extent on the interpretation of data afforded by
the theory itself. In some theories the interpretative
element might be minimised but in Piaget's theory it is
paramount.

CRITICISMS OF PIAGET'S THEORY

In his autobiography (Boring, 1952), Piaget claims that he
could see indications of the idea that was to predominate
his intellectual work for the rest of his life in the very
earliest things that he wrote. This predominant idea was
that intelligence is essentially a biological phenomenon,
and that its development and nature can only be properly
understood in a biological context. This idea, as Piaget
understands it, leads firstly to his claim that empirical
facts and empirical investigations are relevant to the
establishment of philosophical conclusions. Secondly, it
leads to his claim that psychology can provide a causal
explanation for the direction and sequence of human intellectual development. This causal explanation, for Piaget,
would not be different in kind from the causal explanations
advanced by biologists for the direction and sequence of
physical development.

Recent work in both philosophy and psychology has called
into question both of these claims of Piaget's. Some
philosophers regard Piaget's contention that empirical
facts are relevant to philosophical conclusions as a gross
confusion (see Hamlyn, 1971).

On the other hand, some psychologists argue that explanation of human development in terms of logical structures,
developed through a process of equilibration cannot provide
a psychological explanation (see Bruner et al., 1966;
Feldman and Toulmin, 1976).

Piaget's theory, then, has not met with the acclaim that
initially greeted his empirical studies of children.
Recently, within the last five years or so, there has been
increasing criticism of Piaget's empirical work, questioning not only his way of achieving his results but also his
highly interpretative presentation of them. (See Brown and
DesForges, 1979; Donaldson, 1978; Siegel and Brainerd, 1978.)
In the face of this criticism, Piaget consistently maintained
that his critics did not pay sufficient attention to or did
not sufficiently understand his theory. In the early 1960s,
in the foreword which he wrote to Flavell's treatment of
his work (Flavell, 1963), Piaget complained that too much
attention had been paid to the details of the empirical
studies at the expense of the theoretical concepts. And as
recently as 1976, in her foreword to a book of critical
studies (Modgil and Modgil, 1976), Inhelder had the following to say: 'We are somewhat disturbed by the fact that the
replication of our experiments does not always show sufficient understanding of Piagetian theory on the part of the
authors of these new works.' These comments show the
importance that Piaget attaches to his theory. In his view
his experiments must be understood within the framework of
the overarching theory. Otherwise, the results will be
misinterpreted.

Negative results obtained from the attempted replication of
one or another of Piaget's empirical studies do not seem to
carry much weight with Piaget. A serious criticism of
Piaget's claim that sensori-motor activity must precede
concrete operational ability was made by N. Jordan. Jordan
met a person in her early forties who had normal, adult
intellectual capacities but who had the body of a neonate.
Since she had been unable to use her body from birth, she
could never have engaged in sensori-motor activity and yet
she was able to engage in not only concrete operational but
also abstract operational thought. In answer to Jordan's
query, H. Sinclair replied on Piaget's behalf:

Cases such as you quote are not at all exceptional and
do not constitute counter examples to his (Piaget's)
theory. In fact, 'sensori-motor activity' has to be
taken in a very general sense, and does not necessarily
imply using your hands, running around, etc. ... It
implies that activities are assimilated and accommodated,
and this is the case with any child that lives since it
has to eat and drink (involving assimilation and accommodation - and drinks and eats very different things,
and adjusts the movements according to the substance)
and since it has perceptual activity.

Piaget brushes off, then, what would appear to be a serious
criticism of one of his major claims. His view is that
'sensori-motor' activity need not be interpreted so as to
include the things that he usually talks about in his
descriptions, reaching and grasping, eye-hand co-ordination
and the like. All that is essential to the concept of
sensori-motor activity is that there should be some accommodations and assimilations. Other negative results discovered by other empirical observations (Bryant, 1974;
Burton and Radford, 1978) are discounted on the grounds
that the details of the theory are relatively unimportant.
Piaget is not surprised that they might not be correct.
But still he maintains the theoretical framework will stand.
It is the main principles of the theory which he regards as
unshakable.

Piaget's theory is extraordinarily complex. There are two
main reasons for this. The first is that some of his concepts are difficult in themselves. He has been elaborating
his theory for over sixty years and in that time some of
the concepts have changed their meaning and their emphasis.
The second reason is the interrelatedness of the theory and
its all-embracing nature. The major explanatory concepts
of the theory depend on each other for their meaning. A
'valid' structure, for example, is equilibrated. Equilibration implies a balance between accommodation and assimilation. But this balance is assessed by considering the
organisational properties of the structure which make it
'valid'. None of the concepts can be understood in isolation from each other. Piaget often distorts these concepts
or makes them vacuous by trying to use them to account for
all and every aspect of human knowledge. The reply to
Jordan's criticism quoted above is an example of this.

The theory, then, because of its complexity and abstract
nature, is not easy to comprehend. But given this, is
Piaget justified in claiming that he is so rarely understood?

Why do his critics fail to pay sufficient attention to his
theory?

Piaget is led by his concern with philosophy to embed his
cognitive developmental theory in a philosophical theory
about the nature of human knowledge and the human mind.
Because Piaget's philosophical roots lie in the European
rationalism of the late nineteenth and early twentieth
century, this philosophical theory turns out to be essentially rationalist. His Anglo-American critics among both
philosophers and psychologists, do not share this background.
On the contrary, their philosophical roots lie in empiricism
or the later philosophy of Wittgenstein.

This means that the differences between Piaget and his
critics cannot be settled in terms of considerations relevant only to developmental psychology. Their differences
are philosophical. This may help to explain Piaget's
curious imperviousness to criticism of the details of his
investigations. He regards the details as fairly unimportant. What is significant for him is the overarching theory.
And to understand and criticise this requires that one go
into much broader issues concerning the nature of human
knowledge and understanding than his empiricist critics
have thought necessary.

It is perhaps this which Piaget has picked on when he has
accused his critics of failing to properly understand his
theory. Coming from a different philosophical tradition,
they bring to Piaget's theory fundamentally different ways
of viewing the nature of psychological explanation and the
nature of human knowledge.

RELATION BETWEEN PHILOSOPHY AND PSYCHOLOGY

Piaget's attitude towards philosophy and philosophising is
ambivalent. On the one hand he recognises the importance
of philosophical questions and their relevance to the study
of the human mind. But on the other hand, his continental
European background leads him to identify philosophising
with speculative metaphysics. Consequently, while recognising the importance of the philosopher's questions, he
is led to scorn both their methods and their answers. He
complains that while metaphysical speculation can turn up
some interesting views, it cannot lead to the rational
'solution' of problems since 'value and commitment' are
inextricably mixed with the theorising and it is impossible
to obtain an objective viewpoint (Piaget, 1970, p.13). He

believes that his own theory which he characterises as
'constructive' and 'epigenetic' is both scientific and can
solve philosophical problems.

To many philosophers and psychologists educated in the
tradition of philosophical analysis, this looks like a
confusion. In the main, British and American philosophers
and psychologists make a sharp distinction between analytic
and synthetic truths. And they would maintain that it is
the philosopher's job to seek analytic and conceptual
truths and the scientist's job to seek empirical truths.
A related distinction is made by Karl Popper between justification and discovery. This discovery of knowledge he
claims can be the subject of psychological investigation.
But the justification of knowledge is a logical matter.
How a child learns that $2 + 2 = 4$ might be a subject for
psychological investigation but the truth of the proposition that $2 + 2 = 4$ is a matter for logical or mathematical
justification. No amount of psychological evidence can
establish whether or not $2 + 2 = 4$, so psychology is irrelevant to questions of justification.

If these arguments can be accepted it would imply that
Piaget's theory of genetic epistemology (if it is said to
rest on empirical evidence and to involve reference to the
psychological or mental states of individuals) could have
nothing to say to traditional, philosophical epistemology.
It would, in fact, be entirely misconceived.

However, we can look at Piaget's theory in another way.
If he does have a genuine philosophical alternative to
empiricism, rationalism and so on, then we can question
the status of the so-called empirical facts that are
supposed to support it. One can, that is, question whether
genetic psychology is a genuinely empirical undertaking.
It could be the case that what Piaget is doing is what
Popper would accept as genuine epistemology, that is, he
is exploring logical and conceptual relations between
theories, propositions, concepts and so on. It is this
second view which seems to capture more of the spirit of
Piaget's investigations than the former suggestion that
his whole undertaking is misconceived. But it does have
serious consequences for the scientific status of Piaget's
theory. If it is the case that Piaget's theory is a blend
of the empirical and the conceptual then the conceptual
side of the theory will have a degree of certainty and
necessity not shared by the empirical investigations.
Piaget's claim that the invariant order of the stages of
development is necessary does not help his claim that his

theory has empirical significance. Popper has shown that
it is a serious mistake to regard the certainty of a theory
as an indication of its scientific value (Popper, 1959).
Showing that the relationship between the stages is one of
logical implication and so a necessary relationship makes
experimental work unnecessary; a theory based on logical or
conceptual relationships is bound to be confirmed for there
is no possibility of falsification. Piaget's theory is not
a better theory simply because it asserts that the order
of appearance of the stages is a logically necessary rather
than an empirical matter. The necessity of the order of
the stages cannot depend on any empirical facts since these
cannot, by definition, be necessary. It must depend either
on the defining of the higher stages to include the lower
stages. Or else it must depend on the overarching theory
of the determinants of development. Piaget's theory uses
both these reasons in claiming that the sequence of stages
is necessary.

QUESTIONS THAT CONCERN PIAGET

Piaget distinguishes three stages of psychological research.
The first aims to establish general laws, and the second
and third are concerned with causal explanation. He denies
that an explanation can be reached simply by generalising
from data. He says that a law does not explain anything
since all that it does is to verify the generality of a
factual relationship. The elements of a causal explanation
are the deduction of one law from another and the positing
of a substrate 'either actual or "model", concrete or
abstract' (Piaget, 1968, p.161). This substrate is presumed to support the formal deduction of one law from
another and to 'represent' its various connections.
Piaget says that a causal explanation is not appropriate
in mathematics. Although one is not simply confined to
generalising from laws but can show how one law is deduced
from another, there is no necessity to search for a substrate which will provide the reality underlying the
logical deduction, since the only relations relevant to
mathematics are deductive relations. The psychologist, on
the other hand, is searching for causal explanations, so
he needs to supply some real or concrete substrate.

Piaget is hoping to furnish some kind of causal explanation
of the emergence of different forms of thought. He is not
trying simply to generalise from his data but to provide a
theoretical framework within which he can account for the
emergence of these forms of thought. He wants to explain

why it is that understanding develops in the way that it
does; why it is possible to talk of stages of development
and what this signifies for the nature of human knowledge.
In discussing the development of elementary logical and
mathematical concepts he insists that a psychological
explanation is a causal one. He says:

> So, it is clear that a psychology of behaviour thus
> forced to place itself in a genetic perspective, finds
> itself for this reason faced with problems of causal
> explanation. For example, how can we explain that
> these sensori-motor displacements lead to a structure
> involving a direct combination of displacements (AB &
> BC & AC if ABC is not a straight line), an inverse
> composition (return) and an associative one (detour)?
> Is this structure innate? (We have just seen that it
> is not). And if it is not can it be assimilated in a
> simple summation of physical experiences or does it
> result from a progressive equilibrium of sensori-motor
> co-ordination? Why is this structure, once acquired
> through actions, not immediately imposed on the thought
> of the child as soon as the latter is capable of
> imagining displacements? How is it reconstructed at
> the level of thought and why does this reconstruction
> not require an elaboration of the most elementary
> intuitions? ... etc. (Beth and Piaget, 1966, p.158)

These are the kinds of problems that Piaget is wanting to
explain in causal terms. They are questions concerning the
acceptance of norms by the child. We can see, given a
mathematical proof, why one proposition follows from
another. What Piaget is interested in is how children
come to see this. That it is mathematically correct is
not in dispute. The psychological problem as Piaget sees
it is how we come to see the correctness of a mathematical
proof and be convinced by it. On his own view of the
nature of causal explanation he must show:
(a) That the facts he wants to account for are general;
(b) That they can be formally deduced from each other and;
(c) That there is a substrate, actual or model, concrete
    or abstract, which provides the underlying reality of
    the logical deduction.

PIAGET'S TWO KINDS OF EXPLANATION

Piaget uses two different kinds of explanation of the
general facts that he discovers: an explanation in terms
of the biological model of assimilation and accommodation
and an explanation in terms of a probabilistic, structural

model. This is what one would expect given his views on
the nature of causal explanations. The structural model
is offered to show that the facts to be explained can be
formally deduced from each other. The biological model
provides the substrate, the underlying reality of the
logical model. He does not himself distinguish these
explanations as alternatives. He seems to think that he
is offering one explanation of the facts and that the
structural and biological are different facets of one
explanation and add up to a composite view of the development of intelligence. When he can show that the formal
relations between laws follow the actual temporal relations
between events then he achieves his ideal explanation.

Apart from the requirement that any causal explanation
should have a formal and a 'real' aspect, Piaget has several
other reasons for offering explanations in terms of a biological and a structural model. He has, as he explains in
his autobiography, been directed by the single idea that
biological and intellectual functioning are not different
in kind, that intellectual abilities are simply another
'biological device' for adapting to the environment. Since
he sees logic as the essence of intellectual functioning he
naturally tries to show how a biological explanation can be
offered for the emergence of logic. However, the nature of
logic raises questions of truth and validity. Although
Piaget has little to say about truth, he offers his structural model as a counterpart to his biological model. The
first is an explanation of the emergence of logical thought,
the second is offered as an explanation, or at least
explication, of its validity.

It is at this point that Piaget and his critics fail to
understand each other. The critics argue that validity
requires a formal or logical justification and a psychological explanation of it is simply irrelevant. Conversely,
to offer as a psychological explanation some sort of formal
justification is simply inadequate. Piaget, who thinks
that the valid logical structures grow out of the equilibrated action systems of the sensori-motor period and are
consequently representations of reality, makes no such
sharp distinction between formal justification and psychological explanation. The failure in communication between
these two views on the nature of psychological explanation
arises from different philosophical assumptions about the
nature of reality and the relation between knowledge and
reality. Consequently, to understand this disagreement it
is necessary to understand something of the different
philosophical traditions.

SOCIAL NATURE OF MIND

Piaget's identification of philosophy with metaphysical
theorising has led him to neglect the very philosopher with
which most of his critics are familiar. He mentions such
philosophers as Plato, Carnap, Russell and he continually
acknowledges his debt to Kant. But Wittgenstein, perhaps
the most pervasive influence on modern British and American
philosophers, does not get a mention. Piaget believes that
if he can show that logic and mathematics grow out of
natural thought, 'have their origins in the activities of
the subject', then he will have effected a reconciliation
between Rationalism and Empiricism. He himself sees this
reconciliation as being essentially Kantian. He stresses
that the source of structure is the subject himself acting
on external content and he likens this to Kant's view that
the source of structure is the mind itself. Piaget is
claiming to go a step further than Kant in explaining how
this mind develops. However, Piaget, like Kant, overlooks
the social nature of this mind. His model of development
is ostensibly centrally concerned with the individual and
the relationship between the individual and the environment.
Consequently his models cannot account for the achievement
by the individual of a common understanding with other
adults, an understanding which depends on the sharing of
concepts and common ways of seeing the world. It involves
some agreement as to what is valued by human beings as well
as agreement on standards of truth, criteria of meaning and
so on. By underestimating the role of social communication,
Piaget presents the development of understanding in a misleading light as the achievement of a solitary consciousness. Apart from the criticism mentioned concerning Piaget's
refusal to distinguish formal from empirical questions, this
must be the major failing of Piaget's theory. Wittgenstein's
philosophy has tended to show the essentially social nature
of human knowledge and modern psychologists accepting his
philosophical conclusions have investigated the ways in
which children gain access to the social world of human
understanding and knowledge. Piaget acknowledges the need
for the eventual 'socialisation' of the child and his understanding. But his theory, which explains development as
the construction of knowledge by the individual, never
succeeds in explaining how he overcomes his initial isolation and becomes integrated into a shared social world.

AIMS OF THIS BOOK

This book has three aims. The first is to explicate the
key concepts of Piaget's theory within the context of the
philosophical questions that they raise. It is to be hoped
that this will lead to a better understanding of Piaget's
theory and an appreciation of its essential limitations.
The second aim is to sketch out the requirements that any
theory of human development must meet if it is to be philosophically coherent and acceptable. These will be very
general requirements such as the need to take account of
the social nature of knowledge. The third aim is the
underlying one of showing the role that philosophy can play
in ensuring that theories which may have a large empirical
content require also a clear and coherent conceptual base.
Although these three aims underlie all the chapters in the
book, the first three chapters are more concerned with
explication than criticism. Chapters 4 and 7 are concerned
to show the limitations of Piaget's theory and to show how
it can be augmented, corrected or supplanted by the work of
other theorists. Chapter 8 gives a summary of the issues
discussed and further suggestions for developing the relationship between psychological and philosophical studies.

Chapter 1

The biological theory

PREVIEW

This chapter will introduce the central concepts of Piaget's
theory. It will also show how the theory can be initially
characterised as a transformational theory having its roots
in both biological and philosophical presuppositions about
the nature of mind and knowledge. In particular, it will
explain the Kantian notion of the basic categories of
thought and show how Piaget believes that these categories
including quality, quantity, space-time relationships, means-
end relationships and values are laid down during the
sensori-motor stage.

TRANSFORMATION THROUGH EQUILIBRATION

Essentially Piaget's explanation of development postulates
a series of stages or levels of the organism's functioning
in the environment where each preceding stage is a necessary
condition for the subsequent stage. In one of his earliest
works Piaget says (Piaget, 1952, p.1):

Verbal or cogitative intelligence is based on practical
or sensori-motor intelligence which in turn depends on
acquired and recombined habits and associations. These
presuppose furthermore, the system of reflexes whose
connection with the organism's anatomical and morphological structure is apparent. A certain continuity
exists, therefore, between intelligence and the purely
biological processes of morphogenesis and adaption to
the environment.

Piaget is claiming then that development proceeds according
to a series of transformations of one stage into another.
He distinguishes four very broad stages of development:
the sensori-motor stage, the pre-operational stage, the
stage of concrete operations and the stage of abstract
reasoning. Within each of these stages there are several
substages. Each substage is an elaboration of a previous
stage. There is then an apparent continuity between the
stages of biological functioning within the environment and
the later stages of cognitive functioning. If each stage
is a transformation of the previous one then although the
later stages might appear to be totally different from the
earliest stages nevertheless there is a continuum, a chain
of changes. One should, in principle, be able to trace
back the sequence of development through the successive
changes that have occurred, to its origins in biological
functioning.

The possibility of late cognitive functioning can be seen
to grow out of previous organic or biological functioning
through this sequence of transformations. This leaves open
the possibility that all the characteristics of the later
stages might be different from any of the characteristics
of the earliest stages. We can show this by the following
simple diagram:

                 Stage 1   Stage 2   Stage 3

                 A   B   C   D   E   F   G   H   I

There is no break in the continuity between Stage 1 and
Stage 3 but Stage 3 shares none of the characteristics of
Stage 1. On this view, then, although cognitive functioning can be seen to grow out of biological functioning it
need not share any of its characteristics.

The child's earliest psychological means of interacting
with the environment are sensori-motor acts such as sucking,
grasping, or looking at things. Neither perceptual nor
intellectual activity can arise until the child has passed
through a stage of sensori-motor activity that is functionally a precursor to the later activity. The operational
schemes of systems of action that the child develops at
this stage are the precursor of the later intellectual
scheme, not simply in the sense that they come before, but
in the sense that they prefigure the later intellectual
structures. The later structures are derived from action
in the environment. Consequently they must, according to
Piaget's view, be adapted to this environment, they must

fit it since action, to succeed, must fit the environment
and the intellectual structures are derived from successful
action. There cannot then be that divorce between reality
and our conceptual schemes, so commonly suggested by
empiricist philosophers.

Development begins as soon as the stereotyped reflexes
begin to undergo changes as a result of the organism's
need to cope with aspects of the environment to which the
reflexes are not ideally suited. It grows out of this
lack of fit between the primitive reflexes with which the
newly born is endowed and the environment within which he
finds himself: It grows out of the organism's attempt to
adapt itself to its environment. This process of adaptation is for Piaget part of the definition of living organic
life as opposed to non-living inorganic matter. Inorganic
matter is acted on by the environment. Rocks and stones
may have their position and shape altered by winds and
rivers, they may be crushed or buried, heated or frozen.
But they do not contribute anything to these processes.
They are passive, simply acted upon. The organism, on the
other hand, will alter itself in order to avoid annihila-
tion or discomfort.

The adaptation of the organism to the environment comprises
two sub-processes, that of assimilation and accommodation.
The organism assimilates some novel aspect of the environment to its already existing knowledge or capabilities and
then modifies itself, that is, accommodates itself to cope
with the new situation better. Assimilation then is
logically (although not temporally) prior to accommodation.

The function of 'assimilation' is to modify (integrate) the
element incorporated through interaction with the environment and thereby to conserve the structure of the operative
schemes. To assimilate the child restructures the relevant
environmental data so that it becomes coherent with his
existing schemes, that is, so that the data fit in with
what he already knows. This assimilation is the function
that assures that experience will have significance.

The function of 'accommodation' is to modify (differentiate)
and elaborate the child's schemas so that they will be consistent with the character of the external environment.
Accommodation thus integrates new information from the
environment into the child's existing schemas so that they
are modified but not destroyed. Short-term local development is a process by which assimilation and accommodation
are equilibrated. Local disequilibrium occurs whenever one
or the other is dominant.

The mechanism of transformation from one stage to the next
is the process of equilibration, that is, bringing into
balance the functional relationships within the child's
action system which are always in disequilibrium, but more
so, in early life. That is, the child is endowed with
self-regulating biological systems that are directed
towards establishing increasing equilibrium. Development
is the progressive approximation to an ideal equilibrium
state that may never be fully achieved. This is the stable
state of permanent equilibrium of the stage of formal
thought.

The equilibrial level achieved by the child at any moment
may be disrupted by an environmental perturbation whenever
he:
(a) biologically or psychologically recognises that some-
    thing is disturbing him and
(b) lacks the means necessary to deal with the perturbation.

ORGANISMIC MODEL OF MAN

Piaget's theory, then, assumes as a starting point that
human beings are organised totalities capable of initiating
action. This sets him against empiricist theories such as
behaviourism which sees man as a passive mechanism responding in predictable ways to the environment or rationalist
theories such as Chomsky's linguistic theory which views
man as a kind of computer with inbuilt patterns of
processing.

The model or picture that one chooses as one's starting
point in a theory of human development will orient the
rest of the theory in specific ways. By choosing to view
man as an organism, Piaget is favouring a biological
orientation as opposed to, say, a mechanistic orientation.
Organisms are not simply passive recipients of inputs from
the environment but nor are they, even at the purely biological level of functioning, entirely preprogrammed. And
he is emphasising the active role of the subject in his
own development. Knowledge is constructed by the subject
rather than discovered or acquired through passive experience, socialisation or teaching.

Organisms spontaneously initiate their own actions and so
play an active role in their own development. They are
organised totalities of organs and of systems of action
which act in a goal-directed way to interact with and adapt
themselves to their environment. Genetically they are

endowed with, first of all, the necessary physiological structure and the capacity for initial interaction with the environment in the form of the initial reflexes and secondly with the functional capacities necessary to ensure their own development. Development begins as soon as the characteristics of the environment impinge on the child in a way that leads to modification of those inherited initial reflexes.

Development is a process of interaction between the organism and the environment but it focuses on the individual's self-generating rather than upon the environment's socialising influence in the developmental process. It assumes that the person is affected by social (or physical) stimulation only to the extent that he first actively assimilates the stimulation to his schemes. Thus the child does not even clearly distinguish between the physical and the social environment until the fifth sensori-motor stage. During the symbolic operational stage the child increasingly discovers that there is a world external to himself which has physical and social properties that affect him. However he still interprets (transforms) these physical and social properties in accordance with his own schemes: he uses language idiosyncratically at least until the concrete substage and he constructs personally meaningful 'theories' of society even at the formal substage. The environment then is the scene of development and provides the 'nourishment' for the child's development.

It is to be expected that the age at which the child reaches the cognitive substages varies with the child's experiences. It is also plausible that advanced substages may not develop at all in individuals in societies that do not provide the necessary experiences for their development. For example, Greenfield (1966) reports that some unschooled rural Wolof children in Senegal do not develop the concept of quantity conservation whereas all schooled rural children acquire it. Similarly, Kohlberg (1971), in his developmental studies of moral thinking discovered that the two highest stages of moral thought were absent in preliterate or semi-literate village cultures. What the theory insists is invariable is the sequence of the stages and the necessity for each individual to go through each of the stages. The theory does not permit the possibility that the stages might appear in a different or reverse order, or that a child might 'skip' a stage.

Piaget distinguishes between the form and content of knowledge. The forms are progressively constructed by a

person's own actions. Since man's actions develop, the
forms he constructs also develop. The content, however,
is influenced by the particular interactions the person
has with his environment. The forms are determined by the
stage of action to which the person has developed; while
the content varies with the physical and social environment. Piaget stresses continuity in his definition of
alteration. Each new stage is a transformation of the
previous stage. So in this sense, while there is change,
there is also conservation. The structured core of the
previous stage is conserved. This is what Piaget means
when he refers to 'filiations' between stages. When a new
stage is achieved the fundamental structural properties of
the previous stage are conserved and are re-elaborated on
a new plane. The knowledge that the child constructs at
the initial, sensori-motor stage he reconstructs into new,
richer and more comprehensive configurations at each subsequent stage. The developmental process is an autogenetic
internal process of self-differentiation and hierarchic
integration. The person is a self-regulatory organisation
of functional structures that continuously renew and transform themselves by their own actions upon (interaction with)
the environment. These actions lead to a developmental
reorganisation (equilibration) of the person's structures,
which subserve these actions, at a new functional level or
more stable stage of adaptation.

The working relationships among acts constitute the functional structures of the self-regulatory system to which
these acts belong. A system of actions may be considered
as the 'logic' by which actions operate in terms of each
other. The differentiation and hierarchic integration that
characterise the working relationships that develop among
self-regulatory systems of action may therefore be considered to constitute the functional organisation or the
'logic' of the total mental organisation.

The action of the organism is the source of interaction
with the environment. The action of the child is the cause
of both his own psychological phenomena and the behaviour
of the environment. The child's own action is, therefore,
also the cause of his own psychological development.

THE BASIC CATEGORIES OF THOUGHT

In identifying the individual as the source of the organisation of his own knowledge, Piaget is following Kant. Kant,
in reaction to the empiricists who claimed that all concepts

were derived from experience and to the rationalists who
claimed that all concepts were derived from reason or the
mind, argued that there were two sides to knowledge. There
was the sensible side which was supplied by perception and
which had no inherent organisation or structure. There was
also the structured, organisational side to knowledge.
Perception provides the objects that thought is about, but
the understanding provides the structured ways of thinking
about these objects. Kant's major work, 'The Critique of
Pure Reason', lists certain concepts which in his view give
form and organisation to our thinking. He distinguishes
between two kinds of concepts: those that he labels a
posteriori and those that he labels a priori. A posteriori
concepts are those which are somehow abstracted from our
experience. Colour concepts are an example. To call these
concepts 'a posteriori' is emphasising the fact that since
they are drawn from experience they cannot logically precede
it. They come after experience. These a posteriori concepts might be seen as simply reports of experience. To
notice that two objects are the same colour and to refer to
them thereafter as 'white' does not alter the experience in
any way. It merely reflects it.

The a priori concepts, on the other hand, do not merely
reflect experience but organise it. In developing and
applying a posteriori concepts we have to take care that
our concepts conform to and fit our actual experiences.
But in applying a priori concepts, we force the experiences
to fit the concept. An example of an a priori concept is
the concept of cause. Kant follows Hume in maintaining
that the notion of natural necessity which seems to be
part of our concept of causation is not a notion which
could be abstracted from experience. But instead of locat-
ing its source in the imagination as Hume does, Kant claims
that it is a concept which we use not to describe but to
order experience. The two following propositions illustrate
the difference between a structuring, a priori concept and
an empirical, a posteriori one:
(a) Every event has a cause.
(b) Every child likes chocolate.
In the case of (b), if a child were discovered who did not
like chocolate, we might be surprised but we would be prepared to abandon or modify our original claim to say that,
after all, only most children like chocolate. We would
modify our statement to better fit our experiences. But
in the case of (a) we would not do that. If someone pointed
to an event which had no apparent cause, we would not easily
give up our claim that every event has a cause but would
just look harder for the cause. Even if we never found the

cause we would still not abandon our claim but would believe
that this particular cause was very elusive. The concept
of causation then can be seen as a concept that we do not
readily abandon. It is a concept that we use to structure
our experience. When experience does not apparently conform
to it we assume that our experience is too limited rather
than that the concept itself does not fit it.

Kant wanted to distinguish between purely subjective reports
of sensations and genuinely objective judgments. There are
two features which distinguish objective empirical judgments
from perceptual or subjective judgments. The first is that
objective empirical judgments refer to objects, not to subjective impressions. The second is that an objective
empirical judgment, if it is true, is true for everybody,
not just for the person who has the experience. An example
of a subjective judgment might be:
    'This soup feels too hot to me.'
The corresponding objective empirical judgment would be:
    'This soup is hot.'

The difference between the two, according to Kant, is that
in the second one, that of the objective empirical judgment,
we are implicitly applying one of the a priori concepts.

He says in 'Prolegomena' 302:
    If we resolve all our synthetic judgments, in so far
    as they are objectively valid, then we find that they
    never consist of mere perceptions ... but that they
    would be impossible, had there not been added a pure
    concept of the understanding to the concepts which
    were abstracted from perception.

What this 'pure concept of the understanding' is can be
discovered not by looking at the content of the judgment.
That contains only concepts derived from perception. It
can be discovered only by looking at the form of the judgment. By 'form' of the judgment Kant means the way in
which the objective empirical judgment confers objectivity
and generality on the corresponding perceptual judgment.

In the 'soup is hot' example, the difference between saying
that the soup seems to me to be hot and saying that the
soup is hot is that in the first place we are merely report-
ing a sensation whereas in the second we are implicitly
stating that there is such an object as the soup which has
a certain property. The implicit a priori concept in this
example is the concept of 'substance-and-accident'.

It is through the application of these a priori concepts
which are not derived from perception, that our judgments
achieve objectivity. The source of these a priori concepts
is the pure understanding.

Precisely what Kant meant by the pure understanding and
whether his list of twelve a priori concepts is complete
or even correct, are not issues that we need to go into
here. What is important is that Piaget takes on Kant's
distinction between concepts gained through perception
which mirror the sensible content of the world and other
concepts which are not gained through experience, or
through learning of any kind. They are gained through the
process of equilibration and they are applied to experience
rather than being derived from it.

Kant is not much concerned with the psychological origin of
these ideas. He believes that he has shown, by a conceptual
analysis of the notion of a coherent, rational judgment,
that we possess two kinds of concepts, those derived from
experience and those not derived from experience. Occasion-
ally he refers to the a priori concepts as being innate.
But he is concerned with a conceptual analysis of the concepts involved here, not with a psychological investigation
of the origins of our concepts.

 Piaget, while making the same distinction as Kant between
concepts which can and concepts which cannot be derived
from experience is very much concerned with the psychological
origins of these a priori concepts. Piaget's list of a
priori concepts is different from Kant's list. Kant derived
his list from the list of forms of propositions found in
Aristotle's logic. That this was unnecessarily restric-
tive has been pointed out by many critics of Kant. Piaget
derives his own list partly from Kant and partly from his
own idea of what concepts a mature, organised intellect
must possess and apply.

Kant's list includes four basic kinds of concepts: quantity,
quality, relation and modality. Piaget's list includes:
the concept of a permanent object, means-end relationships,
the concept of causality, the concepts of quality and quantity, space-time relationships and a hierarchy of values.
Piaget is not, as Kant was, concerned to produce an exhaust-
ive list of all the concepts that we use to structure our
experience. He nowhere lays down a list of such concepts
as Kant does and would be happy to admit new concepts if
their role in the structuring of experience could be shown.

The notion then that there are two sides to our understanding, an experiential side and an organising or structuring side comes originally from Kant. The notion that knowledge is somehow constructed by the individual out of the application of these a priori concepts to experience also derive from Kant. There are important differences between Piaget's understanding of the relation between these a priori concepts and the objectivity of judgment. One of these important differences is that Kant always insists that if the application of the concepts is to yield an objective judgment then it must be applied to an object given in perception. Piaget denies this important role to perception. This particular problem will be dealt with at greater length in Chapter 5.

Another major difference between Kant and Piaget is that Kant sees the discovery of the a priori concepts of the pure understanding as a strictly logical or conceptual investigation whereas Piaget sees it as a psychological investigation. Kant is concerned with the analysis of the concept of a rational intelligence. Piaget, on the other hand, maintains that the most reliable way to discover what constitutes a rational intelligence is to study one developing.

This digression into Kant's critical philosophy was intended to show the philosophical roots of Piaget's contention that the intellect is structured by concepts which are not derived from experience. Piaget, like Kant, locates the source of the objectivity of knowledge in these concepts. Unlike Kant he proposes to trace their development in the individual mind.

The next section is concerned with Piaget's attempt to show that these structuring or organising concepts are derived from the interiorisation of action. The foundations for these concepts are laid down in the sensori-motor stage and can be discerned in the organisation of the child's actions during this stage.

THE FOUNDATIONS OF THE STRUCTURES OF THOUGHT

The child is endowed at birth with certain primitive reflexes. According to Piaget's theory, development begins when there is a lack of fit between these primitive reflexes and the environment. If the organism is failing to cope with aspects of its environment then it is in a state of disequilibrium and will strive by altering itself or by altering its environment to restore itself to a state of stable equilibrium with its environment.

The organism may, depending on its complexity, have several inbuilt systems for maintaining its temperature, its level of nutrition and so on. Development is the result of the alteration in the functioning of these inbuilt systems as a result of the organism's encounter with some intractable element of the environment with which the inbuilt system is not readily equipped to deal.

An example that Piaget offers is the adaptation of the sucking reflex in the first few days of an infant's life. This reflex, which begins by being released whenever any-thing at all touches the child's lips is not very well developed itself in the sense that it does not achieve particularly well the purpose of keeping the nipple in the child's mouth. Gradually, it comes to be performed better and also becomes more selective. At about the age of three to four weeks the child does not wait for the nipple to touch its mouth but will search for it when anything touches his cheek. He will also, if he is hungry, reject objects which at other times he might suck, for example, his mother's finger. And he achieves in a much more economical way the purpose of keeping the nipple in his mouth.

The child is adapting to his particular environment in the sense that he is improving the fit between his inborn reflex to suck and the features of the particular thing that he has to suck to gain nourishment. Not all breasts are the same size or shape, some babies are bottle fed. The baby will alter his reflex action as a result of contact with the environment.

In this example of the adaptation of the sucking reflex one can see the two processes of assimilation and accommodation at work. The sucking reflex is hereditary but practice within a particular environment is necessary before it functions properly. The reflex accommodates itself to the properties of the objects to be sucked. However, it is the actual contact with the objects to be sucked which leads to improvement in the co-ordination of all the sub-actions which go to make up the action of sucking, for example, searching for and grasping the nipple. New behavioural elements in the sense of well-organised and co-ordinated sucking routines are assimilated into the child's repertoire.

Piaget admits that a physiological explanation describing the adaptation of the reflex in terms of 'irradiation, the prolonged shocks, the summations of excitations and the interco-ordinations of reflexes' (Piaget, 1952, p.31)

would probably explain why the child's searching becomes
more systematic, why a contact which does not set off
prolonged searching at one stage does so a few days later
etc. But he insists that even if a physiological explanation were possible, it is the contact with the environment
which sets off the adaptation of the reflex. In order to
adapt, the reflex must be exercised and it changes as a
result of this use; in other words, whatever the physiological explanation, the reflex adaptation is partly
accommodation.

But the reflex is consolidated and strengthened by its own
practice, and this is one of the cases in which assimilation is most clearly seen:
>   Such a fact is the most direct expression of the mechan-
>   ism of assimilation. Assimilation is revealed in the
>   first place by the growing need for repetition which
>   characterises the use of the reflex (functional assimil-
>   ation) and in the second place by the entirely practical
>   or sensori-motor recognition which enables the child
>   to adapt himself to the different objects with which
>   his lips come into contact (recognitory generalising
>   assimilation). (Piaget, 1952, p.32)
Piaget tries to explain the sense in which the environment
is assimilated to the rudimentary schema, which is what the
altered, adapted reflex amounts to, by describing the
process as one of the feeding of the schema by the 'reality
aliments':
>   This schema, due to the fact that it lends itself to
>   repetitions and to cumulative use, is not limited to
>   functioning under compulsion by a fixed excitant, exter-
>   nal or internal, but functions, in a way, for itself.
>   In other words the child does not only suck in order
>   to eat but also in order to elude hunger, to prolong
>   the excitation of the meal etc., and lastly, he sucks
>   for the sake of sucking. It is in this sense that the
>   object incorporated into the sucking schema is actually
>   assimilated to the activity of this schema. The object
>   sucked is to be conceived not as nourishment for the
>   organism in general but, so to speak, as aliment for
>   the very activity of sucking according to its various
>   forms. (Piaget, 1952, p.35)

Assimilation takes the two forms of increasing generalisation and increasing specialisation. What is being talked
about above is generalising assimilation. The child
extends the sucking action to take in all sorts of objects
to suck. But on the other hand, the child also distinguishes
between the different kinds of objects that it sucks and

they become distinguished as 'objects to suck when hungry', 'objects to suck for comfort', 'objects to suck in general' etc. This is increasing specialisation of the reflex.

Adaptation, however, is only one side of the process of development. The other side is organisation and this other side, the increasing organisation of the reflex, is shown by the fact that sooner or later it reveals something that Piaget calls a 'meaning' for the child. For example, the specific kind of sucking action will vary according to whether or not the child is hungry. It can be said to mean something different to him depending on the circumstances.

The actual direction in which the reflex action develops can be explained in terms of its contact with the environment; its assimilation of new objects to the structure of the reflex and its own accommodation of the reflex to cope better with these new objects and also to perform better the aim of the reflex to obtain food. The performances of the reflex are organised in certain structured ways and these can be interpreted as forming a rudimentary sort of meaning system for the child. Although he cannot understand in any abstract way the relations between different performances of basically the same reflex, we (that is, the adult observer) can say that these different situations mean something different to the child. And what these situations can be said to 'mean' for him directs the way he performs the reflex. So, there is a dual aspect. The actual performance of the reflex forms ways of distinguishing one context of performance from another, this sets up a meaning system, this meaning system directs the next performance which may be in yet another context which may lead to another change in the meaning system, and so on.

All this depends on the fact that the child does actually repeat reflex actions. They are modified as a result of contact with the environment and this could not happen if they were not repeated. Repetition of actions is to be taken as a primary datum, an assumption of Piaget's explanation.

Similarly assimilation and accommodation are basic assumptions of Piaget's theory. The reflex in the first place changes because it assimilates new elements to itself and accommodates itself to external objects. Similarly, later on, the more complex schemata change as a result of assimilating new elements which have some features which were not previously encountered. The schema has to change

itself to a certain extent, that is, accommodate to take in
these new features. So long as there is assimilation of
new elements, changes from one schema to the next and from
one stage to the next are assured. But assimilation and
accommodation are basic facts.

The adaptation of the reflex of sucking to better achieve
the object of gaining nourishment is clearly one of the
most simple kinds of adaptation and Piaget would place this
in the stage of hereditary adaptations. But very soon the
child begins to initiate new kinds of behaviour and this
marks the beginning of the period of acquired adaptations
when the first real schemata are formed.

The main feature of reflex adaptation which limits its
generalisibility is that the action, even in its adapted
form, is still the same action. It does not involve anything except the improved performance of itself. The next
stage, called the stage of secondary circular reactions,
begins when there appears something which is not part of
the original reflex itself. A child who sucks his thumb
whenever it happens to be near his mouth is doing reflex
sucking. But when the child brings its hand up to its
mouth and sucks its thumb, then there is evidence of what
Piaget calls 'acquired adaptation'. The child has learned
something as a function of its own experience, something
which was not present in the original pattern of the physiologically caused reflex. The child has set up for himself
a new structure, the co-ordination of hand and mouth movements. This is not a 'hereditary schema'. It is something
which has been acquired as a function of experience.

This is an example of accommodation leading to an acquired
adaptation. But the same sort of case can be quoted to
show an acquired adaptation depending on assimilation. At
the reflex level the child will suck new objects when they
come into contact with his mouth. The fact that by chance
he sucks an object which he has not sucked before will not
direct his future sucking in any way. But this is not the
case with a schema such as grasping. Successful grasping
requires varying amounts of adaptation on the part of the
child and grasping a new kind of thing will lead the child
to learn. He will acquire a new adaptation as a result of
assimilating the features of a new 'object to grasp'.
However the characteristic advance of this stage is the
co-ordination of vision and prehension. This co-ordination
makes possible and, in that sense, initiates a new kind of
behaviour pattern, the intentional adaptations. This stage
begins as soon as the child shows signs of acting on things

and using the relationships between objects in order to perform more complex actions, rather than simply reacting when
objects act upon him. Until this stage, the child has been
concerned with properties that the objects could be said to
have in relation to himself. The objects were suckable or
not, one could see them or not, they could be touched and
maybe listened to. With the appearance of actions of the
child directed to the actual objects, rather than simply
reactions to the effect that the objects have on him, the
child can discover some more abstract properties that the
objects have as a result of their relations to each other.
For example, they can be distinguished as means and as ends.
The child can come to see the hand as a means for grasping
an object and bringing it up to its mouth.

This is the beginning of the period called, by Piaget, the
sensori-motor period in which the foundations are laid for
the development of all the higher forms of thought. Piaget's
view is basically, as has been said, that one stage is
transformed into the next in a continuous process of development. Since the characteristics of each stage are gradually
transformed, the later stages need not share any characteristics with the earlier stages. However, Piaget distinguishes between, on the one hand, 'characteristics' like the
specificity of the reflex, the lack of generality of the
concrete operational stage and so on and, on the other hand,
the structural properties. He maintains that basically the
same structures make their appearance at each level of
development. At the initial levels of reflex action and
sensori-motor action they will be rudimentary and not very
elaborate, but they will be simplified 'prefigurations' of
later abstract structures. This initial discovery by the
child of the distinction between ends and means is the
beginning of that ability which will later result in the
possibility of intentional action. The action of the child
in reaching for an object and bringing it to his mouth to
suck is a sensori-motor expression of the very beginnings
of a value-system. The hand is not being valued for itself,
but as a means to grasp what is valued, that is, 'something
to suck'.

Apart from the beginning of the understanding of the relationship of means to ends and the consequent rudimentary
beginnings of a value system, the appearance of this kind
of making use of objects rather than simply reacting to them
marks the beginning of the understanding of all the basic
categories of human thought. By the 'basic categories of
human thought' Piaget means concepts such as the concept of
an object, the concept of quantity, quality, means and end

relationships, space and time relationships. The early
learning of the child consists in the gradual sorting out
of these basic concepts by means of which human beings make
sense of their experience. And Piaget claims that the
foundations for all these concepts are laid in this stage
between birth and the onset of language at the age of about
two. Piaget divides this sensori-motor stage into six substages. The first substage marks the transition from the
inherited reflex responses to adapted reflex response. The
second substage marks the move away from reflex activity
towards intentional activity. While admitting that it is
difficult to define what an intentional action is Piaget
attempts to define it as an action which is initiated by
an internal meaning or consciousness of a meaning rather
than by an external stimulus. And it is the using of some
things as means to achieve other things which marks the
beginning of intentional adaptations. A further feature
of intentional action is that it is directed towards the
future. Previously, the child's action has been directed
towards the past, that is, to repetition of previous acts.
As soon as a primitive grasp of the means/end connection
is initiated then the child's action is directed towards
new combinations and actions and in that sense it is
directed towards the future. However, the directing towards
the future is not at this stage, complete. This will only
come about at the fourth stage when the child can apply
known means to new ends. Characteristic of the third stage
is the tendency to repeat actions which the child enjoyed
or which were advantageous to it in some way. They differ
from the repetitions of the first substage in that they
are more complex and are directed towards the action itself,
for example; sucking for the sake of sucking, grasping for
the sake of grasping. The following observations taken
from Piaget, 1952, show the development of some of these
action patterns:

Observation 94 - At 0:3 (5) Lucienne shakes her bassinet
by moving her legs violently (bending and unbending
them, etc.) which makes the cloth dolls swing from the
hood. Lucienne looks at them, smiling, and recommences
at once.... The next day I present the dolls: Lucienne
immediately moves, shakes her legs, but this time without smiling. Her interest is intense and sustained and
there also seems to be an intentional circular reaction.
Observation 94 repeated - At 0:3 (9) Lucienne is in
her bassinet without the dolls. I shake the bassinet
two or three times without her seeing me. She looks
very interested and serious and begins again, for a
long stretch of time, rough and definitely intentional
shaking. That evening I rediscover Lucienne in the act

of shaking her hood spontaneously. She laughs at this
sight.
Here is involved, therefore, the schema described in
the foregoing observation but applied to a new object.
(pp.158-9)

These examples show the generalising assimilation which is
one of the ways in which the child advances. But at this
stage also Piaget detects the first appearance of recognit-
ory assimilation. He notes that regularly when confronted
with certain objects that he has acted on in the past the
child of about five months will not perform the whole
action again but will sketch out the action as if showing
simply that he recognises the object. For example:

Observation 107 - A 0:5 (3) Lucienne tries to grasp
spools suspended above her by means of elastic bands.
She usually uses them in order to suck them, but sometimes she swings them while shaking herself when they
are there. She manages to touch them but not yet grasp
them. Having shaken them fortuitously, she then breaks
off to shake herself a moment while looking at them
(shakes of the legs and trunk). She then resumes her
attempts at grasping.
Why has she broken off in order to shake herself a few
seconds? It was not in order to shake the spools because
she did not persevere and was busy with something else
at the time.... Everything transpires as though the
subject, endowed for a moment with reflection and
internal language, had said to herself something like
this: 'Yes, I see that this object could be swung, but
it is not what I am looking for'. But, lacking language,
it is by working the schema that Lucienne would have
thought that, before resuming her attempts to grasp.
In this hypothesis the short interlude of swinging
would thus be equivalent to a sort of motor recognition.
(Piaget, 1952, p.186)

The final characteristic action of this stage has the rather
clumsy title of 'procedures for making interesting sights
last'. Just as the actions of the second substage prefigure
the final understanding of means/end connections, so the
procedures for making interesting sights last are a preliminary stage in the final understanding of causal connections.
For example:

At 0:7 (2) Laurent is in the process of striking a cushion
when I snap my middle finger against the ball of my thumb.
Laurent then smiles and strikes the cushion but while
staring at my hand; as I no longer move, he strikes
harder and harder, with a definite expression of desire

and expectation and, at the moment when I resume snapping
my fingers, he stops as though he had achieved his object.
A moment later, I hid behind a big curtain and reappeared
every few minutes.   In the interim, Laurent strikes his
covers harder and harder while looking at the curtain -
same reaction while looking at an electric light.   At
0:7 (5) he strikes the side of his bassinet while looking
at the hanging rattles and continues for a long time
despite failure.   At 0:7 (7) he strikes his coverlets
while looking at a tin box on which I have just drummed.
Same reactions until about 0:8.   (Piaget, 1952, p.202)

So, what is happening is that the child is generalising an
action which he has associated with an interesting sight in
the sense that he seems to think his action produces the
sight (although it does not) to a procedure for 'producing'
any interesting sight.   The actions of this third stage
still consist essentially in repeating actions which the
child has just done or is used to doing.   Innovation is by
chance.   The distinction between means and ends has not yet
been made clear.   The action of the child is characterised
by one schema.   At the next stage there will be co-ordination
of different schemata, some of which will be ends and some
means to those ends.

THE CO-ORDINATION OF SCHEMATA

The next stage, substage four of the period of sensori-motor
intelligence is characterised by the child's activity seeking
to obtain a certain effect and trying different means to
achieve this, rather than, as was the case in substage three,
simply trying to prolong an effect which was achieved in the
first case by chance.   For example:
   Observation (2) repeated - At 0:9 (8) Jacqueline tries
   to grasp her parrot which I placed between the entwined
   strings.   She pulls a string from the lower end of which
   her doll is hanging.   She sees the parrot swing instead
   of trying to grasp it, henceforth she merely tries to
   shake it.   It is then that the behaviour pattern we
   shall emphasise here arises and which constitutes a true
   act of intelligent adaptation.   Jacqueline looks for the
   doll at the other end of the string, grasps it with one
   hand and hits its head with the other hand while staring
   at the parrot.   She then does this at regular intervals
   while alternately looking at the doll and parrot and
   each time controlling the result (the parrot swings at
   each stroke).   (Piaget, 1952, p.216)

This observation shows clearly that a distinction is being
made between means and ends. Piaget explains that a few
days before these observations were made Jacqueline had
shaken the parrot to hear the rattle inside it. On this
occasion this is what she wants to do again. Unable to
grasp the parrot, when she discovers that the doll is
connected to the same string as the parrot, she hits the
doll to make it move as a means to shaking the parrot. So
here two distinct schemata, striking the doll and shaking
the parrot, are combined in a means/end relationship. It
is as a result of these sorts of 'experiments', the trying
out of new means to the same end, that increasingly complex
relationships are set up between schemata.

The possibility of relating actions in this way makes
possible the development of the elementary concept of the
permanent object. The child is now able to use one action
in order to achieve another. Therefore he can remove an
obstacle in order to grasp an object which the obstacle
was concealing. This has not been possible until now and
the child, until this stage, behaves as though the object
is being continually made and destroyed as it appears and
disappears.

However, the most important result of this ability to co-
ordinate schemata is the exploration of new objects by
means of the schemata. The child is able, when presented
with familiar objects, to do new things with them by familiar
means. When presented with an entirely new object he cannot
'set himself a goal'. He does not know the sorts of things
he can do. Piaget says that what happens is that the child
will try to apply each of his old schemata in turn to the
new object. This is not the same sort of thing as has
happened already when the child has set a certain schema as
a goal (such as shaking a rattle) and used another schema
as a means. All the schemata have become 'instruments of
comprehension' and the goal is the object itself. For
example:
    Observation 138 repeated - Lucienne at 0:8 (10) examines
    a new doll which I hang from the hood of her bassinet.
    She looks at it for a long time, touches it, then feels
    it by touching its feet, clothes, head etc. She then
    ventures to grasp it, which makes the hood sway. She
    then pulls the doll while watching the effects of this
    movement. Then she returns to the doll, holds it in
    one hand while striking it with the other, sucks it and
    shakes it while holding it above her, and finally shakes
    it by moving its legs.
    Afterwards she strikes it without holding it, then

grasps the string by which it hangs and gently swings it
with the other hand. She then becomes very much interested in this slight swinging movement which is new to
her and repeats it indefinitely. (Piaget, 1952, p.256)

This sort of behaviour might seem to have taken place
already in stage three when the child successively shakes,
sucks and bangs a new object, but Piaget maintains that the
difference is one of orientation. At stage three the
novelty of the object does not interest the child. He
regards it simply as something to practise his schemata on.
At this stage it appears as though the new object presents
a kind of 'problem' to the child. He is trying to understand the nature of the new object not simply trying out
his own schemata.

When application of his own schemata results in a new phenomenon (for example the slight swinging motion of the doll
that Lucienne has discovered) the child does what it has
always done, that is, repeats the action which led to this
interesting, new phenomenon. This marks the beginning of
the active experimentation of the next stage when the child
does things in order to see what will happen.

THE DISCOVERY OF NEW SCHEMATA

The child at the fourth stage is limited to co-ordinating
already familiar schemata whereas the advance of the fifth
stage is the ability to form new schemata as the result of
a sort of active experimentation. An important result of
this is that the child begins to understand the difference
between his own actions and the objects these actions are
performed on. Previously, although accommodation clearly
occurs, assimilation has predominated. The child tries to
assimilate novelty to familiarity and tends to overlook or
minimise aspects which cannot be assimilated. At this stage
if he fails to assimilate an object he appears to try to
find out the respects in which the object is new. So he
will repeat actions which led to a new result but he does
not repeat them as he did at the previous stage, just as
they were. He changes them slightly and so gets even more
new results. These repetitions prefigure later reasoning.
Piaget distinguishes between judgments and reasoning. A
judgment at the sensori-motor level is the simple assimilation of an action to a schema. This has taken place already
at stages three and four. Reasoning is the combining of
several judgments to achieve one overall result. So this
stage marks the beginning of 'reasoned experiment'. As an
example:

Observation 145 - At 0:11 (20) Jacqueline slides a series
of objects along her slanting coverlet. This is an
experiment and not simply repetition because she varies
the objects and the positions. At 1:0 (2) she rolls a
pencil on a table by dropping it just above the surface
or by pushing it. The next day she does the same with
a ball.
At 1:0 (3) also, she takes her plush dog and places it
on a sofa, obviously expecting a movement. As the dog
remains motionless, she places it somewhere else. After
several vain attempts she pushes it gently, while it is
several millimetres above the material, as though it
would roll better. Finally she grasps it and places it
on a slanting cushion, so that the dog rolls. She then
immediately begins all over again. Experimentation certainly exists. But in the last attempt definite pre-
vision can be seen. (Piaget, 1952, p.271)

It is at this stage that accommodation and assimilation,
which have been more or less undifferentiated until now,
are gradually distinguished from one another. Until now,
assimilation has predominated and the child has only
accommodated when forced by some intractable characteristic
of the reality he needs to assimilate - but at this stage
he becomes more and more interested in the external results
of his actions. His attention is gradually turned away
from his own schemata to the external environment and he
begins to take much more account of the features of the
external environment which he cannot assimilate. Accommodation becomes important for its own sake. This leads to an
increase in the objectification of the world. An object
that one can swing, grasp, drop, roll etc. gradually ceases
to be simply a part of an action sequence and becomes
regarded as a centre of interest in its own right and
gradually as a centre of force, so prefiguring the concept
of causation. For example:
One recalls (in Observation 140) how at 0:10 (2) Laurent
discovered in 'exploring' a case of soap, the possibility
of throwing this object and letting it fall. Now, what
interested him at first was not the objective phenomenon
of the fall, that is to say, the object's trajectory,
but the very act of letting go. He therefore limited
himself at the beginning to reproducing the result
observed fortuitously which still constitutes a 'secondary reaction'. On the other hand at 0:10 (10) the
reaction changes and becomes 'tertiary'. That day,
Laurent manipulates a small piece of bread (without any
alimentary interest; he has never eaten it and has not
thought of tasting it) and lets it go continuously. He

even breaks off fragments which he lets drop. Now, in
contradistinction to what has happened in preceding
days, he pays no attention to the act of letting go
whereas he watches with great interest the body in
motion; in particular he looks at it for a long time
when it has fallen and picks it up if he can.
(Piaget, 1952, p.268)

MENTAL EXPERIMENTS

By the end of substage five, the child can use the means
which it has already developed for one purpose in order to
achieve another purpose and also achieve purposes which
have been already attained in one way, by other means.
The advance of substage six is that the child is able to
invent quite new means to cope with new situations without
active experimentation. Formerly, the child 'discovered'
new means by a process of trial and error. At this stage
the child seems able to invent new means with no physical
movement at all. He begins to show signs of using images
and symbols which he can combine with no physical movement.
Although this ability does allow the child to do a great
many new and different things Piaget does not think that
this step forward is different in kind from other steps.
The child has not developed a new sort of capacity to
represent things symbolically to itself. This symbolising
is no more than a thorough knowledge of all the schemata
he has acquired at previous stages. Because he is so
familiar with them the child can organise them quickly and
pick out which one he needs. It is an internalised sort
of experimentation, not something which is different in
kind from physical experimentation just as reading silently
to oneself is a refinement of reading aloud and not something different in kind.

As an example of the kind of operation that goes on at this
stage Piaget quotes the solving of an elementary problem by
Lucienne; she has already emptied a chain out of a box
without a lid by turning over the box and has pulled a chain
out of a half shut matchbox by putting her finger in it.
So she has developed these two schemata. Now she is presented with a new situation:
    Observation 180 - Lucienne 1:4 (0). I put the chain back
    in the box and reduce the opening to 3mm. Lucienne is
    not aware of the functioning of the opening and closing
    of the box, and has not seen me prepare the experiment.
    She only possesses the two preceding schemata; turning
    the box over in order to empty it of its contents and

sliding her finger into the opening to make the chain
come out. It is of course this last procedure that she
tries first. She puts her finger inside and gropes to
reach the chain, but fails completely to make the chain
come out. A pause follows during which Lucienne mani-
fests a very curious reaction which bears witness not
only to the fact that she tries to think out the situation and represent to herself through mental combination
the operations to be performed but also to the role
played by imitation in the genesis of representations,
Lucienne mimes the widening of the slit.
  She looks in the slit with great attention then several
times in succession she opens and shuts her mouth, at
first slightly and then wider and wider! Apparently
Lucienne understands the existence of a cavity. The
attempt at representation which she thus furnishes is
expressed plastically, that is to say, due to inability
to think out the solution in words or clear visual
images, she uses a simple motor indication as signifier
or symbol.... Soon after this phrase of plastic reflection Lucienne unhesitatingly puts her finger into the
slit and, instead of trying as before, to reach the
chain she pulls so as to enlarge the opening.
(Piaget, 1952, pp.337-8)

The importance of this stage is that it marks the move from
material to formal thinking. Piaget maintains that this
move could not be explained without the previous assimilatory activity at the level of motor intelligence. The
difference between material and formal thinking is that
whereas material thinking requires some perceptual or actual
content to set it off - formal thinking is the combining and
comparing of schemata without the need for any perceptual
content. What is present is a kind of mental representation
of some object or action; for example, Lucienne's imitation
of the box opening shows some representation or symbolising
of what she wants. But the role of this representation is
not simply to act as a memory of previously performed acts.
It can only lead to invention if it is derived from the
schemata. It is not simply a mental image or other aid de
memoire.

THE CONCEPT OF THE PERMANENT OBJECT

The kinds of things that the child can be said to know at
the stage of sensori-motor operations are rough and ready
classifications of things according to his own possibilities
for action. But these rough classifications serve to define

some elementary 'concepts', for example, the concept of the
object. For Piaget, what would count as 'having' a mature
concept of the 'object' is that an object be seen as an
entity which exists independently of the subject and moves
in a space common to it and the subject. So a child with
this kind of concept will believe that an object continues
to exist when he is no longer acting on it or perceiving it.
A necessary corollary to this is the realisation that the
self is only one object among all the others that exist.
If these criteria are acceptable for the understanding of
the concept of an object these young infants do not possess
this concept and they develop an understanding of it very
gradually. Piaget suggests that the way the very young
infant sees objects is as an extension of his own action,
perhaps even the product of his own effort to see. He does
not distinguish himself as subject from what is surrounding
him. The child will continue to look in the direction in
which an object, which was for the child a pleasant sensation, disappeared with apparently the expectation of seeing
it reappear. But this does not suggest more than that he
is trying to encourage a pleasant sensation to return, not
that he can understand that the object is existing independently of himself and will come back again. This state of
affairs will persist throughout the first two stages of the
sensori-motor period. At the third stage the child's
actions have developed more co-ordination and he begins
to anticipate where an object which has disappeared will
reappear, for example, when an object drops to the floor,
the infant will look at the floor, not simply stare at the
place from which it fell. He will also search in a desult-
ory fashion for an object which has disappeared. But this
search is soon abandoned if the object does not reappear
quickly. It seems as if the object at this stage is still
no more than an experience for the child, and what he is
trying to recreate or recapture are experiences rather than
searching for independent objects.

Later during this stage the child can find an object which
he has abandoned for something else and is also capable of
recognising an object when only a part of it is in view.
But still Piaget thinks that what the child is doing is
repeating an action; he is doing again something that he
did before rather than finding an object. When he recognises an object when only a part of it is showing, the
child behaves as though he believes the object is being
continually made and destroyed. When he can see only a
small part he fails to recognise the object at all; if he
sees a larger part he recognises it; then, if more of it
is concealed again, he fails to recognise it. These

reactions do not add up to evidence of the possession of
the concept of a permanent object as Piaget has defined it.
He says:

> Everything occurs as though the child believes that the
> object is alternately made and unmade.... When the child
> sees a part of the object emerge from a screen and he
> assumes the existence of the totality of that object,
> he does not yet consider this totality as being formed
> 'behind' the screen; he simply admits that it is in the
> process of being formed as it leaves the screen.
> (Piaget, 1951, p.31)

In the final part of this stage the child can remove objects
which prevent his own perception, for example, he can remove
a blanket from his face but he does not remove obstacles
which are placed in front of the objects he is trying to see.
He understands something about his own actions, his own
perception is blocked by an object which is touching him
and he can remove it but he does not understand that an
obstacle can be placed in front of an object without
thereby destroying the object.

At Stage Four the child begins to search for objects which
have been hidden but he does this only if he has actually
seen the object being hidden and then only where he saw it
being hidden in the first place:

> The procedure is as follows, at least in the most
> characteristic period of the stage. Suppose an object
> is hidden at point A: the child searches for it and
> finds it. Next the object is placed in B and is
> covered before the child's eyes; although the child
> has continued to watch the object and has seen it dis-
> appear in B, he nevertheless immediately tries to find
> it in A! (Piaget, 1951, p.50)

As an example of what happens:

> Gerard at thirteen months knows how to walk and is
> playing in a large room. He throws the ball, or rather
> lets it drop in front of him and, either on his feet or
> on all fours, hurries to pick it up. At a given moment
> the ball rolls under an armchair. Gerard sees it and
> not without some difficulty takes it out in order to
> resume the game. Then the ball rolls under a sofa at
> the other end of the room. Gerard has seen it pass
> under the fringe of the sofa; he bends down to recover
> it. But as the sofa is deeper than the armchair and
> the fringe does prevent a clear view, Gerard gives up
> after a moment; he gets up, crosses the room, goes
> right under the armchair and carefully explores the

place where the ball was before.   (Piaget, 1951, p.59)

Piaget suggests that what these examples mean is that the
object is not yet for the child clearly distinguished from
its context:

> Hence there would not be one chain, one doll, one watch,
> one ball etc. individualised, permanent and independent
> of the child's activity... but there would exist only
> images   such as 'ball - under - the - arm - chair',
> 'doll - attached - to - the - hammock', 'watch - under
> - a - cushion', 'papa - at - the - window'. (Piaget,
> 1951, pp.62-3)

At Stage Five the child overcomes his dependence on previous
search patterns and learns to search for an object only where
it last disappeared. But he can do this only if he actually
saw the object disappear into that place. If one hides an
object in one's hand and then puts it behind a screen the
child will search in the hand for the object and he will
not look behind the screen. It is only at Stage Six when
some kind of representational or symbolic action becomes
possible that the child can manage invisible displacements
of objects, for example:

> At 1:7 (20) Jacqueline watched me when I put a coin in
> my hand and then put my hand under a coverlet. I with-
> drew my hand closed: Jacqueline opens it, then searches
> under the coverlet until she finds the object. I take
> back the coin at once, put it in my hand and then slip
> my closed hand under a cushion situated on the other
> side (on her left and no longer on her right); Jacqueline
> immediately searches for the object under the cushion.
> I repeat the experiment by hiding the coin under a
> jacket; Jacqueline finds it without hesitation.
> (Piaget, 1951, p.79)

Piaget thinks that this kind of behaviour presumes the
possession of a concept which measures up to the criteria
that he has suggested for the concept of an object. The
child seems to presume the continued existence of an object
even when it is moved from place to place without the child
actually seeing it. The different stages in the development
of an understanding of the permanence of an object correspond to the six substages of the sensori-motor period. And
the child seems to have found out, by his own actions, something about the world, that is, that there are objects which
exist independently of his perception of them. But here
Kant's distinction between the unstructured data of perception and the organisation of objective experience must be
kept in mind. The permanence of objects is not either for

Kant or Piaget a 'given' of experience. For Kant it is a
concept which we need to experience the world in a coherent
way: for Piaget it is an understanding achieved only after
a large amount of experience and action in the world. It
is a 'construction' derived from the exercise of the understanding. The child also develops at this time rudimentary
spatial and temporal concepts and the gradual freeing of the
concept of causality from an analogy with human action. It
can be seen that all these concepts depend to a great extent
on each other and consequently their development at more or
less the same period is not mere chance. This suggests, as
will be discussed later, that the sequence of development
that Piaget discovers should be understood not so much
with reference to the empirical data and in terms of a
temporal sequence, but rather with reference to the interconnections and relationships between the concepts themselves,
that is, in terms of a conceptually or logically connected
sequence.

From this brief description of the sensori-motor period one
can begin to see the sort of relationships that Piaget sees
as holding between the different stages of development at
this level. The stages grow out of each other in the sense
that the initial innate reflexes are improved and extended
by practise. Their sphere of action extends to take in more
and more features of the environment which are amenable to
the sort of action that the reflex comprises. The reflex
itself is altered by these repeated contacts with different
features of the environment until its character is quite
changed. Gradually different reflexes are 'co-ordinated'
to fit better both with each other and with the specific
characteristics of the environment. A simple 'structure'
is being built up in the sense that the child is becoming
capable of performing series or groups of actions which can
be seen as a whole to have a different character from the
constituent parts. The action, or totality of actions, for
example which comprises reaching for something, grasping it
and putting it into the mouth expresses a certain primitive
level of purpose or intention which is not expressed by
random sucking, finger curling, or arm stretching. What
development seems to amount to at this level is the gradual
gaining of control over the child's immediate environment
through the co-ordination of actions which are, at first,
not much more than simple reflexes, not particularly well
adapted to the specific features of the environment and
consequently not particularly successful in achieving their
ends. This gradual improvement and co-ordination of action
eventuates in the expression in the child's behaviour of
something that we might begin to recognise as intention,
meaning, understanding.

A study of the sensori-motor stage reveals what Piaget identifies as the structuring and ordering concepts and shows where his interest in development lies. Piaget is not interested in problems that we might label 'problems of content'. He is not interested, for example, in how the child comes to identify, classify, name and so on, an object like 'cat'. He is interested in cases of long-term development from the concrete to the abstract, from the subjective to the objective reasoning processes that underly the acquisition of knowledge. For any theory of the acquisition of knowledge an important problem is how the whole thing gets started in the first place. Eschewing innate knowledge, Piaget begins with only a few primitive reflexes and provides a very plausible, very interesting description of the gradual changes in behaviour across the six substages of the sensori-motor period, ending with the achievement of symbolic representation which is the essential starting point of intellectual development. The sensori-motor period provides the essential link between the biological and intellectual levels.

With the onset of the stage of concrete and later formal operations Piaget's biologically based theory becomes less and less plausible. We will leave detailed discussion of these stages to the chapters dealing with Piaget's structuralist theory. The structures typical of the stage of concrete operations are the famous 'grouping' and the structures of conservation. The operations at the concrete operations stage must, as the name suggests, be performed on concrete objects. But once the structures of this stage have been developed, the child becomes capable of attending to these operations themselves rather than the objects that were operated on. He becomes able to perform operations on operations. This is the distinguishing feature of the stage of formal operations.

The most important characteristic of the stage of formal operations is that it concerns verbal statements that are no longer linked to concrete objects. Replacing objects by verbal statements that no longer need representation means that children at the formal stage can reason about unrealised possibilities. Piaget chatacterises this stage as the stage at which what is real becomes only one example of what is possible. There is a reversal between the importance of the real and the possible.

SUMMARY

Piaget's theory is concerned with the development of thought
from concrete to abstract, simple to complex and subjective
to objective. It represents this development as a continuous series of transformations from simple hereditary reflexes
to the operations of formal thought. There are no revolutionary changes, only the gradual evolution of abstract,
objective understanding.

The increasing structure and organisation of understanding
is what confers objectivity on an initially subjective
experience. The concepts which constitute this structure
are derived from the structures discernible in the child's
actions during the sensori-motor period. The same structures
are re-elaborated at levels of increasing abstractness and
generality. These structural concepts perform the same
function in Piaget's theory as the a priori concepts of the
pure understanding in Kant's critical philosophy. They
provide the form of experience. In Kant's theory they can
never provide the content of experience since that is
supplied by perception. In Piaget's theory, they do supply
the content at the higher levels of development when it
becomes possible to perform operations on operations.

Chapter 2

Functionalism and biology

PREVIEW

The aim of this chapter is to show the roots of Piaget's
biological approach to cognitive development. The implications of this view for the nature of the human mind and
human knowledge will be drawn out. Finally, the problems
that such a view raises for understanding human development
are discussed.

MIND AS A FUNCTION OF THE ORGANISM

Piaget's theory of intelligence is firmly grounded in
biology and he begins his explanation of the functional
invariants of intelligence with an example of these same
functional invariants at work in a biological context. He
does not think that there is simply an analogy to be drawn
between biological functioning and intellectual functioning.
He thinks that there is a complete 'isomorphism' between
the two and that intelligence is simply the most useful and
highly developed adaptation device that the organism has.
The hypothesis that intellectual functioning has the same
essential characteristics as biological functioning (the
only essential characteristics of the two being organisational properties and assimilatory and accommodatory
activity) is what leads him to assume that talk of the
assimilation of reality elements into the cognitive structure
and accommodation to reality will make sense in the context
of a theory of intelligence.

In his earlier works Piaget talks about 'intelligence', in
later works he refers more often to 'knowledge' or 'under-

standing'. By these terms he is referring to aspects of 'mind'.

'Mind' is to be distinguished from 'brain' in that the brain is a part of the body, a physical entity. It can be studied in the same sorts of ways as other physical organs such as the heart or the kidneys. Brains can be removed from skulls, dissected and observed. None of these things is true of 'mind'. In talking about a person's mind we are talking about his beliefs and knowledge, his feelings and intentions. We normally study these things by talking to people, drawing inferences from their behaviour, generalising from what we know of them in the past.

Piaget clearly recognises this distinction between mind and brain and sees psychology as the study of mind and physiology as the study of brain. Having recognised the distinction it is clear that there is a close connection of some kind between the mind and the brain. Brain damage leads to loss of memory, inability to think coherently and so on. Lobotomy, the severing of the prefrontal lobes, leads to the inability to feel strong emotions. Emotions are associated with physiological changes in the brain and the rest of the body. The close connection is obvious but what puzzles philosophers is what kind of a connection it is. The mind and the brain are not simply different things, they are different kinds of things. As Ryle would argue (1949), mind and body are in different categories. What sort of connection can there be between them?

Stated in other words, the problem is: What is the relation between thoughts, feelings and actions and the electro-chemical activity of the brain that we know accompanies thoughts, feelings, actions? Philosophers have made many attempts to specify this relationship. So far, none of them has been completely satisfactory. The most obvious first step is to view the relationship as a causal one. This immediately runs into difficulties. What is the direction of the causal relationship? Does the brain activity cause the thoughts or do the thoughts cause the brain activity? We tend to think of our beliefs as justified or unjustified. Does it make sense to ask of events which have been caused, whether they are or are not justified? What kind of causal relation is this between two such different kinds of things?

Alternative views include among others the identity hypothesis which is the view that thoughts are nothing but brain activity, and the parallel hypothesis that thoughts and brain processes simply parallel each other.

Piaget's own clear preference is for a form of parallelism.
He believes that there is a level of objective meaning
structure where the relations holding between propositions
are relations of logical implication. An example would be
the objective meaning system of mathematics. The relations
holding between the propositions of mathematics are logical
relations which remain valid even though many individuals
may not understand or accept them. The study and justification of these relationships does not make any reference to
any individual's beliefs.

This level is paralleled by the actual thought structure
of individuals. That is, the belief structure of individuals is on a different level from the logical structure of
the meaning system. It may conform to it or not. When the
structure of the belief system reflects that of the logical
system, then Piaget would say, thought has become objective
and valid. What I have called the belief system, Piaget
calls the 'mental organisation' or 'mental structure'.

This level of mental structure is paralleled in its turn by
the level of cerebral or physiological structure. Piaget
thinks that this hypothesis of parallelism is made plausible
by the fact that both mental and neuro-physiological structures can be represented or modelled by abstract logical
structures. That is, the mental and neuro-physiological
structures can be described in formal terms derived from
the level of logic. For Piaget, this shows that the structural features of all these levels are identical.

Mind emerges in this view as a function of the organism
serving adaptation to the environment. Piaget is led to
this view of mind by his biological orientation and the
functionalist philosophy that the theory of natural selection inevitably leads to.

PIAGET'S FUNCTIONALISM

In characterising mind as a function of the organism Piaget
is placing his own theory within the broad spectrum of
theories which can all be labelled as functionalist.

Functionalism is not, at least in so far as Piaget uses it,
a theory. It is an approach to theorising. It is an
assumption that is logically prior to Piaget's theorising
about development. The first assumption that he makes is
that the organism is an organised system. To a certain
extent, the decision to demarcate certain elements as

forming a system, is a matter of convenience. Buddhist
mythology presents everything as being part of one great
system. Science has to carve out of this total connectedness, smaller units for study. In fact, the system that
Piaget demarcates comprises not simply the organism but the
organism in interaction with the environment.

The second assumption Piaget makes is that all the components of the system function to contribute to the maintenance
of the whole. It is this assumption which characterises
his systems approach as functional. With these assumptions
one can see how Piaget is led inevitably to the view that
mind or consciousness serves the function of adaptation.
In a functionalist theory, each of the components of a
system functions to subserve the maintenance of the whole
system. Mind, therefore, since it is a component of the
system, must contribute to its maintenance which in the
case of biological organisms involves its adaptation.

Functionalist theories fall into two major types, the
mechanistic and the biological. Piaget's theory falls
clearly within the biological type. Biological functionalist theories have several features of their own which are
well exemplified in Piaget's theory. For example, they
assume a system to have a basic organising principle of
goals and self-regulating mechanisms; that the system is
a fairly stable and enduring unit able to maintain itself
in a state of equilibrium with respect to the forces
acting on it and that the direction of change or development is inherent rather than rational or chosen.

Functionalist theories by their very nature, are concerned
with structures. Most functionalist theories can be
characterised as 'functional-structural'. Functionalism
is concerned with the ways in which the components of a
system interact. It is argued that these interactions
can often be specified by showing them as changes in the
structural relationships between those components. Conversely, structural change can be explained by emphasising
the functions of the components of the system and showing
how the change contributes to the maintenance of the whole.
Abrahamson (1978) characterises the relation between
structure and function as a 'chicken and egg dilemma'
He says:
    Structural-functionalism is created by assuming that
    if structure is organisation in space, then function
    is organisation in time. Any system, it is assumed,
    'must fuse the two ... so that its function can main-
    tain its structure' (Yates et al., 1972, p.123). Or,

is it the other way around; namely that its structure
must maintain its function? Raising this question
makes it apparent that structure and function present
some aspects of a chicken and egg dilemma (Ibid., p.13).
It is not surprising, then, that Piaget's theory relying on
a functionalist approach to mental development will utilise
the concept of structure to the extent that he does. Over
the many years during which Piaget was developing his
theory his emphasis shifted from its stressing of the
functionalist to a stressing of the structuralist aspects
of his theory. He became less concerned with showing that
mind and intelligence subserve the adaptation of the organism to the environment and more concerned with describing
the structure of rational thought. The same shift of
emphasis can be discerned in his theory from the functionalist descriptions of the sensori-motor and pre-operational
stages to the structuralist descriptions of the concrete
operational and formal operational stages.

LINKS WITH THE THEORY OF EVOLUTION

Many of the views on the nature of the study of mind that
Piaget supports derive from the biological theory of
natural selection. Piaget himself sees problems in both
a Lamarckian theory stressing the malleability of the
organism and the Darwinian theory stressing the element of
preformation and chance in selection. He claims that a
synthesis of the two theories is necessary incorporating
new ideas about growth and organisation and biological
causality in general. He quotes Waddington as a biologist
who has filled in many of the 'gaps' in classical theory.

Among the ideas to be found in Piaget and traceable back to
their origins among the Victorian biologists is in particular the idea that child studies can throw light on human
psychology, that the study of child development is in fact
an essential prerequisite to understanding adult forms of
thought.

Before the advent of evolutionary theory, there was no
reason to suppose that either child or animal studies would
have any relevance to the study of adult psychology. But
the basic message of evolutionary theory is that all things
evolve continuously from lower to higher, from simple to
complex. Originally this was meant to apply to anatomical
development. But it was not long before the biologists
themselves were suggesting that it could fruitfully be
applied to mental as well as physical development. If we

view the higher mental processes in the light of the lower
ones, and if the direction is said to be from simple to
complex, then the higher mental processes will be seen as
more complex forms of the lower ones. It then becomes
worthwhile studying the lower processes in order to better
understand the higher ones. Thinking along these lines
led to the establishment of the science of Comparative
Psychology. Stanley-Hall in 1891 founded the Journal of
Genetic Psychology. Earlier George Romanes had justified
the study of animal intelligence on the grounds that the
aim was to trace the 'probable genesis of mind from non-
mental antecedents' (Romanes, 1882, p.457). Darwin himself
claimed that we really know things only when we trace their
development (Darwin, 1859). In the 1870s Ernst Haeckel
appended to Darwin's theory the view that ontogenesis re-
capitulates phylogenesis, that is: the view that the development of the individual follows the evolutionary development of the species. Originally, again, this view was
intended to apply to the anatomical aspect of development.
But it was soon extended to the psychological aspect.

All these ideas can be rediscovered in Piaget; the recapit-
ulation hypothesis (Piaget, 1970a, p.13); the view that
intelligence must be traced back to its source in non-
intelligent antecedents (Piaget, 1952) and the view that
the study of lower processes or forms of thought is
essential to understanding later, higher forms (Piaget,
passim).

The theory of natural selection also leads inevitably to
the major point of Piaget's theory, that intelligence
serves the function of adaptation. Romanes defines mind as:
'the extent to which the organism learns to make new
adjustments or to modify old ones in accordance with
experience' (1888, p.62).

E.R. Lankester in 1900 claimed that: 'Adaptation by means
of mental process must take the place of adaptation of
bodily structure' (1900, p.625).

Mind and intelligence then came to be seen as adaptive
devices by means of which an organism which has reached
some sort of limit in anatomical adaptation can continue
to adapt.

Piaget in his autobiography (Boring, 1952) explains how he
arrived at the view (from his own early studies of mullusks)
that adaptation and its counterpart, organisation, were the
fundamental processes that could explain all biological
functioning and how he eventually came to the view that

they could also account for the nature and existence of
consciousness or mind.

Piaget began his academic life as a biologist and it is
understandable that a biologist would offer this kind of
explanation of mind, but he is not simply offering a model
of intellectual development based on an analogy with biological development. He is claiming that in so far as
structure and function are concerned (although not where
subject matter is concerned) intellectual functioning and
biological functioning are the same.

MIND AS ADAPTIVE DEVICE

He argues that the nature of man's understanding is connected with a certain general heredity possessed in common
with all other living organisms. It is due to the nature
of the organism as such. That is, the nature of intelligence and reason is the same whether it is found in a jelly
fish or a nuclear physicist; it is a result of the nature
of the organism and the nature of the relationship between
the organism and the environment. He says:

> The 'specific heredity' of mankind and of its particular
> 'offspring' admits of certain levels of intelligence
> superior to that of monkeys, etc. But, on the other
> hand, the functional activity of reason (the ipse
> intellectus which does not come from experience) is
> obviously connected with the 'general heredity' of the
> living organism itself. (Piaget, 1952, p.2)

The features of intelligence which are a result of this
general heredity are not particular ideas or specific forms
or structures. They are functional features. The organism,
if it is to continue to be such, must survive and to do
this it must adapt itself to its environment. Similarly,
Piaget suggests, if our understanding of our environment is
to increase then it must 'fit' the environment. We cannot
push reality into rigid moulds of our own invention. We
must adapt our intellectual concepts to fit reality. So
adaptation is one of the features of both biological and
intellectual functioning which is owed to this general
heredity.

Conversely, the organism would be unable to adapt itself
physically to the environment if it did not have a certain
degree of organisation. For example, it would be unable to
nourish itself, and so survive, if it possessed nothing
corresponding to a mouth and digestive organs. Again Piaget

suggests that the case of intellectual functioning is
parallel. The intellect must have a certain degree of
organisation (and this means that it must be organised in
a certain way) if it is going to be able to function at all.

Adaptation would not be possible without these organisational structures since assimilation is the assimilating
of new elements to already formed structures. But the
structures are to be distinguished from the functional
invariants since they are formed and not a priori given
and they are very different at different stages whereas
the functions always remain the same.

In Chapter 1, the distinction was made with reference to
Kant between a priori and a posteriori concepts. Kant
argued that a posteriori concepts, since they were derived
from perception, should fit experience whereas the a priori
concepts which were not derived from perception structured
experience and so made experience conform to themselves.
Piaget is here maintaining the distinction between the
concepts concerned with the content of experience, concepts like red, warm, and so on and the structuring concepts like cause, quantity and so on. But he maintains
that even the structuring concepts must conform to
experience and are in fact derived from it although in a
very complex way. It is not a question of imposing a set
of structural properties on an infinitely malleable set of
perceptions. It is a question of developing a structural
system in conjunction with the intractable elements of the
environment which impinges on the individual. An important
part of this environment is the child's own actions. Given
the physiological and physical make up of a human child,
given the intractable features of an environment which
contains hard objects, people, events and so on, these
actions will only be able to accomplish certain things.
They will only be combinable in certain ways. It is this
give and take between individual and the environment which
leads to the development of structures which organise but
do not distort experience.

ADAPTATION AND ORGANISATION: INNATE FUNCTIONS

The physiological structure of the organism which provides
the initial organisation and the functional invariants of
adaptation and re-organisation which are innate, define
the relationship of the organism to its environment when
it is born. Clearly, then, they will direct the early
experience of the child. The stereotyped reflex actions,

however, stemming from the physiological structure soon
change and give way to more complex, better adapted
activity. Their influence on the child is short lived,
but the functional invariants of adaptation and organisation continue to orient the whole of the child's subsequent
development. Piaget says:

> If there truly exists a functional nucleus of intellect-
> ual organisation which comes from the biological
> organisation in its most general aspect then it is
> apparent that this invariant will orient the whole of
> the successive structures which the mind will thus work
> out in its contact with reality. (1952, p.3)

Given the method of functioning and given the nature of
reality, the general nature of the knowledge possible for
human beings is predetermined. This is the case because
the basic explanation that Piaget offers for the development of intelligence is the transformation of one stage
into another. On traditional behaviourist explanations of
learning, although there has to be some unlearned ('instinctive', 'reflex') activity, to allow the learning process to
start, the characteristics of what is innate are not particularly important and do not have any influence beyond the
starting point of learning. Learning is explained in terms
of the piling up of associations, atomic 'bits' of experience. It is a cumulative process. Piaget denies that
learning can be cumulative and says that learning occurs
when the way in which thought and action is structured at
one stage changes in a qualitative way. The later structures are transformations of the earlier structures. The
transformation is brought about by experience. So the
nature of the later structure will be determined partly by
experience and partly by the nature of the previous structure. The reflexes are the first primitive action systems
and as a result of contact with the environment they are
changed until they gradually become less rigid and stylised
and eventually can be seen to be qualitatively different,
that is, a different stage or transformation appears.
Since this new structure is a transformation of the previous,
innate structure, it retains some of its properties. But
gradually, as stage succeeds stage, the specific properties
which characterised the reflex, for example, its specificity,
are lost. However, its most general, abstract properties,
that is, its organising ability still remain. In this sense
the innate structures orient the successive structures.

The innate functions of adaptation and organisation provide
the principles of transformation. Consequently they have a
much more direct effect on later structures than the innate

reflex structures do. One can see that as one structure is
transformed into the next there will eventually be very
little that is characteristic of the reflex action present
in the later 'thought' structures. But as transformation
explains each step between stages and transformation is
explained in terms of adaptation and organisation, the
features of these invariant functions will direct all
structures. Consequently what is 'innate' for Piaget is
important in a way that it is not for a non-genetic learning theorist. But what is 'innate' is a way of interacting
with the environment, not any specific piece of knowledge.

THE ISOMORPHISM BETWEEN BIOLOGICAL AND INTELLECTUAL FUNCTIONING

The sensori-motor period, providing as it does the transition from biological functioning to cognitive functioning,
shows the continuous chain of transformations that the
child's activity undergoes from the simple reflex response
to the inception of representational thought at the beginning of the preoperational stage. We can see how the
later more complex, cognitive abilities can grow out of
the initial biological capacity. He makes a distinction
between the 'way of functioning' and what it is that the
functions are being performed on, that is, the subject
matter of the functioning. It is the subject matter of the
functioning which identifies the level of functioning. In
biological functioning the subject matter will be food,
warmth; in sensori-motor functioning, the subject matter
will be actions; in cognitive functioning the subject matter
will be beliefs, ideas, values. But whatever the subject
matter, the functioning itself will always be the same process; it will have certain invariant, unchanging characteristics. The direction that is given to development by the
inherent characteristics of functioning itself, Piaget
refers to as orthogenesis.

This inherent direction is towards increasing differentiation and specification of the initial primitive action system. This increasing differentiation and specification
results in the emergence of novel and increasingly discrete
action systems that are also increasingly integrated within
themselves such that the most advanced (differentiated,
specialised, and internally integrated) systems hierarchic-
ally integrate (functionally subordinate and regulate) the
less developed systems. That is: one side of development
is progressive differentiation and specification, the other
side is progressive hierarchic integration and centralization.

What this means, in effect, is that the organism has certain
specific ways of interacting with the environment, that is,
accommodation and assimilation. The way in which accommodation and assimilation work are by altering the nature of
the structure that the organism is applying to reality in
order that the organism may assimilate more of it and
organising features of the environment so that they will be
more readily assimilable. The nature of the structures
that the organism is applying to reality can be altered in
two ways: (1) by becoming increasingly more microscopic,
that is, by making increasingly more specific distinctions
as with a child who calls all people mama, then learns that
some of them are dada, and then gradually learns that only
one of them is mama, (2) by becoming increasingly more
macroscopic in the sense of more abstract and general.
Thus particular objects or events can come to be seen as
instances of a more general class or principle.

We can see from the description of these stages that there
is a continuous chain of transformations from the simplest
reflex responses of the new born to the sophisticated thinking of the adult. In a sense then, we can readily accept
that the later intellectual structures 'grow out of' the
earlier biological structures if no more is meant by this
than that there is no break in the chain of transformations.

But Piaget wants to claim far more than this. Piaget makes
not only the uncontroversial claim that intellectual processes somehow grow out of or evolve out of biological ones.
But he makes the further claim that there is an isomorphism
between biological and intellectual functioning. By this
he seems at least to mean that the concepts that we use to
understand, describe and explain biological phenomena can
with equal application be used to understand, describe and
explain intellectual or cognitive phenomena.

His explanation of cognitive development as due to transformations of the subject which come about through 'compensation resulting from the activities of the subject in
response to external intrusions' (Piaget, 1962, p.101) is
supposed to gain its sense from the use of those concepts
in biology. The question is whether there is sufficient
analogy between Piaget's explanation and the homeostatic
mechanisms that maintain biological equilibria by compensating for biological changes, to give any sense to Piaget's
own explanation. In other words, when Piaget uses words
like assimilation, accommodation, equilibrium and the like,
what does he mean? He would argue that we can find out
what these terms mean by looking to biological explanations

which employ these terms since the meaning in both the
biological and the cognitive context will be the same.
But the question is, are these two contexts sufficiently
similar to permit the same concepts to be employed with an
unchanged sense? Piaget does not give any thorough or convincing examples of the workings of these processes in
biology. One example that he does give describes the
changes that occur in the eye as a result of the assimilation of light:

> Let us take for example the eye which develops under
> the influence of the use of vision (perception of
> lights, forms, etc.). From the physiological point of
> view it can be stated that light is nourishment for the
> eye. Light is absorbed and assimilated by sensitive
> tissues and this brings with it a correlative develop-
> ment of the organs affected. Such a process undoubtedly
> presupposes an aggregate of mechanisms whose start may
> be very complex. But if we adhere to a global descrip-
> tion, that of behaviour, and so of psychology - the
> things seen constitute nourishment essential to the eye
> since it is they which impose the continuous use to
> which the organs owe their development. The eye needs
> light images just as the whole body needs chemical
> nourishment, energy, etc. (Piaget, 1952, p.42)

One can begin to see from this sketchy example what Piaget
has in mind. The organ develops as a result of functioning
and whatever is necessary to its functioning properly (and
not to the general functioning of the organism itself) is
regarded as nourishment for that organ. The parallel process during the sensori-motor period is the practice of a
particular schema. It is the practice of that schema,
rather than any overall need that the organism has, which
leads to the development of the schema. This makes the
explanation of the assimilation of light by the eye depend
on the analogy with the assimilation of food by the organism. In fact, although he never himself gives a detailed
description of it, Piaget obviously has in mind, as an
example of biological adaptation, the taking in of food by
the organism. He continually uses words like 'nourishment',
'reality aliments' and the like to suggest the process of
adaptation in both biological and intellectual functioning.

In the process of assimilating food we can see the distinction that Piaget makes between assimilation and accommodation. The organism first of all has to be an organism of
the type that can assimilate that kind of food. An amoeba,
for example, is in no position to ever contemplate a plate-
ful of steak and chips. But given that the initial

organisation allows for the assimilation of that kind of
food by the organism, still the organism has to accommodate
itself to the features of that particular kind of food. The
food substance has somehow to enter the organism so it must
open its mouth or whatever corresponds to a mouth. If the
substance is hard the organism must chew it, must swallow
it, and it must possess the right kinds of digestive juices
to deal with the particular chemical properties of the food.
The organism, then, must alter its own state in order to
assimilate the food.

Conversely, the food itself will be altered until eventually
it will lose all its former characteristics and become part
of the substance of the organism itself. Hard food will be
chewed until it is soft, swallowed, broken down by the
digestive juices and its component elements converted into
energy, muscle, blood or whatever.

The process is consequently one of mutual modification of
the organism and of the environment, in this case represented
by food substances, with which it has to cope. The distinction between assimilation and accommodation is a conceptual
distinction in the sense that we can understand the difference although we never observe two distinct processes. In
any process of adaptation there is never assimilation without accommodation and never accommodation without assimilation.

Adaptation is what Piaget calls the 'dynamic' aspect of
intellectual functioning. Any intellectual act in which
assimilation and accommodation are in some sort of balance
or equilibrium is an intellectual adaptation.

Intellectual functioning, as well as biological functions
like digestion, is also characterised by organisation as
well as adaptation. Adaptation and organisation are the
two sides of the same coin since adaptation presupposes
some underlying organisation and organisation or structures
are formed through adaptation.

Digestion is a process which can only be carried on within
a certain structure. Each of the organs involved has its
own place and functions within the general structure. If
that structure breaks down or becomes radically disorganised
then digestion cannot be carried on. Piaget thinks that
cognition is something which is organised in the same sort
of way as digestion can be said to be organised.

In talking about intellectual functioning, assimilation
refers to the structuring of objects that goes on when we
understand something. To understand something involves
fitting it into the context of the understanding that we
already have. We cannot understand something unless we
already have a background knowledge and can fit the new
information into the intellectual structure that we have
already learned. In this sense, in the sense that we are
fitting a new object into an already existing structure,
we are structuring it. We are finding out, by trying to
fit it into the knowledge that we already have, what properties it has relative to other things that we already
understand and we are finding out where it fits in. Piaget
represents this as a process of actually changing an object.
The specific properties of this organisation change greatly
as development progresses but there are always certain
stage-independent characteristics. All intellectual
organisations can be conceived of as structures (that is,
totalities) of systems of relations among elements. Acts
are also organised in terms of means to ends. With this
basic potential for organisation the organism builds up its
successive cognitive structures by the processes of assimilation and accommodation. Assimilation in this context refers
to the fact that every act of intelligence, however rudimentary (primitive perception to hypothetico-deductive
reasoning) presupposes an interpretation of something in
external reality; that is, an assimilation of that something to some kind of meaning system in the subject's
cognitive organisation.

In Piaget's terms: to adapt intellectually is to assimilate
something in terms of some enduring structure or organisation within oneself. But no matter how much of the adaptation process consists of assimilating the elements to old
structures, some of it must be accommodating to reality.
Reality cannot be infinitely malleable and certainly no
intellectual development can occur unless the subject in
some way adjusts the structures that he has already developed
so that new elements will fit into them without completely
changing their nature. These two aspects of adaptation are
in fact simultaneous and indissociable. As in the case of
the ingestion of food the incorporation of reality aliments
always implies both an assimilation to structure and an
accommodation of structure. To assimilate an event it is
necessary at the same time to accommodate to it and vice
versa. At different levels of development these two aspects
of adaptation are in varying degrees of balance with regard
to each other. A state in which the two processes are
completely belanced is said to be a state of equilibrium

where the organism is making the best use he can of his
past knowledge and the information he is receiving from
the environment. It is at a stage like this that he 'pene-
trates deeper into reality' because he is neither being too
egocentric and forcing elements into structures where they
do not really fit (thus causing some of their characteristics
to be overlooked) nor is he trusting too much to sensory
evidence, but can use what he has learnt from past activity
in the world.

CRITICISMS OF THE BIOLOGICAL MODEL

It is difficult to defend a view that the concepts of
assimilation and accommodation are suggested in any simple
way by his experiments on children. They are at the basis
of his theory of development in that they are the basic
mechanisms of his epistemological view. I think that Piaget
realised that with these functional invariants he was doing
philosophy and not psychology. The fact that he attempts
to defend these concepts by comparing them with other epist-
omological views such as classical empiricism and Kantian
a priorism suggests that he was attempting to set out the
philosophical presuppositions of his theory rather than the
empirical concepts of it. That he should attempt to do
this is a merit. Too many psychological 'theories' deduce
general laws about the behaviour of organisms without giving
any indication of the kind of organism they suppose themselves to be dealing with. Piaget states clearly that the
organism he is discussing is in progressively more intimate
and active contact with his environment and possesses
certain mechanisms which permit, direct and extend this
interaction.

Intuitively, this sounds plausible but the enormous difficulty of finding ways of measuring the balance of assimila-
tion/accommodation without introducing norms makes it more
or less useless as an explanatory concept both practically
and theoretically. Piaget's method seems to be a mixture
of experiment and a priori reasoning. To a certain extent,
his experiments show the increasing decentration of the
child's thought, for example, he ceases to think that an
event in his environment which is caused must have been
caused by him, and his increasing independence of immediate
perceptual data, for example, his increasing assurance in
stating that the mass of a lump of dough has not been
changed even when its shape has and it 'looks bigger'.
But when Piaget extracts from (or imposes on) these activities certain logical and mathematical structures and refuses

to acknowledge that the state of development of the child
is a state of equilibrium until the child's activities can
be shown to conform to the logical structures, then he seems
to be defining the balance of assimilation and accommodation
by means of external norms. This will be discussed in
greater detail in Chapter 4.

Another difficulty with the assimilation/accommodation
view as a theory of experience is in separating out those
elements of experience which are due to assimilation and
those which are due to accommodation. Admittedly Piaget
time and again insists that in any interaction with the
environment both assimilation and accommodation are in-
separable. But if the conceptual distinction can be made
so far as the function of the two activities is concerned
it should be also possible, one would expect, to make it as
far as the content of the two activities is concerned. In
the biological example one can see fairly clearly which
aspects of the ingestion-of-food process are due to the
accommodation of the organism to the particular character
of the food and which aspects due to the changing of the
food by the organism. But even in the simple cognitive
examples the distinction is less easy to make. For example,
in talking of the perception of a red cushion by a subject
one could say that the cushiony aspect of it was a more
intellectual, structured characteristic and would be more
on the assimilation side whereas the redness of it was
certainly something imposed on us by the object and to
which we had to adapt ourselves. But even in calling the
colour red, even in recognising that it is a colour, we
are assimilating it to some meaning system, to some schema.
It is not simply something imposed by reality.

One might argue that the problem lies not so much in appre-
hending which aspects of an experience are due to assimilation and which to accommodation as in explaining it.
Putting things into words is organising those things according to the structures that are available to us in our
language. As soon as an experience is put into words, then
it is assimilated to the structures of language. Perhaps
we could have unassimilated experiences so long as we did
not try to describe them. Our language cannot describe unassimilated reality. Piaget would argue that these difficulties were simply a sign of the intimate connection
between accommodation and assimilation. But this is not
enough. We can agree that there is an intimate connection
between the two and still want to know more about it than
Piaget tells us. It is important for him to be able to say
which aspects of our experience are the incorporating of

new elements into schemata and which are accommodations to
intractable elements of external reality. At some points
he seems to be wanting to say that those aspects of our
experience concerned with assimilation are the structural
aspects of it, whereas the aspects concerned with accommodation are more concerned with the content.

What this seems to imply is that the act of organising and
structuring the incoming reality 'aliments' from the environment is actually changing them. This is also implied, of
course, by the analogy with digestion. Incoming aliments
are undoubtedly altered and eventually lose their own
character altogether becoming absorbed into the organism.

While it is clear that the developing child must accommodate
his beliefs and expectations to the environment, it is not
so clear why or how he would change the incoming information
from the environment. One can understand that he might
ignore some of it or be unable to comprehend it and so pay
it no attention. But in what sense can he be said to alter
it to make it fit into his schemata?

The connection between Kant and Piaget has already been
made. To understand the sense in which Piaget is claiming
that the incoming information from the environment is changed
during the process of assimilation, it is necessary to consider Kant's claim that 'perceptions without concepts are
blind'. Kant claimed that knowledge involves 'two elements:
firstly the concept through which an object as such is
thought (the Category), and secondly the perception in
which it is given' (Kant, 1929, 117, B146). If we perceive
an object in the sense that it stimulates our senses we
cannot be said to know anything about it unless we also can
judge it as being an instance of some concept. Knowledge
is, for Kant, 'applying concepts to the data of perception'.

Kant was attempting to show the close connection between
perception and thinking which he felt had been overlooked
by the empiricist philosophers like Hume. Far from gaining
knowledge directly from perception of the environment, Kant
claimed that perception provides only the conditions for
the application of concepts whose source is the pure understanding. Only the two elements together yield knowledge.

Kant does not, however, present the applying of a concept
to perceived reality as altering or changing that reality.
Reality is what it is and merely recognising it as such
does not make it into something different.

Piaget, on the other hand, does see the assimilation of
reality aliments to a schema as altering those reality
aliments. If we are to understand assimilation in the way
in which it is understood in biology, then the assimilation
of food in digestion results in the total loss of identity
of the original input. Can this be what happens when we
learn something about our environment and fit it into our
web of knowledge and previous experience?

Piaget is representing the gaining of knowledge as the
result of an interaction between something which is objective (external environment) and something which is subjective (mental structure or schemata). The offerings of the
environment must be processed by the individual and fitted
into the mental structures that he has developed before he
can make any use of them. Whether the result of this process is to count as objective knowledge or not depends, for
Piaget, on some intrinsic features of the schemata. If the
schemata are reversible, operational structures having a
high degree of abstraction, then the result is said to be
objective knowledge. If the child is at a lower level of
development, then his viewpoint is distorted by his own
egocentricity and his own over-reliance on perceptual data.

The understanding of structural frameworks corrects the
distorted picture of the world that the peculiarities of
our perceptual system induce. It is interesting that
although he goes along with the empiricist principle that
without experience there can be no knowledge, Piaget's
final view is very different from that of the empiricists
who hold that experience is the source of all our knowledge.
He regards the increase in abstract knowledge and the
increase in the organisation of the environment according
to abstract concepts as a way of approaching a truer description and a better understanding of reality. The
empiricist viewpoint leads in general to the position that
the further away our knowledge gets from 'simple perception', the more abstract and organised it becomes, the less
likely are we to have a true picture of the world. Piaget
thinks that the comparative dependence of the young children
on the data of sense perception leads to a distortion
of reality which is only corrected by the realisation of
the necessity of logical and mathematical constants. What
Piaget calls the 'phenomenism' of the young child, its
dependence on sense perception for information, gradually
gives way to 'construction'. The child relies more on its
knowledge about the structure of the world than on sense
perception, the 'evidence of its own eyes' (Piaget, 1950,
vol.III, pp.295-306).

There are two main problems here. The first is that this
view, with its 'inherent' direction of development and its
acceptance of the evolutionary dictum that 'ontogeny recap-
itulates phylogeny' is suggesting that the child's inherited
capacities are sufficient to lead it to construct one and
only one conception of reality; to reconstruct time and
again, the same concepts of space and time, the same concepts of measurement and number, the same concepts of
causality as generations before. This is to recapitulate
not the biological history of the race, but the cultural
history. And the child is supposed to do this all alone,
with no help from the culture.

Hamlyn has argued persuasively (a propos of Chomsky) that
any picture of 'the child as a solitary inquirer attempting
to discover the truth about the world ... with no-one to
help him' must be rejected (Hamlyn, 1973). He refers to
the distinction made by Hebb between early learning and
late learning. Later learning is based on prior knowledge
and understanding and is typically swift and sudden but
early learning which involves the slow sorting out of basic
categories and distinctions which are made by human beings
in their ways of understanding the world is not only slow
and gradual but relies heavily on the establishment of
personal relationships with other human beings who not only
know what the world is like as seen through human eyes but
who also care that the child should come to see it that
way too. This problem will be discussed at greater length
in later chapters. It would seem more reasonable to assume
as Toulmin argues: 'that whatever general "native capacities"
a child possesses are capable of realizing themselves in a
wide range of different specific ways (or none) depending
on the particular cultural context within which he has the
opportunity to exercise them' (1971).

The second major problem is the representation of the gaining of knowledge as an interaction between something objective and something subjective. Piaget describes what we
might call 'having a concept' as being in possession of a
particular, subjective mental structure. The fact that all
subjects at the same level of development are presumed to
possess identical mental structures does not make the structures any the less subjective since they have their origins
in the subject's own consciousness. The objectivity of
thought does not depend on any intrinsic features of the
thought itself but refers to the openness of that thought
to inspection and criticism by others. Piaget himself sometimes admits the role played by discussion and the airing
of views in the development of objective thought. But

because he does not think that social influences can have
a very marked effect on the child until at least the age
of eight or nine, the benefits gained from discussion are
very late in appearing. The explanation of the development
of the logico-mathematical structures of thought makes no
reference whatever to the effect of criticism by or discussion with others.

This problem, too, will be taken up again in later chapters.
Both these problems grow out of the biological functionalist approach that Piaget adopts towards his explanation of
mental development. While that approach may have its
advantages in emphasising the connectedness and continuity
of human development it is most acceptable only as far as
the period of sensori-motor activity. Even at that stage,
at least one of the basic concepts, that of assimilation,
cannot be directly transferred from the biology to the psychology. As higher levels of development are achieved, the
strain between the nature of rational thought and the biological concepts which are used to describe it will become
more obvious.

SUMMARY

The essentially biological bias of Piaget's theory is more
obvious at the earlier stages of development, the sensori-
motor and pre-operational. He uses several analogies taken
from biology and describes learning at this stage as the
processes of assimilation and accommodation. In describing
the later operational stages, less emphasis is placed on
adaptation and far more on the organisation of understanding. However, Piaget claims that even at the highest level
of functioning intellectual activity is an extension of
biological activity. It performs the same function (that
of adaptation) in essentially the same way by means of
organisation, assimilation and accommodation.

Unlike many psychological theorists Piaget has set his
theory into a detailed epistemological background. Whatever
the shortcomings of the assimilation/accommodation model,
it is at least explicit and describes the sort of creature
Piaget envisages the human organism to be. And with this
conception of the kind of device that he sees himself to
be dealing with, all the other main points of Piaget's
theory would seem to follow. It does make sense, with
this conception of the organism/environment relationship,
to claim that a child cannot be influenced by certain kinds
of stimuli yet (he lacks the structures with which to

assimilate them) but he will be influenced by them later
(when he has developed the relevant structures). With this
view it makes sense to see development as a step by step
process of structural changes, each structure building on
the previous one and yet going beyond it. The interaction
between the organism and the environment is always insisted
on and Piaget's account never allows this relationship to
degenerate into a passive organism controlled by an external
stimulus as, for example, the behaviourist account does.

However, although Piaget's account of the sensori-motor
stage offers an interesting account of the transition from
biological functioning to some kind of mental functioning,
his concepts become more and more inappropriate as higher
levels of mental development are reached. His concepts of
assimilation and accommodation finally must be recognised
as giving a misleading view of intellectual development.

Structuralism and logic

PREVIEW

Chapter 3 addresses the most central notion in Piaget's
theory, that of a structure. It is difficult to see how
any theory which purported to describe the growth of
knowledge in an individual could be without it. In Piaget's
theory, cognitive structures lie between the general invariants of function and the specific variants of content.
They form a bridge between the data of perception on the
one hand and abstract thinking on the other. However
critical one may be of the particular structural analysis
that Piaget has made it must be acknowledged that he has
insisted on the central importance of the concept for a
psychological theory in an area where its central position
has sometimes been overlooked. The gaining of knowledge
involves the connecting of ideas, beliefs and information
into some kind of coherent, structured pattern.

PIAGET'S STRUCTURALISM

The particular structuralism that Piaget puts forward relies
heavily on a formalisation of the child's inferred mental
structures. The earliest structures that possess enough
generality to permit them to be described formally are the
structures of the stage of concrete operations. The
structures of this stage correspond to what Piaget calls a
'grouping'. This is a concept derived from a combination
of some of the properties of mathematical groups and some
of the properties of mathematical lattices.

Piaget believes that the structures of pure mathematics are
simply more abstract and general versions of those early
structures of the natural thought of the child. There is
consequently a genetic relation between the abstract structures of pure logic and mathematics and the lower level
structures of the concrete operational stage which are
derived in their turn from the action systems of the sensori-
motor stage.

The question of the ontological status of these 'thought
structures' naturally arises at this point. Must the
structures be seen as merely heuristic models whose justification lies in their usefulness for predicting the
course of development? Or can we accept Piaget's claim
that to say that structures only exist in the mind of the
psychologist 'would be like saying that the child can eat
and breathe but that his stomach and lungs only exist in
the mind of the physiologist' (Inhelder and Piaget, 1979,
p.169).

Piaget recognises structure at many different levels. The
physiological and neurophysiological structures of the
organism provide the infrastructure for the psychological
structures of the mind which in turn provide the infrastructure for the logical structures of knowledge.

Piaget is not a neurophysiologist, so apart from his view
that neurophysiological structures underlie the structures
of consciousness he has no further interest in them. Conversely, he does not claim to be a professional logician,
so his interest in the logical structures of logic and
mathematics is concerned with seeing how far those structures correspond to the psychological structures of the
developing subject.

His interest in the psychological structures of behaviour
is confined to those actions which either are or will become
interiorised in the form of operations. He says:
>   In the case of those actions which will become interior-
>   ised in the form of operations, the schemes of actions
>   then include their most general characteristics, that
>   is to say the characteristics of co-ordination as such.
>   In fact actions such as combining (or separating),
>   ordering (in one direction or in the complementary
>   direction), putting into correspondence etc., actions
>   which form the starting point of the elementary operations
>   of classes and relations, are not simply actions capable
>   of being performed on external objects; they are primarily
>   actions whose schemes express the general co-ordinations

of all actions, for every action (from simply reflexes
to actions which are learned such as picking a flower
or lighting a pipe) presuppose at least one of the
co-ordinations consisting of the ordering of successive
movements of the combining of elements etc.
(Beth and Piaget, 1966, p.235)

If Piaget's subject of study is only those actions which
will later reappear as operations, he is concerned only
with a small part of the behavioural repertoire of the
child. He is in fact concerned with what he calls the
'epistemic subject'. He maintains that it is legitimate
to talk about such a thing as the epistemic subject because
the mechanisms by which understanding develops in individuals are the same regardless of ability or culture. Knowledge of the structure of the world develops from the
initial awareness of the ways in which actions can be co-
ordinated. This 'logic of action' is not something which
could be different from one individual to the next. Consequently, there is a distinction between the person
viewed as a psychological subject with his own particular
experiences, prejudices, likes and dislikes and the person
viewed as an epistemic or knowing subject. The subject of
the knowledge of the epistemic subject is what Piaget calls
the 'logico-mathematical' structure of the world. This is
the same for everyone and knowledge of it is acquired
through the common processes of assimilation and accommodation. Piaget says:

There is the psychological subject centred in the
conscious ego whose functional role is incontestable,
but which is not the origin of any structure of general
knowledge; but there is also the 'epistemic subject'
or that which is common to all subjects at the same
level of development, whose cognitive structures derive
from the most general mechanisms of the co-ordination
of actions. (Beth and Piaget, 1966, p.308)

Piaget is prepared to recognise that the particular age at
which a child reaches a certain level of development is
dependent on previous education, culture and ability. It
may differ fairly widely from child to child, even within
the same cultural group. The level of development is
defined by the actions that the child can do not by the age
he has reached. Piaget is not even concerned with everything that his group of subjects have in common at a certain
level of development. He is concerned only with those
actions which are of the kind that he calls 'logico-mathematical'. Paralleling the distinction between the psychological subject and the epistemic subject is the distinction

between the actions and experience characteristic of these
two subjects. An example of logico-mathematical experience
is the ordering of a group of objects. What the subject is
concerned with here (in so far as he is performing logico-
mathematical actions) is not the nature of the objects or
any particular characteristics that they might have, it is
his own actions in doing the ordering and the objective
result of his own actions, that is to say, the fact that
what was a group is now an ordered set. A psychological
concern with the same action would mean introspection of
the subjective characteristics of the action, for example,
whether the action was hard or easy to perform, whether the
subject enjoyed doing it or not.

These sorts of considerations do not enter into logico-
mathematical activity, or at least, into those aspects of
activity which are relevant to the development of logico-
mathematical thought. What is important in logico-mathematical activity is the results of the actions and, again,
only those results which are 'objective' and 'necessary'.
Piaget says:
> On the other hand, logico-mathematical experience is
> not concerned with action as an individual process but
> with its results as objective and as necessary.
> (Beth and Piaget, 1966, p.234)

The main features of Piaget's concept of the epistemic subject are not derived from his observations of children.
They are derived from his view of the nature of human
understanding and what is to count as the understanding of
elementary logical, mathematical and physical concepts.
He is interested in only a very small part of the behaviour
of the children he uses as subjects and this part is
characterised not by the intrinsic features that it has
itself but by the objectivity and necessity of its results.
It is the fact that a certain action has an objective result
which is seen by the observer to be necessary and which will
later be seen by the subject to be necessary which identifies
it as a logico-mathematical action and, consequently, an
action of the epistemic subject.

It can.be seen that it is not by chance that the structures
which a child develops through logico-mathematical activity
are common to all subjects at the same level of development.
They must be common because it is only those structures
which can be seen as leading to a valid understanding of
the logico-mathematical structure of experience which are
going to be attended to.

Piaget is interested in the actions of the epistemic subject
rather than those of the psychological subject because his
primary concern is the emergence in the individual of an
understanding of what he calls 'valid forms of thought'.
He believes that the validity of a form of thought is something intrinsic to that form and that it is connected with
its degree of structure and organisation. Talk about knowledge and understanding implies standards of truth and
correctness which are over and above an individual's own
belief that he knows or understands something. These standards of truth and correctness are public standards. One
cannot simply develop one's own criteria for validity, truth
and correctness. Their development can be traced through
the cultural history of the society and the individual must
conform to them if he is to be credited with valid knowledge.
An individual must learn to conform to these public standards. This involves bringing his own views, which as Piaget
points out, are initially distorted by his egocentrism, into
line with those of others.

Piaget represents this process as the progressive construction by multiple individuals, of identical mental structures.
In spite of his suggestions that explanations of the development of understanding might be offered in terms of educational
and linguistic pressures, he himself seriously underestimates,
not to say neglects, any social, linguistic, or educational
pressures particularly at the young age. The explanation
he offers is in terms of 'structures resulting from the
subjects' actions or operations themselves, arising from
successive stages of equilibrium reached during development'.

The question is whether a theory of development couched in
such terms could account for the individual's gaining access
to the intersubjective standards and criteria which define
the objective forms of knowledge. In this chapter we will
look mainly at the concept of structure itself. The next
chapter will deal with the equilibrium model and Chapter 5
will explore the concept of objective knowledge.

THE SCHEMA

The first recognisable structures that 'result from the
subjects' actions or operations themselves' are the elementary schemata of the sensori-motor stage. The schema is a
concept of central importance to Piaget's theory since it
is the sensori-motor precursor of the cognitive structures
which characterise the later stages of intellectual development. Although the concept of a schema is independent of

any particular stage and is likely to be used as a synonym
for 'structure' at any stage it is used most extensively
and consistently with reference to the sensori-motor period.

Firstly, the schema is defined by the behavioural patterns
which it refers to. But although it is defined by the
behavioural patterns it refers to it is not right to say
that it is just these patterns. Piaget's view of what
constitutes an explanation in psychology is that it is
necessary not only to show how one general law of development can be deduced from others but also to provide some
model, some substratum which would 'represent' the formal
explanation: the schema is that substratum. Piaget would
say that an infant who performs an organised sequence of
grasping behaviours is in fact applying a grasping schema
to reality not that the behaviour itself constitutes that
schema (Piaget, 1952, pp.405-07; Piaget, 1957a, pp.46-74).
But, he is applying it to reality and that is something
else than just behaving in ways which can be described
according to the schema. The implication is that the child
as a result of assimilation/accommodation now has a certain
cognitive structure which he will apply on more than one
occasion. He not only does behave in certain ways, he is
more likely to in the future; he has a certain structure.
Piaget says:
> One can conceive of intelligence as the development of
> an assimilatory activity whose functional laws are laid
> down as early as organic life and whose successive
> structures serving it as organs are elaborated by inter-
> action between itself and the external environment.
> (Piaget, 1952, p.359)

There are certain characteristics that a behaviour sequence
must possess if it is to be called a schema. The schema
does apply to behaviour sequences of widely different
complexity and generality. Compare, for example, the simple
sucking sequence of the new-born child with the complex
schemata involved in playing a game of football. But to be
called a schema at all, a behaviour sequence must be organised into a totality. It must have a certain cohesiveness
and it must, as a unit, be fairly stable. A behaviour
sequence which is not repeated by the child does not count
as the application of a certain schema. Piaget says:
> As far as 'totality' is concerned, we have already
> emphasised that every schema of assimilation constitutes
> a true totality, that is to say an ensemble of sensori-
> motor elements mutually dependent or unable to function
> without each other. It is due to the fact that schemata
> present this kind of structure that mental assimilation

is possible and any object whatever can be incorporated
or serve as aliment to a given schema.
(Piaget, 1952, p.244)

One can see this 'ensemble of sensori-motor elements mutually dependent or unable to function without each other',
in any behaviour sequence which counts as the application
of a schema to reality. For example, an elementary schema
of grasping consists of interconnected reaching, finger
curling, and retracting which together make up a stable,
identifiable unit. Piaget also describes the schema as a
sort of sensori-motor concept: 'The schema, as it appeared
to us, constitutes a sort of sensori-motor concept, or
more broadly, the motor equivalent of a system of relations
and classes' (Piaget, 1952, p.385). What the significance
is of calling the schema a kind of concept is not quite
clear but it seems to be referring to the fact that the
schema identifies a class of action sequences which might
all differ from each other to a certain extent but which
all have what Piaget calls the same 'meaning' for the subject. One can imagine, for example, that a series of
applications of the grasping schema might all differ
slightly from each other depending on the nature of the
object to be grasped, the physiological condition of the
infant etc., but a grasping schema is said to be applied
whenever sequences which all have the same 'aim' or 'end'
for the subject are performed.

The schema then, is said to be a sort of concept because
it has a certain degree of generality; it affords principles for distinguishing one kind of behaviour sequence
from another; and it describes what an object 'means' for
the child. An object like a rattle attached to a cot which
a child can grasp and shake but cannot, perhaps, suck
'means' whatever the child can do with it, that is, it
means 'something which can be grasped and shaken but not
sucked'.

Because of this 'meaning', a schema can be described as a
way of seeing the world, a certain aspect on the world.
But it is a fluid, dynamic 'way of seeing' which is always
likely to be changed by experience. The schema is a
plastic way of organising experience, it is not a rigid
mould into which experience is poured. The schemata are
'mobile frames' successively applied to various contents,
and the schemata are created by the activity of the child
in the environment.

The schemata, then, can be seen as structures which the
child can use to organise his actions in the environment.
They are not simply descriptions of the child's behaviour
offered by a sophisticated observer. They are meant to be
structures that the child has developed and that he can
bring to bear on his own experience. However, the child
is not himself aware that that is what he is doing.

OPERATIONAL THOUGHT

Although the child would seem to have made a fair amount
of progress by the end of the sensori-motor period, the
'concepts' that it has are very elementary; his experience
is very limited. The beginning of development involved a
slow sorting out of basic concepts like those of space and
time, object and causality. It is not until he begins to
think 'operationally' that his development begins to proceed more quickly. For operational thinking the ability
to symbolise and understand signs is necessary and the
development of this skill is the main characteristic of
the stage of preoperational thought. Genuine operational
structures make their first appearance at the stage of
concrete operations.

Piaget claims that in the subject's activities there are
two kinds of structures: those with laws of combination
peculiar to the system as such and those structures capable
of exhibiting the same form regardless of their content.

An example of the first type of structure is the perceptual
Gestalt which gives rise to perceptual illusions in spite
of the fact that we understand that these are illusions
and know how the object should look. But the perceptual
illusion is not the only Gestalt that Piaget thinks affects
the subject's activities. He also includes wholes such as
the geometrical form immediately organised and standing out
against a background. These structures are distinguished,
for Piaget, by their non-additive combination and their
irreversibility. By their non-additive combination Piaget
means that they cannot simply be added together as numbers
can to produce an objective sum. For example, if to line
A one adds another line A' shorter than A, A will be overestimated in relation to A'. As far as the perceptual
Gestalt is concerned $(A+A') \neq A+A'$.

Gestalts are also irreversible in the sense that once one
has seen a Gestalt one cannot 'unsee' it and one cannot
turn the Gestalt around and see it another way as one can

either add or subtract numbers, count from right to left
or left to right, roll out or squash up a piece of dough,
etc. They are due to the peculiarities of our own perceptual systems, and any explanation of them must refer to
physiology.

The kind of structure that Piaget is interested in is of
the second kind. Those structures which exhibit the same
form regardless of their content also tend to take on
additive and reversible forms of combination. In
'Structuralism' (1970c), Piaget characterises a structure
as a system of transformations which includes laws and is
conserved or enriched by the interplay of its transformations. The transformations take place within the system.
The structure is a totality which undergoes transformations
and is self-regulatory.

In cognitive structures the elements forming the content
of the structure are perceptions, memories, concepts, operations, structures or 'un objet quelqu'onque' in logic and
mathematics. The relations between the elements giving
the form to the structure can be spatio-temporal, causal,
implicative, etc. The form then is constituted by the way
in which the elements are related to each other. The
content is constituted by whatever it is that is being
related.

This distinction between form and content might at first
sight appear simple. But confusions can arise because what
was form at one level of development can become content at
the next level. At the level of sensori-motor intelligence
the content is objects like the blanket-to-suck, the doll-
to-swing. The form is constituted by relations between them
springing from the child's power for action; for example,
the doll can be swung, sucked, shaken. Here observables
give the content and the general co-ordination of actions
give the form.

At the stage of concrete operations the content is still
provided by objects, at least, initially. The child in
order to count needs beads, sweets, matches to count with.
But the form is now provided by the logico-mathematical
framework that the subject has developed for himself. For
example, in a structure like conservation the operations
of identity, reversibility and reciprocity are the form
while the 'observables', for example, quantity of liquid,
weight, number of objects, are the content.

At the next stage, that of formal operations, the operations
of identity, reversibility and reciprocity become the content for the higher level, more abstract reasoning of the
stage of formal, mathematical thinking.

An example of the kind of structure that Piaget is concerned
with which illustrates the additive and reversible nature
of cognitive structure is, for example; at all levels of
development there exist classificatory forms of behaviour
either as forms of classification or else inherent in
other activities. Either the subject will actually divide
a number of objects into collections or else he will act on
them in some way which implies certain classifications, he
might try to grasp them and then they will be divided into
objects which can be grasped and objects which cannot be
grasped. Clearly, at all levels, these classifications
cannot exist independently of each other. From the very
beginning there is some sort of rudimentary system of relations between the classes. At the sensori-motor level this
already shows itself. If a new object is given to a baby
of 8-10 months, it will be successively seized, shaken,
sucked, rubbed against the edges of the cradle, etc., as if
(in Piaget's words) in order to understand its nature, the
child successively incorporates it into its own successive
schemes of action. Between these schemes there are many
structural relations, for example: everything which can be
grasped can be seen but the converse is not true; everything
which can be heard can be seen but the converse is not true;
there are objects which can be seen and grasped at the same
time; others which possess the first property without the
second; others the second without the first and others
neither of the two and so on. There is, in short, what
Piaget calls a 'schematism of sensori-motor action' which
has a certain classificatory structure, however elementary.
At other points he refers to this as 'the general mechanism
of the co-ordination of actions'. This structure is not the
result of any idiosyncracies that the child might have.
What Piaget is concerned with is what is common to all
normal children at this stage and any deviations from the
normal classificatory scheme which might be the result of
physical deformity, for example, are not dealt with.

What Piaget is dealing with in fact is what he calls 'the
logic of action'. Later abstract logic such as that of
logical or mathematical systems is seen as a refinement of
this much earlier, more primitive but structurally similar
logic of action. This classification of actions and the
relationships between them does not depend on any of the
characteristics of the child. Even when the child has

outgrown the tendency to try to suck everything that it can grasp it will still be true that whatever can be grasped can be sucked. Piaget is concerned with 'objective relations' between actions. At all levels these classifications will exhibit their laws of structural wholes and the organisation tends more and more to show two general characteristics: a certain additivity (A + A = B) and a certain reversibility (B - A' = A) making these systems not only more flexible but also more intelligible than simple Gestalts. Piaget's concept of objective knowledge begins to emerge here. In the first place, he means not simply what is actually common to a certain number of children but what must be common, that is the 'logic of action' that we have described. And on the other hand by 'objective' he means 'intelligible'. He does not mean intelligible in the sense of simple to understand but in the sense of there being something there to understand. The simple Gestalt is inexplicable except perhaps on physiological grounds, but the structure of classification systems is explicable in terms of the logic of actions and the kinds of operations that are concerned here. There is certainly an advance in the complexity of the content with these reversible structures compared with the simple perceptual Gestalt. But it is not because of this fact that they are said to be more intelligible. It is because the complexity is a complexity of structure which can be explained in terms of relations between parts and according to structural laws.

THE EARLIEST STRUCTURES - GROUPINGS

Mathematics and logic are autonomous and normative in the sense that they are not describing any actual thought processes but are prescribing what rational, logical thought should look like. According to Piaget, psychology seeks causal explanations of the positions that logicians and mathematicians are led to adopt as a result of their purely logical and mathematical researches. Psychology attempts to show in terms of genetic processes how 'pure' logic and mathematics is possible. Instead of trying to find the most general characteristics of structures as the logician or the mathematician might do, Piaget is interested in showing the genesis of structures. What he tries to do is to find out the characteristics of the first organised actions that could qualify as structures at all. The simple schemata could be said to have some of the properties of structures but their application is too restricted and their structural properties too particular for them to be seen as structures in any clear and general sense. The

first appearance of any system complex and general enough
to be called a structure is at the level of concrete operations. Piaget defines an operation as an action which
either is or is capable of becoming interiorised and which
is reversible and co-ordinated into a structural whole.

By 'becoming interiorised' Piaget means that the action is
one which could eventually be performed in thought rather
than in overt action. Reversibility implies, roughly, the
ability to 'return' to one's starting point. Originally
Piaget claimed that this ability did not appear until the
level of concrete operations was achieved. But he later
realised that children are able, well before this stage,
to return to a starting point. They can find their way
home from a friend's house, for example, they can dress and
undress dolls, build towers of bricks and knock them down.
What is special about the reversibility of the concrete
operational stage is that the child is paying attention
not simply to the result of his action, that is, the fact
that he started off from home and how here is is again.
At the concrete operational stage the child is paying
attention to the process of the action itself. He sees an
action such as dressing and undressing a doll as a doing
and an undoing. The preoperational child sees it as two
distinct actions with two distinct results. The first
action starts off with an undressed doll and concludes with
a dressed one. The second action starts with a dressed
doll and concludes with an undressed one. The concrete
operational child sees that it is the same action performed
in two different directions. He is capable of understanding the concept of returning or undoing.

Operations are actions which either are or will be interiorised, that is, performable in thought or using a model or
analogue and which show operational reversibility. Concrete
operations are those which occur in the manipulation of
objects. And all the structures at the level of concrete
operations can be reduced to a single model which Piaget
calls a 'grouping'. The 'grouping' is not a mathematical
structure since it is lacking in logical generality because
of the multiple restrictions imposed on it by the lack of
generality of its content (it describes the structure of
concrete operations which are always performed on actual
objects and so are constrained by the properties of those
objects). Piaget gives a formalisation of the grouping
(Piaget, 1937a and b) which shows that it shares some of
the properties of the mathematical group and some of the
properties of the lattice. A group is an abstract system
which has a set of arbitrary elements and a specified

operation performed on these elements such that the following conditions hold:
  1 COMBINATION - Any two elements in the system can be
  combined by means of the specified operation and they
  will yield another element of the system. Thus A op B
  = C and C is an element of the group.
  2 ASSOCIATIVITY - (A op B) op C = A op (B op C) that
  is, combining C with the product of B and A gives the
  same result as combining with A the product of C and B.
  3 IDENTITY - Among the set of elements there is one
  which when combined with any other element in the system
  leaves that element unchanged. If we call this element
  0 then A op 0 = A.
  4 REVERSIBILITY - For each element of the group there
  is another element called its inverse. When these are
  combined they yield the identity element. A op A' - 0.

The set of positive and negative whole numbers under the
operation of addition forms a familiar group. If we take
the four characteristics of a group then:
  1 COMBINATION - any integer added to any other yields
  an integer.
  2 ASSOCIATIVITY - 2 + (3 + 4) = (2 + 3) + 4
  3 IDENTITY - There is one identity element 0 which when
  added to any other integer leaves it unchanged so 4 + 0
  = 4.
  4 REVERSIBILITY - There is one inverse for each element
  which when combined with that element yields the identity
  element so 2 + (-2) = 0.

Not all sets of elements with an operation form groups.
For example the set of positive whole numbers under the
operation of addition violates the reversibility condition
since there are no inverses.

A lattice is a different kind of structure from a group.
Whereas a group is essentially an algebraic structure, a
lattice is essentially an order structure. A lattice
consists of a set of elements and a relation (not an operation) which can relate two or more of these elements. The
elements might be the set of classes in a hierarchy of
classes and the relation might be that of class inclusion.
Let this relation be symbolised by ζ and we have the class
of say, mammals including the class of humans, so M ζ H.
In logical symbolism we have:

$$H + M = M$$

$$or\ H \cup M = M$$

The smallest class which includes both the elements that
are related is called the least upper bound of the two
elements.   The largest class which both the elements contain is called the greatest lower bound.   In this case it
is humans since 'mammals' contains 'humans' and so does
'humans' but 'humans' does not contain 'mammals'.

So, a lattice is a structure consisting of a set of elements
and a relation such that any two elements have one greatest
lower bound and one largest upper bound.   It is not only
class hierarchies that exhibit this lattice structure but
it is a particularly suitable structure for representing
some of the properties of logical operations concerning
classes.   Since these are the most important characteristics
of the period of concrete operations, properties of the
lattice are combined with properties of the group to make
up the 'groupings' which describe the concrete operations.
Because of its roots in concrete action the generality of
the grouping is restricted in the following ways:

1   In a group any two elements of the system A and B will
produce by their combination A op B (where op is the direct
or inverse operation of the group) a third element C of the
system without passing through the intermediates between A
and B.   In a grouping, things proceed in a step by step
way, all the elements must be passed through, they can only
be combined contiguously.

2   A group is associative whereas a grouping is not always.
In fact there are many exceptions to the general rule and
although Piaget shows that these exceptions can all be
handled with the aid of a few special rules (Piaget, 1949,
pp.100-3), the necessity for this shows that the grouping
lacks the simplicity of a mathematical structure.   This
structure however has a certain degree of generality and is
found in eight distinct systems all represented in different degrees of completion in the behaviour of the child of
7-8 to 10-12 years of age, and differentiated according to
whether it is a question of classes, relations, additive
or multiplicative classifications, symmetrical (biunivocal)
or asymmetrical (univocal) correspondances.

		Classes	*Relations*
Additives	{ asymmetrical	I	V
	symmetrical	II	VI
Multiplicatives	{ co-univocal	III	VII
	biunivocal	IV	VIII

Grouping I is when the grouping structure is said to have

the same relationship to the child's actions as the group structure has to the sets which form groups. That is, it is a set of rules governing operations of a certain type such that if they are to count as being of that type they must conform to these rules. So Grouping I is a set of rules governing the operations involved in forming a hierarchy of classes and the operations that it is possible to perform on the elements of their hierarchy once it has been formed. If one has, for example, the following hierarchy of classes:

Trout included in Fish included in Animals, included in Living Things, one can then do several things with the elements. One can consider the class of Trouts or one can ignore it and think only of its supraordinate, that is, Fish. One can symbolise considering the class by + and ignoring it by -. So we have the operation of addition and its inverse. However, Piaget does not describe the elements of a system as isolated classes. The elements are equations and the operation is that of combining these equations. To explain this better it is necessary to use some of Piaget's symbols. For example, let us say that A is the class of trout. Then A' will be the class of all edible fish that are not trouts and B will be the class of all edible fish. So we can have an equation like $(A + A' = B)$. To go further, if B is the class of all edible fish then B' will be the class of all fish that are not edible and C will be the class of all fish and so on. We can now have two equations $(A + A' = B)$ and $(B + B' = C)$. Any number of equations can be formed in these ways, for example $(B - A - A' = C)$; $(B - A = A')$ etc. and then they can be combined in such a way that they exhibit the five properties of Grouping I;

I COMBINATION: The product of combining two elements of the grouping is itself an element, for example $(A + A' = B) + (B + B' = C) = (A + A' + B' = C)$.

2 ASSOCIATIVITY: The product of a series of elements does not depend on the way in which they are grouped, for example $(B - A' = A) + (C - B' = B) + (D - C = C)$ and $(B - A' = A) + (C - B' = B) = (D - C' = C)$ are both equal to $(D - C' - B' - A' = A)$.

3 IDENTITY: Piaget gives the identity element as the sum of two null classes $(0 + 0 = 0)$.

4 REVERSIBILITY: For each element there is an inverse which combined with it yields the identity element. For example: $(A + A' = B) + (- A - A' = -B) = (0 + 0 = 0)$.

So far the properties of the grouping have not distinguished it from the group but the fifth property is one which is

derived from the lattice. It is this property which is
rooted in the nature of the entities that are being dealt
with and which restricts the generality of this structure.
In the group structure the elements have no properties not
defined in the axioms of the group. They can simply be
added up, for example 2 + 2 + 2 = 6. But this cannot be
the case with the addition of classes. Classes have a
property that is not defined by the properties of the group
A + A + A = A NOT 3A; A + B + C = C not something greater
than C. What this means is that the grouping possesses
elements which sometimes do the same job as the identity
element. In a lattice of classes a unique lowest upper
bound can be found for any pair of classes, consisting of
the logical sum or union of these classes. For example if
A + A' = B then A + B = B and A + C = C and A + D = D etc.
then A in this case is doing the job of an identity element
with respect to B, C, D and all their supraordinate classes.
A is also an identity element with respect to itself since
A + A = A. So in addition to the general identity element
0 + 0 = 0) we have;
    5 SPECIAL IDENTITY: where every class is an identity
    element with respect to itself and with respect to its
    supraordinate classes. For example: (A + A' = B) +
    (A + A' = B) = (A + A' = B).

It is this lattice-derived property which, although it is
essential to characterise the grouping as concerned with
classes, restricts its generality. For example it is this
which restricts the associativity of groupings:

In the case of Grouping I for instance:
    (A + A' = B) + (A + A' = B) + (- A - A = B) ≠ (A + A'
    = B) + [(A + A' = B) + (- A - A' = - B)]
since the left hand side of the equation adds up to 0 while
the right hand side adds up to (A + A' = B).

Grouping I is that of simple inclusions which succeed in
forming a hierarchy of classes. For example, Trout included
in Fish included in Animals included in Living Beings.
Until about nine years of age most children have difficulty
in understanding relationships between classes. Piaget
cites as an example the instance of a child who could not
understand that a member of the class 'Genevans' could also
be a member of the class 'Swiss' (Piaget, 1928):
    Ober 8.2: 'I live in Freiberg which is in Switzerland
    but I am not Swiss. It is the same thing for the
    Genevans.'
    'Are there Swiss people?'
    'Yes.'
    'Where do they live?'

'I don't know.'
Another experiment which Piaget performed at a later stage
with Inhelder shows that children will agree that collections
of roses, tulips and other flowers are all flowers but they
will assert that if all the flowers die then the roses (or
tulips) will still live. They appear to attribute a separate
entity to the subclasses from that of the main class.

Grouping II is that of vicariances. This corresponds to the
ability to substitute for each other different things which
have the same end result. For example, in arithmetic
children constantly use such relations as 15 = 10 + 5 = 3 +
12 = 14 + 1.... Use of different coins to make the same sum,
of experiences with weights, capacities and lengths of time
induce understanding of these relationships if the substitu-
tions are seen in practice. Other kinds of subdivisions of
classes are constantly being used. Piaget says that they
correspond to 'vicariances' because once the first category
has been selected then the second must be complementary,
for example, the Swiss plus all the foreigners in Switzerland,
subdivisions of the class of children into boys and girls,
over eight and under eight, people into male or female,
white or black, etc.

Grouping III is that of a table with two or more entries.
When a child arranges objects into subclasses by considering simultaneously shape and colour, he will arrive at four
subclasses which can be described in terms of both characteristics at once, for example, red squares, blue squares,
yellow squares, red circles, blue circles, yellow circles.
This is a multiplication of classes.

Grouping IV is that of classifications corresponding to a
genealogical tree. In this case the children are called
upon to group individuals by making one term correspond to
several others instead of one to one. For example, a family
of brothers and their sons may be arranged in a family tree.
In such a case the relationship between the brothers is
symmetrical but the relation between father and sons is
asymmetrical.

Grouping V is that of seriations, that is, a sequence of
transitive, asymmetrical relations. This requires the
ability to assemble relationships which express differences.
For example, the children may be asked to order things
according to diminishing size.

Grouping VI is that of combinations of symmetrical relationships. By about six years old the children realise
that a distance is unaltered in whichever direction it is

measured (although they may be confused if the distance to
be measured is between a tall tree and a short one). At
about eight most children realise that if there are two
brothers then each is brother to the other. Similarly
they begin to understand such relations as friends,
enemies, partners in a game, two factors of a number etc.

Grouping VII is that of multiplications between two seriations concerned either with the same relation (serial
correspondence between two distinct rows of objects
according to the same relation, for example, larger and
larger dolls corresponding to longer and longer sticks) or
two distinct relations (for example, objects to be placed
in order according to their weight and volume at the same
time). A particular case is of some importance here. If
there are two rows A_1, A_2, A_3 ... and B_1, B_2, B_3..., there
is a one to one correspondence which is important in the
child's construction of the concepts of time. A child must
be able to match an increase in sequence of ages with a
decreasing sequence of birth dates to arrive at an objective
concept of age. This is a concept which does not appear to
develop until about the age of nine although the ability
to match, for example, beads in one to one correspondence
appears quite early. Understanding of one to one correspondence in general precedes the development of concepts
of conservation, for example, conservation of number is
not understood by children who cannot copy a line of
counters accurately.

Grouping VIII corresponds to the genealogical relations
already shown under IV but is the classification of terms.
It is concerned with the multiplication of the various
symmetrical and asymmetrical relations which define the
classes in hierarchies such as 'family trees', relations
like 'father of', 'cousin of', etc. For example, 'If A is
father of B and B is first cousin of C, then A is father
of the first cousin of C and thus uncle of C.'

MATRIX STRUCTURES

This description, however, is of the very earliest appearance of anything which can be called a structure. Piaget
says that he has only described the most general features
of the elementary structure of the 'grouping' which is
merely to indicate under what common forms the earliest
operational structures are manifested. He now intends to
classify these operational structures not in terms of their
most general features but in terms of their most important

characteristics, that is, those characteristics which will play a part in the construction of later structures as the restrictions typical of the early grouping are removed.

The 'later structures' that Piaget has in mind are the matrix structures brought to light by the Bourbaki school of mathematicians. Their method of regressive analysis has so far according to Piaget's interpretation, brought to light three fundamental matrix structures.

1 Algebraic structures of which the prototype is the 'group'.

2 Structures of order an important type of which is the network or lattice which deals with such relations as x R y (x is at the most equal to y).

3 Topological structures which deal with the concepts of neighbourhood, unit and continuity.

From these matrix structures we can derive all others by differentiation or by combination. Finally we arrive back at the particular theories of classical mathematics by specifying the elements with which the differentiated or multiple structures deal.

Having characterised the matrix structures through the application of mathematical methods, Piaget believes that the next task is to establish whether there is any relation between them and the structures of the actual actions and operations of the subject. In asking whether these structures correspond to anything in the subject's actions and operations, Piaget says he is asking whether in the spontaneous co-ordination of his operations (insofar as they are interiorised actions) the subject exhibits co-ordinating structures having some relationship with the matrix structure.

Piaget claims that there is a genetic relationship between the matrix structures and the elementary 'grouping' structure which characterises the concrete operational stage.

From the retrospective viewpoint of the later constructions, the groupings can be divided according to two principles. The first concerns which of the two distinct forms of reversibility (inversion or reciprocity) they make use of and the second concerns whether they start from discrete elements and combine them into wholes of increasing types or whether they start from wholes and divide them up into decreasing types. If the form of reversibility employed is inversion then the operational structures correspond to the later abstract algebraic

structures. If the form of reversibility employed is reciprocity, then the operational structures correspond to the
later order structures. Both of these kinds of structures
concern discrete entities. When inversions are added the
result is an annulment. When reciprocals are added the
result is either an equivalence or the relation with which
we started unchanged. Inversion is the form of reversibility characteristic of the additive system of relations.

Over and above the actions or operations affecting discrete
objects and consisting of collecting or ordering them and
so on, there are actions and operations concerned with the
separation and recombination of objects themselves as continuous wholes. They are the operations relative to space
and time. Structures concerning operations on wholes
correspond to topological structures.

The highly abstract matrix structures which emerge in a
structuralist interpretation of pure mathematics are,
according to Piaget's theory, more complex and abstract
forms of these elementary groupings. The groupings are
the forerunners, the ancestors of the abstract mathematical
structures. The mathematical structures are linked to the
groupings by an unbroken chain of transformations. The
groupings have certain features which restrict their generality. For example, the elements can only be combined contiguously, and therefore step by step. This restriction
is the result of the fact that the child does not at this
stage distinguish between the form and the content of his
actions. The structure lacks generality because it is
applied only to the objects which are being manipulated in
concrete operations.

Because of its lack of generality, the grouping is not of
interest to mathematicians but Piaget claims that as a stage
in the development of general, abstract structures it has
enormous significance to the psychologist. The combinations
of a step by step form express the beginnings of deductive
power, not yet freed from concrete manipulations and only
proceeding thus by means of contiguous overlappings without
achieving a combinatorial system.

Hypothetico-deductive operations at the following level will
exhibit the fundamental new characteristic of a combinatorial system. However, basically the same structure is being
re-elaborated and re-constructed at each level of thought.
The adolescent at the level of formal operational thinking
is enabled to develop structures of a greater degree of
abstraction and generality because he no longer is concerned

with the manipulation of concrete objects. The subject
matter of his thought at this level is the structures themselves which organised his thought at the concrete-opera-
tional level. This subject matter does not restrict him
to step-by-step combinations. Structures themselves can be
multiplied together as well as added together. The different levels of thought are distinguished by the abstraction
and generality of their subject matter rather than by any
fundamental difference in the structures that they bring
to bear on that subject matter. The structures are simply
increasingly more abstract and general versions of the
'grouping' which in its turn is simply the interiorisation
of the structures of sensori-motor action.

CRITICISMS OF PIAGET'S LOGIC

Piaget's logic is unorthodox in the sense that he invented
a new kind of structure, the 'grouping' which is a combination of some of the features of the group (in the sense of
Klein's theory of groups) and some of the features of the
lattice (as developed by Birkhoff). He invented this
structure not because it would add to the strength or
clarity of his logic but because he wanted to use logical
symbolism to characterise the elementary structures of
thought and these because of their lack of generality,
could not be described as either groups or lattices.
Piaget thinks it important to describe the elementary
structures of thought in these terms of abstract mathematics because he thinks that learning and thinking proceed
by the 'emboîtment', the integrating of smaller, less
general and less abstract structures into a wider, more
general and abstract hierarchical system. The exposition
of mathematics by the Bourbaki school of mathematicians
represents it in part as just this sort of study. Piaget
then is attempting to show that all thought proceeds by
means of the sort of integration that is found in structuralist expositions of the nature of mathematics.

Piaget has been soundly criticised for his view that the
mother of structures found in the Bourbaki mathematics
have their counterpart in the seriations, classifications
and number, and the topological structures of the child's
thought. Two kinds of criticism are made. The first kind
concerns his interpretation of mathematics itself and the
second kind concerns his claim that the abstract structures
of mathematics have their parallel in the thought of the
child.

The first kind of criticism claims that Piaget uses technical mathematical terms loosely and ambiguously. A typical
criticism was made as early as 1952 by Kneale:
>   The difficulty is rather in understanding his use of
>   such abstract words as 'operation' and 'structure'. It
>   seems spurious, for example, to speak of (vp) and (p)
>   as the fundamental interpropositional operations (p.331)
>   and it is not clear to me when or in what circumstances
>   I am supposed to perform these operations, if indeed
>   there are such. Perhaps the argument would have been
>   easier to follow if M. Piaget had written less about
>   the detailed application of his notion of a groupement
>   and more about his philosophy of logic. In particular
>   he might have helped the reader by trying to relate his
>   own views about the psychology of reasoning to modern
>   linguistic theories of logic. (1952, p.92)

More recent criticisms on the same lines have been made by
Freudenthal (1973) and Rotman (1977).

It would be helpful to have more discussion on Piaget's
view of the relationship between the psychology of reason
and the abstract structures of mathematics and logic
because this might help to clarify the role that the concept of a grouping is supposed to play. When mathematicians write of 'groups' or 'lattices' they are trying to
study in abstract fashion certain structures or patterns
of organisation which may be realised in very different
materials. As Piaget says (1949, p.91) the system of
operations each of which consists in adding an integer,
positive or negative, is a group in the technical sense
because the application of two such operations in succession is equivalent to an operation of the system, every
such operation can be annulled by an inverse, there is a
single operation (+0) which makes no difference and the
operations can be combined according to the associative law.
But, as Kneale points out in his review, the system of all
possible translations of a rigid body in space is also a
group in this sense. The whole point of introducing this
technical terminology is to get away from the individual
features of these systems and to study only those features
that they have in common. The idea of a grouping, as
Piaget himself admits, has no interest for the mathematician
since its generality is restricted by the nature of the
objects it is concerned with. He claims that it is only
'of interest for a logic which tries to express the mechanisms of the most elementary operations of the mind' (Piaget,
1949, p.97).

Piaget then accepts the criticisms aimed at him by those
who accuse him of using mathematical terms loosely. But
he insists that what he is concerned to do is to formalise
natural thought and that this cannot be done by conventional
logic. He is concerned to formalise the natural thought of
the child because he wants to show how later formal thought
is derived from earlier natural thought.

The main feature of natural thought which makes its formalisation by conventional logic impossible is its dynamic
character. To describe dynamic psychological processes of
structural transformation, Piaget only had available the
formalisations of algebra and logic. And he had to deform
these because they are ill suited to the representation of
dynamic, self-regulatory systems.

Piaget must believe that while the grouping expresses the
mechanism of the most elementary operations of the mind,
the abstract structures of logic and mathematics express
the mechanism of the most sophisticated operations of mind.

DO STRUCTURES EXIST?

Piaget makes many attempts to explain the sense in which
mental structures exist. They are not observable but are
inferrable from the overt behaviour of the child, what he
does and says. When the child becomes capable of doing
something he very rapidly settles into very consistent
procedures. The adult observer may then formalise a
description of what he does and these procedures and so
'construct the structure'.

Piaget says:
> The structure is indeed constructed by the observer, but
> it is not at all a product of the observer's thought; it
> is the description of the actions which the subject
> knows how to do independently of what he thinks or says
> about it. (1977)

In the article (Inhelder and Piaget, 1979) a comparison is
made: saying that structures only exist in the mind of the
psychologists 'would be like saying that the child can eat
and breathe but that his stomach and lungs only exist in
the mind of the physiologist' (p.169).

If we describe biological functioning we can name the organs
which function. We can show how they are structured in
relation to each other and which parts contribute what to

the functioning. We can distinguish functions because we
can see both the beginning and the end of a process. We
say for example that digestion is a biological function.
This is a judgment about the various processes that go on
in an organism. We have picked out various things that
happen in an organism and seen that they are connected in
two ways: (1) they contribute to the sustenance of life of
the organism, and (2) they are the transformation of one
kind of material into another kind. There are connections
all during the processes both from one part of the process
to the next and between the different organs which perform
parts of the process. There are tangible objects and
tangible material which is transformed and there are
observable processes which can be characterised as being
processes of digestion, processes of physical maturation,
etc.

Piaget does not ever produce a sufficiently detailed and
clear account of the nature and functioning of the intellectual structures. In the first place his account relies
on concepts drawn from biology. This begs the question
of their applicability to the context of intellectual
development. We want to know whether the two contexts are
sufficiently similar to allow the use of the same terms.
In the second place he relies on concepts which while they
may be imaginative and suggestive are far from clear. The
concepts of equilibrium, reflective abstraction and transformation are such concepts.

If Piaget were suggesting simply that there is an analogy
between intellectual and biological functioning then one
could argue about how illuminating and useful such an
analogy would be and about the points of similarity and
difference between the two things. But he offers the 'isomorphism' between the two as an explanation of the nature
of intellectual functioning. In the physical sciences if
a model is claimed to represent the actual mechanisms of
reality great care is taken to provide transformation rules
from the level of the model to the phenomenon requiring
explanation. If there are points where the model does not
fit the facts then limits are drawn to the usefulness of
the model and one says that the model only represents some
of the aspects of the real mechanism or only represents it
to a certain extent. But in order for this to be possible,
the model has to be clear and detailed in the first place.
This cannot be said for Piaget's theory.

Piaget's claim of an isomorphism between biological and
intellectual functioning reifies the mental structures.

His theory suffers from the defects that Ryle pointed out
in any view that presents the intellect as some kind of
special organ:

> We hear stories of people doing such things as judging,
> abstracting, subsuming, deducing, inducing, predicating,
> and so forth as if these were recordable operations
> actually executed by particular people at particular
> stages of their ponderings. And, since we do not wit-
> ness other people in the act of doing them, we feel
> driven to allow that these acts are very subterranean
> happenings, the occurrences of which are found out only
> by the inferences and divinations of expert epistemo-
> logists. These experts seem to tell us that we do these
> then somewhat as anatomists tell us of the digestive and
> cerebral processes that go on inside us without our
> knowledge. So our intellects must be fleshless organs
> since these para-anatomists tell us so much about their
> clandestine functionings. (Ryle, 1949, p.269)

This is precisely what Piaget is trying to tell us about
the development of the child's intelligence. The child is
not aware that he is developing schemata and he is not
aware of the characteristics of these schemata. Nor can
they be seen and touched as can the organs involved in
physical processes. They can only be discovered at all by
the 'inferences and divinations' of the genetic psychologist.
Ryle argues that thinking objectively and validly should be
regarded as an achievement rather than a process. Earlier
in this chapter objective knowledge was said to involve
intersubjective standards of truth and validity. 'Valid
thinking' is thinking which meets these standards. It is
not thinking which necessarily involves a particular process.
What Piaget appears to be describing is the successive
results of thinking rather than any process of thinking.
He is describing the structure of intersubjective knowledge
rather than the structure of the individual mind.

THE NEGLECT OF CONTENT

If this contention that Piaget is describing the structure
of objective knowledge rather than the structure of mind is
correct, then another criticism which is often made of
Piaget is explained. He is often accused of being concerned
only with the ideal competence of a subject rather than the
subject's actual performance. In the discussion of the
grouping, it was pointed out that the content of operations
at the level of concrete operations restricts the generality
of the grouping structure. The operations are carried out

on concrete manipulable objects and the features of the
objects themselves restrict the range of operations that
can be performed on them. The content in this case is
restricting the development of the structure. Apart from
this concession to the importance of features of the content
of thought, Piaget largely ignores it. He has been accused
of concentrating too heavily on the significance of abstract
logical structures for cognitive development and ignoring
the effect of concrete content and context. (See, for
example, P.C. Wason, 1977.) Empirical studies have shown
that people have much greater difficulty in applying
logical thought in situations which are unfamiliar to them.
According to Piaget's theory, one case of the application
of a logical structure should be as easy or as difficult
as any other. The familiarity or otherwise of the content
is not taken into account. Piaget, consequently, tends to
overestimate the rationality of human thinking. Even the
mistakes that children make, irrational as they at first
appear, are shown by Piaget's theory, to be the inevitable
result of the application of the particular 'logic' that
the child has.

Piaget overestimates the importance of logic for human
development partly because he is more concerned with the,
perhaps unrealised, potential of the human mind than with
its performance in any specific situation. But he also
overestimates its importance because his evolutionary view
leads him to see intelligence inevitably progressing from
'lower' to 'higher' forms through self-regulating processes,
culminating in the 'stable equilibrium' of the level of the
purely abstract structures of logic and mathematics.

STRUCTURES AND PROCEDURES

In his later work Piaget distinguishes between two kinds of
knowledge: the know-how which leads to the successful performance of some action and the understanding of how that
performance was achieved which makes possible the description of the action (Piaget, 1976 and 1978).

He introduces the term 'procedures' for the organised series
of steps that the subject uses in order to attain a specific
cognitive goal.

Procedures lead to the solution of problems - to knowing
how to do something. They have only been described in
Piaget's most recent articles (for example, Piaget, 1979),
but they are closely linked to the logico-mathematical

structures of the earlier work. In his later work Piaget
insists even more strongly on the fact that these structures
transform reality. He even goes so far as to call the
structures themselves 'mechanisms' which a subject uses to
transform reality (Piaget, 1975, p.165). The old structures
come close to what are now called 'procedures' but Piaget
seems to have adopted a computer programming approach to a
description of action now rather than the static descriptions of action in terms of mathematical formalisations.
The abstract formal models which he uses to describe the
equilibrated structures failed to characterise the dynamism
of the continual establishment and unbalancing of the structures. Piaget several times expressed approval of the
computer programming analogy of the human mind partly
because it offers a way of characterising development as a
series of stages or steps towards some goal. He did not
himself develop his theory to any great extent in this direction. But its concept of 'procedures' is a move towards
this. Procedures and structures, then, are essentially the
same. The concept of procedures, however, attempts to cope
with the dynamism of development in a way that the static
concept of structures fails to do.

SUMMARY

The concept of structure dates from Piaget's earliest
researches into biology. All organisms have a certain
morphological structure. But this concept has changed
throughout the years from a biological to a logical to a
more psychological concept. In his concern to show how the
abstract structures of mathematics grow out of the structures of natural thought, he attempted to formalise the
structures of natural thought and failed in this attempt
either to produce a convincing formalisation or to characterise their dynamism. In Structuralism (1970c) Piaget
characterises a structure as 'a system of transformations'.
He uses the terms system and structure more or less interchangeably. Transformation refers to two different kinds
of change. In one example, that of a group of displacements
where returning from B to A is 'the transformation of the
direct operation' is where the original state is transformed. So reversibility, composition and addition are
transformations because the operations of negating, compos-
ing and adding transform the original state of the objects
that the negating, etc., are being performed on. But on
the other hand there is transformation as transforming an
operation, that is to say, an 'operation on operations' as
when, for example, two operations are combined to give a

third and so they become sub-operations of the super-
operation.

Piaget's view that the role and nature of the cognitive
structures can be understood on the analogy with the role
of the physical organs in biological functioning was
rejected. The reasons were that the structures can only be
regarded as the achievement of thinking, as structures
describing objective knowledge, not as the cause of valid
thinking.

Piaget's use of the concept of a 'procedure' is similar to
his use of the concept of a structure but with an increased
emphasis on the role of the structure in transforming
reality.

Chapter 4

The equilibrium model

The subject of this chapter will be the equilibration model.
It is the explanation that Piaget offers for the transformation of one stage into the next. It has connections both
with Piaget's biological functionalist theory and his
structuralist theory.

The equilibration model purports to be a scientific, causal
explanation showing the 'mechanism' of transformation from
one stage to the next. This chapter will consider first
of all what features a scientific, causal explanation would
be expected to have, secondly whether Piaget's explanation
has those features and thirdly whether one would, in any
case, expect a theory of human development to be scientific
and causal.

EMPIRICAL V. LOGICAL TRUTH

It is tempting to think that the more irrefutable a scientific theory is, the better. But there is a distinction to
be made between a theory's never having been refuted and
its being irrefutable in principle. Karl Popper has argued
that theories which are irrefutable in principle do not
have any scientific interest.

Popper's argument rests on a distinction which has been
made in many different ways since the beginning of philosophy, but which essentially points to a difference between
matters of fact and logical or conceptual truths. Very
roughly, statements of fact are true if what they state

corresponds to some state of affairs in the world whereas
logical or conceptual truths result from the connection
between concepts in our language or in the logical system
that we are using. One well-known formulation of this
distinction was made by Kant (1929). He distinguished
between analytic truths and synthetic truths. He defines
a proposition as being analytic if the predicate concept
is 'contained in' the subject concept and synthetic if the
predicate concept is not contained in the subject concept.
What this implies is that the truth of analytic propositions can be discovered simply by 'analysing' the proposition. The predicate is simply an amplification of the
subject. The synthetic proposition, however, is formed by
a synthesis of ideas which have no conceptual connection
with each other. To see whether or not they really go
together we have to consult the state of affairs that they
describe.

More recently Kant's original rather vague criterion has
been replaced by more precise ones. Carnap, for example,
defines analytic sentences as those sentences which, if
true, are true in virtue of their logical forms and the
meanings of the logical and descriptive terms occurring in
them. On the other hand the 'truth or falsity of a synthetic sentence is not determined by the meanings of the
terms, but by factual information about the physical
world' (Carnap, 1966, pp.259-60).

Various other modern formulations, for example, W.V. Quine
(1953), A.J. Ayer (1956), D.W. Hamlyn (1970) have formulated
the distinction in such a way as to draw out the difference
between something's being true in virtue of the meanings
of the words involved and something's being true in virtue
of the way things are in the world.

An example, given by Quine and used by many other philosophers, of an analytic proposition is the proposition:
     'No bachelor is a married man.'
Since 'bachelor' and 'unmarried man' are synonymous, the
proposition can be translated into:
     'No unmarried man is a married man.'
This is clearly and irrefutably true and is so in virtue of
the meanings of the words employed.

An example of a synthetic proposition would be:
     'This pencil is yellow.'
Whether this proposition is true or not will depend on how
the pencil actually is, some feature of the world, not on
the meanings of the words in the proposition.

Although the distinction is denied by some (for example, W.V. Quine, 1953) its opponents do not succeed in making out a convincing case for its abolishment. They do succeed in showing that the distinction is not so clear cut as was previously thought and that not all propositions are identifiable unproblematically as either analytic or synthetic (for example, H. Putnam, 1962).

Popper relies heavily on this distinction in developing his criterion of falsifiability for distinguishing between scientific and what he calls metaphysical theories.

The main argument of Popper (1959) is that: 'empirical falsifiability is the criterion of the empirical and scientific character of theories.' Popper's original formulation of this falsifiability criterion arose from his desire to distinguish between, on the one hand, theories such as those of Freud and Marx which while claiming to be scientific seemed to be able to explain any and every happening in a vague and general sort of way, and, on the other hand, theories such as Einstein's theory of relativity which made surprising and testable predictions.

Popper's notion was that while theories like those of Freud and Marx were interesting as imaginative and suggestive ways of looking at man they were metaphysical rather than scientific. They offered a picture of man, an orientation to man to the acceptance or rejection of which, scientific evidence of what people actually did was more or less irrelevant.

PIAGET'S THEORY A MIXTURE OF EMPIRICAL AND ANALYTIC

This is the kind of position that some critics of Piaget have suggested that he is in. Critics such as Hamlyn (1971) and Mischel (1971) have argued, for reasons rather different from Popper's rejection of Freud's and Marx's theories, that empirical evidence is irrelevant to the establishment of the major points of Piaget's theory. They argue that his theory amounts to a description of the structure of human knowledge rather than a description and explanation of the structure of the human mind.

These criticisms are levelled at Piaget from two directions. It is argued, first of all, that the relations between many of Piaget's so-called 'stages' are logical relations and that it does not require empirical evidence to discover that if A is a part of B then the child must be able to

do A before he can do B properly. This amounts to the
criticism that many of Piaget's so-called empirical discoveries are in fact disguised analytic truths.

The other direction of criticism is to make the claim that
Piaget's apparently causal explanation of human development
is not in fact causal at all but is merely a laying out of
the relationships between different concepts and different
parts of human knowledge, relationships which a child has
to learn. Piaget is accused then of dressing up an epistemology as a psychology. The further criticism is added that
it would not be appropriate anyway for a story about human
development to be a causal story.

Piaget himself offers contradictory accounts of what his
theory is supposed to be doing. In Beth and Piaget (1966)
he says:
> The knowledge that transitivity corresponds to a formal
> 'norm' does not help to explain why it imposes itself
> at 7-8 years of age as a norm accepted by the subject.
> In fact, we shall have to understand why it does not
> impose itself beforehand and how the subject has become
> aware of it. Now, from the genetic viewpoint, it is
> again a problem of causal explanation, whether we solve
> it by appealing to educational or linguistic pressures
> or whether we see it as a structure resulting from the
> subject's actions or operations themselves, arising
> from successive stages of equilibrium reached during
> development. (Beth and Piaget, 1966, p.158)

He is suggesting here that his theory is a causal theory
on a par with accounts of equilibration and homeostatic
mechanisms in biology. At other times he suggests that a
causal explanation is not appropriate for psychology.
What is required is an explanation based on 'implications'.
He says:
> Neuro-physiology is exclusively causal while psychology
> is based on implication. The reason is that the data
> of neuro-physiology are concerned with physio-chemical
> states which can be given purely causal explanations,
> while states of consciousness and mental behaviour
> cannot be given causal explanations but constitute only
> systems of signification or significant actions which
> are interrelated by 'implications' in the broad sense
> of the term. A healthy psychology consists, in this
> case, in the replacement of the imprecise and incomplete
> implications of consciousness by logico-mathematical
> implications which constitute a coherent body of knowledge
> and which are adequate representations of experience
> (1969: xxiii)

Piaget's aim seems to be to produce a causal explanation
of the development of understanding. But not only does he
want to show how one stage in development leads to another
(which is what he is trying to do with his biological
equilibration model), but also wants to offer an explanation of why the child accepts at one stage as a necessary
truth something which at an earlier stage he would have
rejected as untrue. He wants to see not only what the
direction of development is but also why it should be like
that. And he supposes that he can provide a psychological
explanation for this too, but that it will be in terms of
implications. He believes that his assimilation/accommoda-
tion model can explain the fact that understanding and
intelligence do develop and can describe the mechanisms
that lead to its development. But he also wants to explain
the force that the knowledge which is new at each different
stage exerts on the child. The child accepts that certain
propositions which he formerly rejected are necessarily
true. Why does he now accept what he formerly rejected?

Piaget asserts many times that he recognises the autonomy
of logic and mathematics and that his own explanations of
the psychological possibility of formal modes of thought
are in no way meant to supersede formal analyses of the
nature of logical and mathematical entities and theories.
He thinks that his psychological arguments for why it is
that we accept some things as necessary truths should run
alongside formal arguments for validity but, on the other
hand, he thinks that his own arguments could lead to a
revision of views of the nature of mathematical and
logical entities and theories. He says:

> Our role ... consists of looking for the psychological
> explanation which, as we shall see, will continue to
> transform itself into a psychological correspondance
> (in the sense not of an uncursion into the problem of
> validity but of a causal explanation of the process
> leading to some step in thinking) of the position
> which the logician is led to adopt by virtue of the
> autonomous development of research into foundations ...
> a correspondence between the implicatory structures
> employed by logicomathematical activity and the causal
> or genetic structures discovered by psychology would be
> very instructive for general epistemology.... We
> should have to reconsider all the problems of Platonism,
> conceptualism or nominalism and of a priorism and
> empiricism, if we could show experimentally that the
> intrinsic features of logic have their origin in the
> activity of the subject. (Beth and Piaget, 1966,
> pp.135-6)

There seem to be two distinct questions here which Piaget
conflates. If he believes that his findings will lead him
to reconsider the problems of Platonism, conceptualism and
nominalism then he must believe that he is concerned with
describing the nature of the form of understanding of logic
and mathematics. However, Piaget equates this question
with the question of how genetically this understanding
comes about. The first of these questions is non-empirical.
In order to describe the form of understanding of logic and
mathematics what is required is an analytic study of logic
and mathematics. But the possibility of posing the second
question presupposes that an answer has been found for the
first question. Since Piaget does not distinguish these
two questions he fails to see the logical priority of the
first question. Consequently, his developmental theory
which is an attempt to answer both questions at once is a
confusion of the empirical and the non-empirical.

To understand better the view that Piaget's equilibration
theory is a mixture of empirical and analytic claims we
will have to consider in greater detail both the equilibration model and Piaget's views on the nature of psychological
explanations.

PIAGET'S VIEW OF PSYCHOLOGICAL EXPLANATION

In the natural sciences nomological explanation, that is,
explanation of a single event by fitting it into a lawlike
generalisation, is sometimes considered to be a sufficient
explanation. In this case, a phenomenon which was perhaps
thought to be anomolous, is shown to be an example of a
generalisation which is universally true in a lawlike way.
Philosophers of science have generally had difficulty with
distinguishing between lawlike generalisations and accidental
generalisations. An important difference between these two
which has been stressed by Nelson Goodman (1955, Chapter 1)
is that lawlike generalisations can, while accidental generalisations cannot, support counter-factual conditionals.
The explanatory power of lawlike generalisations as opposed
to the lack of explanatory power of accidental generalisations, Goodman argues, is closely related to their use to
support counterfactuals. However, it would seem that both
their ability to support counterfactuals and their explanatory power derive from the large amount of background knowledge both factual and empirical which they assume or which
could, if demanded, be brought forward to support them.
This point is made clearly by Hempel. He says:

> A statement of universal form, whether empirically
> confirmed or as yet untested, will qualify as a law if
> it is implied by an accepted theory...; but even if it
> is empirically well confirmed and presumably true in
> fact, it will not qualify as a law if it rules out certain
> hypothetical occurrences ... which an accepted theory
> qualifies as possible. (1966, p.58)

The complexity of the relationship between laws and theories
cannot be entered into here (for a fuller discussion see
E. Nagel, 1961, Chapter 4). However, a brief look at the
literature on this relationship will show that lawlike
generalisations which do have explanatory power are not the
same as simple empirical generalisations supported by
repeated observations; that is, simply because 'that is the
way things have always been observed to happen' is not an
explanation of any event or sequence of events in the way
that fitting it into a pattern of theoretically supported
laws is an explanation.

A scientific explanation, then, is generally thought to
require some kind of accepted background theory which can
be used to support it. It is also a requirement, as Popper
has argued, that the connection between the event to be
explained and the explanation is a connection with some
empirical content, that can be tested by some kind of
reference to experience.

The same point was made much earlier by Hume (1888) in his
analysis of causation. Hume's first criterion for a causal
explanation was that the connection between a cause and its
effect is not one of logical necessity. Consequently, the
relation between the explanans and the explanandum cannot
be one of logical inference.

Hume's analysis of causation which was the inspiration for
Hempel's later covering law model of explanation leaves
largely unaccounted for the explanatory force of scientific,
causal explanations. Harré has criticised the empiricist's
account of causation and scientific explanation on just
these grounds. He argues (1960) that the aim of a scientific
investigation is to uncover the 'hidden mechanisms' which
make things work as they do. When these are too difficult
to discover we content ourselves with models and analogies
but always the intention is to find out how things really
work.

A part of Harré's criticisms of positivist theories of
scientific explanation are met in the more recent theories

of the empiricists by the stressing of the background theory
which supports any simple scientific explanation. The explanatory force then is accounted for by the fact that the
explanation is fitting the event into a generally accepted
picture of the way things are rather than simply showing
it to be an instance of a more general class of facts.

These views on the nature of causal, scientific explanations
have been advanced by philosophers concerned with the
natural rather than the social sciences. Causal explanation in the social sciences raises special problems of its
own. Before exploring some of these we will look at Piaget's
own view of psychological explanation. The following
exposition is taken mainly from Piaget (1968) but discussions
can also be found in Piaget 1950, 1953, and 1957a.

Piaget distinguishes three stages of research:

1 First of all there is the establishment of general
facts or laws. In this connection it must be realised
that experimental findings always end in establishing
laws. Even the third stage which consists of introducing
a substrate, or model and a sum of relationships between
critical laws, comes back to establishing or assuming
more laws, because these relationships continue to be
altered by laws. However, the law in itself does not
explain anything since it is limited to stating the
generality of a factual relationship. Explanation
begins only with the co-ordination of laws and that co-
ordination may occur in the following two complementary
ways.

2 Simple generalisation is not enough. A new element
which is not contained within the idea of law must be
introduced. That is deductive argument by means of
which one distinguishes the law requiring explanation
from laws which are assumed to explain it. Explanation
presupposes a system of laws among which one can be
constructed or reconstructed deductively from the others.
But the deduction of a law from a collection of other
laws does not constitute a 'causal' explanation.

3 The deduction of the law requiring explanation from
the system of laws which account for it does not remain
simply ideal or logical, but it can be applied to a 'real'
or 'model' substrate which is assumed to support such a
deduction and 'represent' its various connections.

Piaget goes on to explain that the ideal in causal deduction
in psychology, as elsewhere, is a deductive argument applied
to the production of phenomena. This argument, he claims,
is all the more satisfactory if deductive steps correspond
to the links between the subject matter of the theory so
that the order of the explanation reflects that of the
antecedents and consequences involved in the actual or
temporal unfolding of events. He says:

> Causal explanation will succeed insofar as each trans-
> formation involved in the relations between the object
> corresponds to a transformation or operation in the
> deduction; this last being copied from reality. Cause
> sees ratio, said Descartes: the cause is a logical co-
> ordination (2) 'projected' onto a real co-ordination (3).
> (Piaget, 1968, p.161)

Piaget claims that this description of the nature of causal
explanation accounts for the two characteristics of explanation as opposed to simple generalisation: (a) the necessity
of relations between causes and effects which arise from
their deducibility and (b) the reality of the causal tie
underlying the measured phenomena which is assured by the
model acting as a substrate of the deductive argument. He
then goes on to outline seven kinds of explanation which
continue to be used in psychology, identifying two kinds
of explanation that he uses in genetic explanation (involving equilibration mechanisms) and an explanation based
on abstract models. Piaget outlines the advantages of the
explanation based on abstract models as follows:

1 An abstract model can be used when the real substrate
is unknown. It suffices to account for observed laws
by seeking what the various conceivable substrates have
in common, and so, it will be applicable whichever of
the possible substrates turn out to be the real one.

2 It makes precise, imprecise deductions.

3 It enables one to discover new relations between
general facts or laws which were not previously compar-
able.

4 It can supply causal links which were previously overlooked. The example he gives is of the application of
'game theory' originally developed in economics, to the
discrimination of objective indices and of 'noise'.
(Tanner, W.P. Jr. and Swets, J.A., A decision making
theory of human selection, 'Psychol. Rev.', vol.61,
1954, pp.401-9)

However, Piaget's last justification of the use of abstract
models does sound, as he himself says, like a vicious circle:
    As neurology (a factual science) cannot explain why
    2 + 2 = 4 or why A = A (equivalences whose necessity
    rests not on facts but on deductive principles) the fact
    remains that the implications of consciousness, while
    reflecting organic connections could not be understood
    in developmental terms without resorting to abstract
    models whose very force depends on their deductive
    necessity. But isn't this a series of vicious circles,
    since these models are the products of certain deliber-
    ate actions and since they are used in neurology, which
    is expected to explain psychological facts? (Piaget,
    1968, p.182)

Piaget attempts to show that since the relationship between
the implicative structures of consciousness and the causal
structures of neurology is parallelism, the vicious circle
can be avoided. He tries to specify the meaning of this
parallelism in the following way: the idea of causality
does not apply to consciousness because one state of consciousness does not 'cause' another, but implies it according to other categories. Among the forms of explanation
that he has distinguished, he claims only abstract models
apply to consciousness because they can disregard the real
substrate. Since none of the characteristics of physical
causality apply to consciousness it must arise from
'original and specific categories which by their very
nature ignore material facts' (Piaget, 1968, p.187).
These categories Piaget identifies with what the philosopher would want to call conceptual or (loosely) logical
relations. The examples he gives are: 2 + 2 = 4 does not
cause, but implies the truth of 4 - 2 = 2; the value
attributed to an aim or moral obligation is not the cause
of the value of the means or of an action connected with
the obligation. He concludes that the kinds of connections
appropriate to states of consciousness are implicative
not causal. So by a parallelism between the facts of
consciousness and physiological processes he means an isomorphism between the implicative systems of meanings and
the causal systems of matter.

But he also introduces a third level intermediate between
the physiological structures and the implications of consciousness. This is the level of the psychological structures discussed in the last chapter. Only by looking in
detail at Piaget's equilibration theory can we see whether
the relation between the psychological structures is meant
to be a causal relation or an implicative relation.

THE EQUILIBRATION MODEL

Piaget analyses the process of the development of understanding into a homogeneous and continuous equilibration
process giving rise to heterogeneous and discontinuous
states of equilibrium. The states which are said to be in
equilibrium are what Piaget means by 'structures'. The
concept of equilibration is not concerned with any particular stage of development but is concerned with the transition from one state to the next.

Essentially a system in a state of equilibrium is one which
possesses some sort of balance or stability with respect to
the forces acting upon it or within it. In a system which
does not possess any mechanism for maintaining the state of
equilibrium, this may very well be short-lived. But there
are many simple systems which do possess mechanisms which
guarantee the maintenance of a state of equilibrium. For
example, a system controlled by a simple thermostat maintains itself in a state of equilibrium because each change
in the environment is compensated by a change in the thermostat which causes a change in the system. This notion of
equilibrium is easy to understand and has been used with
some success in cybernetics and some branches of physics as
an explanation of 'self regulating' systems. It is also
used with some sort of explanatory force in biology to
explain the self-regulating mechanisms of biological organisms (for example, homeostasis). But Piaget is talking
about cognitive systems. More particularly, he is dealing
with systems of actions either internalised or external
which the subject carries out in a very complex, social
world of people, objects, relations, ideas.

The process of equilibration involves the adopting of
successive 'strategies' on the part of the subject such
that the consequences of adopting one strategy increase
the probability of his adopting the next until he reaches
the last strategy and succeeds in establishing a more
stable and permanent cognitive equilibrium than was achieved
by any of the preceding strategies. For example, in learning that the amount of water remains the same when it is
transferred from a short wide glass to a tall thin one, the
child first reasons on the basis of one of the two transformed dimensions (for example, it's taller); then he
notices that the other dimension has also changed, it is
narrower. For a while he will oscillate between paying
attention to the increased height or to the decreased width.
Eventually, he ceases to pay attention exclusively to one
or the other and begins to consider them together. Then he

is likely to discover 'the interdependence of the two
transformations'. The child now 'starts to reason about
the transformations', and the probability increases that
'he will discover that the two variations are inverse to
each other ... the child now finds a reversible system'
(Piaget, 1967a, pp.154-7). The child is not necessarily
clear about what he is doing. He is not yet self-conscious
enough to realise that he is rejecting and adopting different strategies but Piaget insists that it is always the
'failures or insufficiencies' of one strategy that lead to
the adoption of another, more 'equilibrated' strategy
(Piaget, 1957a, pp.58-9). These failures must be noticed
in some way by the subject himself since an unnoticed failure would not lead the child to change his strategy at all.
Piaget explains the abandonment of one strategy in favour
of another in terms of 'considerations by the subject',
his 'choice of strategies', his 'doubts' and 'reasoning',
what he 'conceives', 'asks himself', 'imagines', 'discovers',
etc. (Piaget, 1957, pp.62-72).

This process of adopting more and more successful strategies
to cope with cognitive perturbations is what Piaget calls
the process of equilibration. It is his explanation for
cognitive development. Beginning with the infant's earliest
actions, 'every schema tends to assimilate every object',
but meets 'the resistance of objects to assimilation'
(Piaget, 1959, p.43). This produces 'perturbations' that
the child equilibrates by accommodating to the features of
the object which initially resisted assimilation. As new
structures develop, the child can notice problems that could
not ever arise for it before it had those structures. In
coping with these new problems he constructs more adequate
structures. Cognitive development then 'consists of reactions of compensation to perturbations (relative to previous
schemas) which make necessary a variation of the initial
schemas' (Piaget, 1959, p.50).

Piaget thinks that this explanation can be understood as
the same kind of process as those found in mechanical and
biological systems where the adaptation of the system to
external intrusions of the environment is accomplished by
self-regulation of the internal activity of the system
itself. However, there seem to be important differences
between on the one hand the awareness of the child that his
strategies for coping with the environment are not succeed-
ing and his consequent attempt to try other strategies and
on the other hand, the response to a rise in temperature
of a mechanical system fitted with a thermostat or the
response of a biological organism with some kind of homeo-

static control system to such a temperature change.   The
major difference, as Piaget himself describes his equilibration theory, is that the subject in cognitive equilibration
is aware of what he is doing, and he is aware of the significance of environmental events for his own intentions.
The relation is not one between an environmental event and
a responding mechanism but one between an interpretation of
an environmental event and a particular subject.

BIOLOGICAL EQUILIBRATION

In comparing his concept of equilibration with mechanical
and biological homeostatic systems, Piaget is not primarily
thinking of systems as simple as the control of a boiler by
a thermostat.   He compares cognitive equilibration with the
concept of 'homeorhesis' developed by the biologist
Waddington, rather than the simpler concept of 'homeostasis'.
Piaget says:

> It goes without saying that these regulatory mechanisms
> in knowledge at all levels, raise the problem of their
> relationship with organic regulations. At every stage
> of development of the living structure it is clear that,
> in fact, the essential question is that of the regulat-
> ing mechanisms. At the physiological level of the
> synergy of functions, the problem underlying all these
> questions is that of homeostasis; the equilibrium of
> each open system and the hormonal or nervous regulations
> which ensure co-ordination in the whole living entity.
> At the stage of ontogenetic development the central
> problem is that of the dynamic equilibrium of 'channeled'
> formulations - 'homeorhesis', which Waddington has
> rightly differentiated from homeostasis. (1971, p.12)

Waddington explains the concept of homeorhesis as follows:

> As a matter of fact, if a process of embryonic develop-
> ment is disturbed, it usually returns to normality some
> time before reaching the adult condition: its trajectory,
> that is to say, converges not merely to the normal end
> state, but to some earlier point on the path leading
> towards the end state.... Such a system exhibits a
> tendency towards a certain kind of equilibrium, which
> is restored after disturbance; but this equilibrium is
> not centred on a static state but rather on a direction
> or pathway of change. We might speak of such an equili-
> brium-property as a condition of 'homeorhesis', on the
> analogy with the well known expression heomeostasis
> which is appropriate when it is an unchanging state
> which is maintained. (1957, p.32)

Waddington goes on to name this 'pathway' to which the
organism returns after disturbance a 'chreod' suggesting
that there is some causal necessity built into this particular pathway. Different parts of the organism are more
or less canalised among these pathways and the degree of
homeorhetic control varies also from individual to individual and species to species.

 In Waddington's theory he gives importance to the fact
that selection in evolution acts directly on the phenotype
and only through the phenotype is the genotype altered.
The phenotype is an organism's morphological structure and
behaviour patterns, whereas the genotype is its stored
genetic information. Waddington points out that any one
genotype is sufficiently flexible to allow for the development within certain limits of a number of structurally and
behaviourally different phenotypes. Which one will develop
depends on the interactions between the developing organism
and the environment.

The genotype is more like a schematic blueprint than a
detailed map of the phenotype and has the capacity to
develop different self-regulating phenotypes that have
their own particular ways of accommodating to features of
the environment.

Organism and environment together form one system. The
phenotype is a result of a self-regulating developmental
process which is limited by the possibilities inherent in
the genotype but which, within those limits, can take
account of environmental changes and accommodate to them.

To illustrate the way in which the developmental potential
and the environment interact Waddington sketches a meta-
phorical 'epigenetic landscape'. He asks us to imagine a
ball (which may be representative of the cell, the organ,
the organism, the individual or the species). This ball
is moving in a landscape of hills and valleys. Clearly a
rolling ball will move more easily downhill than up and
will roll along the valley floor rather than along the tops
of the hills. The valleys represent 'chreods' as necessary
paths. The ball may potentially travel along any one of
these but may be travelling along only one at any one time.

The properties of the chreods themselves lead to some
accommodations with the organism as it passes. The valley
depth represents the degree of difficulty the ball would
have in leaving one path to follow another.

The developmental facts that the metaphor is intended to
bring out are, for example, that a single cell may have the
capacity to develop into either muscle or nerve tissue.
But it cannot do both at the same time. As differentiation
proceeds (as the ball rolls along the valley floor and
accommodates its movement to better cope with the particular
features of that floor) so it becomes increasingly difficult
to change paths. The location and depth of the valleys
represent the probability of one developmental process
giving way to another. At certain points different valleys
connect with each other and these connections represent the
critical periods during development at which sudden changes
can occur.

A real ball pushed up a hill will roll back into the valley
again. It may roll a little up the opposite hill. But
eventually, losing momentum, it will continue on its path
as if it had not been interrupted. In this way it compensates for the perturbation and preserves its initial direction. It does not return to its initial state but to its
initial direction. This is why Waddington refers to this
kind of compensation as homeorhesis in contrast to homeostasis which leads to the preservation of the original
state. The explanation of the tendency of organisms to
return to a chreod after disturbance depends on genetic
factors which are the result of evolutionary change. He
says:

> It is important to realise that the comparatively simple
> orderliness of the epigenetic landscape ... is a property
> of a higher order dependent on an underlying network of
> interactions which is vastly more complicated. The
> cells proceeding along any developmental pathway must
> have a metabolism of some corresponding complexity....
> In well-studied forms such as Drosophila we know that
> the development of any given organ such as the wing is
> influenced by very many genes which operate in sequence
> and in many cases interact with one another. Since each
> gene must be regarded as a distinct chemical entity, the
> path of development as it is observed by the anatomist
> must be viewed as the resultant of all the very numerous
> processes in which these genes are involved in the cells
> concerned. (Waddington, 1957, p.35)

In biology the explanation for the direction of development
is causal in that it is to be explained in terms of the
chemical activity within the individual and the chemical
constituents of the genes. The particular chemical constituents of the genes and the ways that they interact can,
according to Waddington, be explained causally in terms of

the effect of evolution on the epigenetic landscape. The direction of development, the chreod, depends on previous chemical activity within the gene as a result of the pheno-type's interaction with the environment.

COGNITIVE EQUILIBRATION

In spite of many similarities of approach between Piaget's and Waddington's theories, Piaget's conception of equilibra-tion cannot, as he claims, be understood in the same way as Waddington's concept. Piaget claims that progress in dev-elopment follows an invariant order. He outlines the following principles for development:
1 All development proceeds in 'one' direction.
2 Progress in development follows an invariable 'order'.

This is from:
     (i) subjective to objective
    (ii) concrete to formal
   (iii) whole to part
    (iv) particular to general
     (v) simple to complex
   (vi) from simple associationism to an understanding
       of causal and other types of implication.

But where does this direction come from? In Waddington's theory of biological development the epigenetic landscape which determines the direction of development is structured by an underlying network of complex chemical interactions. In Piaget's theory the direction seems to be imparted to development by a number of different influences. In the first place since one of the ways in which development occurs is by the integration of two or more subordinate structures to form a superordinate structure there is an invariant direction imparted by the logic of this.

One of the most important features of Piaget's concept of development is the alternation between the progressive differentiation and integration which operates both within and between stages. He says:
> Overall structures are integrative and non-interchange-able. Each results from the preceding one, integrating it as a subordinate structure, and prepares for the subsequent one, into which it is sooner or later itself integrated. (Piaget and Inhelder, 1973, p.153)

At the sensori-motor stage, for example, looking and listen-ing are co-ordinated into 'things heard', which is in turn a subordinate level in means/end relationships and so on.

Obviously, co-ordination of two subordinate actions cannot
occur to form the superordinate action until the child can
perform the two subordinate actions. The child cannot, that
is, combine listening with looking until he can do each
independently. So if in deciding what is involved in being
able to do C, C is defined in such a way that it implies
the co-ordination of subordinate actions A and B, then it
is a logical not an empirical matter that C follows the
acquisition of A and B.

In other words, the notion of hierarchic integration implies
that there is a logical sequence to the stages of development. If each stage is defined in such a way as to incorporate the lower stage or the higher level tasks used to
test development level have been defined in such a way as
to incorporate the lower level tasks then the claim for the
invariance of the sequence of developmental stages has the
force of an analytic claim.

As Popper has pointed out, scientists aim to establish
empirical, not logical, connections. They are concerned
to discover why things are as they are when they could
well have been otherwise, not to establish analytic truths
which could not have been otherwise.

In commenting on some of Piaget's findings, Flavell and
Wohlhill comment:
> The existence of these relations poses something of a
> conundrum for the developmental psychologist, however.
> We are accustomed to thinking of ourselves as students
> of nature, not of logic, and we seek to discover,
> rather than reason out, the developmental connections
> between acquisitions. If someone predicts that a pair
> of acquisitions A and B emerge in a fixed and invariant
> order for all children, our immediate inclination is
> to want to test the proposition empirically. In the
> case of acquisitions linked by implicative mediation,
> however, it is hard to see any justification for any
> kind of empirical test. (1969, p.86)

Piaget himself seems to be unaware that his comments on the
'necessity' of the order of the stages might be ambiguous.
He says, for example:
> If we restrict ourselves to major structures, it is
> strikingly obvious that cognitive stages have a
> sequential property, that is, they appear in a fixed
> order of succession because each one of them is

necessary for the formulation of the following one.
(Piaget, 1970c, p.71)

It is not clear here, or in many of his other uses of
'necessary', whether he means actually necessary in the
way in which it is necessary to break eggs to make
omelettes or logically necessary in the way in which the
co-ordination of two sub-processes requires that the two
sub-processes be available to the child.

A second source of the direction of development is provided
by the overarching framework of Piaget's general theory.
He assumes the existence of the organism as a structured
whole interacting with an environment to which it must
adapt if it is to survive. It has only two 'mechanisms'
to effect this adaptation and these are assimilation and
accommodation. If there is to be progress at all then
assimilation must be assimilation of more and more features
of the environment. Progress is constituted by increasing
'openness' to the environment. Piaget believes that inevitably this progress towards increasing 'openness' must result
in the logico-mathematical structures. Because of their
abstraction and generality they are the most 'open' to the
environment and 'multiply the field of' the possibilities
of assimilatory activity (Piaget, 1971, p.123)

Increasing accommodation, on the other hand, must result in
the development of the abstract structures because its
tendency is to make the organism more and more independent
of the vicissitudes of the environment. The development of
physiological mechanisms for the maintenance of internal
temperature, for example, decreases the organism's dependence
on environmental temperature. The logico-mathematical
structures of thought constitute an abstract internal world
independent of the environment.

One can see the direction given to development by the processes of assimilation and accommodation by looking at the
characteristics that Piaget considers important in contrasting cognitive levels.

Cognitive states of equilibrium can be compared and contrasted in four different ways:

1 'The Field of Application'
This is the class of objects or properties that the
equilibrated action system (that is, schema) accommodates
to and assimilates. The field of application of the
schemes developed in earliest perception is very small,

comprising only the immediate perceptual field of the
subject. It is obviously much larger for a concrete
operational classification grouping, for example, since
this comprises all the objects subsumed by the classes
and subclasses, to which the grouping structure is
applied.

2 'Mobility'

This refers to the spatio-temporal distances which the
actions of the system can cover. A single perception
is not mobile at all. Representational thought is
potentially much more mobile than sensori-motor activities and perceptions. The difficulty here is really to
see just what Piaget is talking about, and why he wants
to call it mobility. It seems to be more or less
complexity of content.

3 'Permanence'

This property and the next (stability) which are closely
related both concern the resistance of the system to
change of state when there are changes of input from
the environment. A system is said to be in permanent
equilibrium when the elements on which the subject's
actions are performed do not mean anything different to
the subject when he pays attention to other elements.
A system is changed when new elements are met with which
cause a certain change in the way of thinking of the
child. This change in the way of thinking may then be
applied to the old elements and they will be seen in a
new light. A system is said to be in a state of permanent equilibrium when the formation of a new system does
not invalidate the meaning of the old schema. A simple
classificatory system will provide an example. If
humans are understood to be a subclass of mammals, then
they will still be a subclass of mammals even when
mammals are shown to be a subclass of animals and consequently, human beings are also shown to be a subclass
of animals.

4 'Stability'

This is the most important factor of the four for the
explanation of development and understanding. It refers
to the system's capacity to compensate for and cancel
out perturbations which tend to alter the existing state
of equilibrium. For example, perceptual and preoperational thought structures are systems of less than stable
equilibrium because they are only partly under the
influence of knowledge gained in other ways, for example,
the fact that one knows that two lines are of the same

length does not mean that one will not still look longer
than the other if one is drawn with outward pointing
arrows at the ends and the other with inward pointing
arrows (The Müller-Lyer Illusion). On the other hand,
the reversible operations of concrete and formal operational structures guarantee complete stability. Each
+A has its -A which annuls it; each p has its reciprocal
q which compensates it. The crucial importance of this
for the definition of the concept of equilibrium is
shown by the fact that, throughout his writings, Piaget
uses equilibrium and reversibility interchangeably.
They are not however theoretically identical. A structure is in equilibrium because it is reversible. Reversibility is a necessary by-product of the equilibration
process. A cognitive system which is strongly equilibrated must contain the balancing and compensating
functions of one or more of the forms of reversibility.

The theoretical concepts that Piaget uses then to describe
the process of development necessitate that the direction
of development should be towards the development of increasingly general and abstract structures because these are the
most stable and the most 'open' to the potential implicit
in the environment.

The first explanation of the direction of development which
refers to increasing hierarchic integration of subordinate
structures into superordinate structures is based on the
definitions of the developmental stages. Consequently,
Piaget's claim for the invariance of the sequence of stages
is based on analytic truths. His second reason for the
direction of development is based on the meanings given to
the major theoretical concepts of assimilation and accommodation. The direction of development towards increasing
abstraction and generality follows from the overarching
framework of Piaget's theory and is consequently not
empirically but conceptually based.

IS PIAGET'S THEORY CAUSAL?

So far, the explanations put forward by Piaget to account
for the direction of development have involved conceptual
rather than empirical considerations. But what of the
equilibration account itself with its story of cognitive
perturbations and compensations? Mischel (1971) argues
persuasively that this account provides a conceptual framework for fitting in the empirically discovered details of
what children specifically do at these different stages.

He says:

> When we say that inconsistencies need to be removed,
> perplexities need to be clarified, dissonant cognitions
> need to be adjusted to fit better, novelties need to be
> assimilated to what is known, and so forth, we are not
> enumerating empirical discoveries but are stating the
> prescriptions that guide directed thinking. (Mischel,
> 1971, p.342)

Mischel goes on to argue that to say that problems need
solutions, that cognitive concepts need to be resolved
(equilibrated) and so forth is to state the norms that
govern the social practice of 'directed thinking'.
Piaget discusses the 'process' of equilibration as if he
were presenting an empirical theory about the workings of
the mind, a theory which is continuous with biological
theories about organic processes of assimilation and
accommodation. Mischel, on the other hand, wants to suggest
that Piaget's general account of equilibration, or the way
in which a child's awareness of cognitive perturbations
motivates his intellectual development and functioning,
does not constitute a theory to be confirmed or refuted by
the facts:

> It is an analysis, or rational reconstruction of how
> we think in accordance with the norms that govern
> directed thinking - an analysis which Piaget uses as
> a framework for an empirical mapping of the stages
> through which the child passes in coming to think in
> accordance with the norms of adult logic. (Mischel,
>   1971, p.343)

When a child realises that nothing has happened to cause a
diminution in a quantity of lemonade when it is poured from
one container into another he has not been caused to
believe that the amount has been conserved. He has come
to realise it, to understand it. Piaget's explanation in
terms of assimilation and accommodation suggests that once
a child has come to see the truth of conservation he cannot
'unsee' it. This clearly is true. But he has not been
caused to see it in the way that his having drunk a bottle
of sherry might 'cause' him to deny conservation. He has
come to see that there is no good reason why the quantity
should have changed and it is this reasoning which affects
his beliefs, not a causal process. There is an essential
difference between being compelled to do something in the
sense of 'cause' and being compelled to accept something in
the sense that the arguments in its favour outweigh arguments against it. In the second case, one is only
'compelled' at all if one subscribes to a certain degree

of rationality, if one understands the concepts employed
in the arguments, if one chooses to pay attention to the
arguments. In a sense, one can say that one is compelled
to accept the arguments through one's own free choice.   In
the case where one is caused to do something, for example,
fall over a cliff as the result of a push, one has no free
choice in the matter. There is an essential difference
between being 'caused' to do something in a mechanistic
sense and being compelled to believe, admit or understand
something because the reasons for it are convincing.

Seen in this way, Piaget's account of the interests, con-
flicts, modes of conduct and reasoning that are typical of
children at different stages of development is empirical.
But his overarching theory, his general account of more and
more equilibrated structures is not an empirical theory.
What Piaget says about 'environmental perturbations' and
the achieving of 'equilibrium' cannot be explicated, as
Piaget hoped with reference to the use of these concepts
in biology. It can only be made meaningful by applying our
normative concepts of consistency, objectivity, validity
and so on to the child's efforts to understand a culturally
defined subject matter.

Certain things that Piaget says suggest that he would not
reject this interpretation. For example, when he claims
that he is dealing with the epistemic rather than the psychological subject. Talk about the actions of the epistemic
subject is not talk about the real activities of any actual
subject but is a way of talking about abstract logico-
mathematical relationships.

But there are other places where Piaget insists that the
equilibration model provides a causal theory about actual
mechanisms whose operations can be understood as a continu-
ation of the equilibrating mechanisms of organic processes.
He thinks that it provides an empirical, scientific theory
of the operations of the mind.

While most philosophers and many psychologists would want
to make a sharp distinction between these two interpretations
of Piaget's theory, he himself would claim that they were
simply complementary aspects of one thing. Piaget can maintain this view because he holds that 'logico-mathematical
systems' since they can trace their development back to the
successful actions of the sensori-motor period, are adequate
representations of reality. And he holds that a causal
explanation is a projection of these structures onto reality.
Consequently, he can maintain that the same causal explanation

can have both a formal structural aspect and a material
causal aspect   Piaget says:

> There need be no conflict between physio-chemical causal-
> ity and psychological implication any more than between
> physical and material experience and the logico-mathemat-
> ical deductions used to explain it: there is an isomorph-
> ism between causality and implication ... and the future
> harmony between causal physiology and analyses based on
> implication should be sought on the basis of the relation-
> ship now existing between experimental or causal, and
> mathematical or implicative, physics. (1969, p.xxiii)

PIAGET'S CONSTRUCTIVISM

Piaget characterises his own view as 'constructive'. The
'isomorphism' of causal and implicative systems seems to be
a direct result of this constructivism. We have shown
already how Piaget traces the abstract structures of logico-
mathematical thought back through the stages to their roots
in the interiorised actions of the sensori-motor stage.
The 'systems of implication' that Piaget talks about are
mental structures resulting from the interiorisation of
action.

The subject has himself constructed these logico-mathematical
structures. He himself is their source. Therefore they
must be adequate representations of reality since experience
must conform to them. In just this way did Kant argue that
experience must conform to the Categories of the Pure
Understanding. If an 'experience' did not conform then it
was not something which could be experienced by us. We
experience things only when we apply the Categories to the
data of perception. We contribute these organising concepts
to our experience, therefore it logically must conform to
them.

Similarly, for Piaget, to become an object of experience
for us, that is, to be assimilable, something must conform
to the structures that we have developed. If it does not
conform it simply does not form part of our experience.
Reality, in so far as it can form part of our experience,
must conform to the structures that we apply to it.

A causal explanation is the result of 'projecting' our
logical co-ordinations onto material substrates. The structure of reality revealed by the causal explanations of
natural science must be isomorphic with the structure of
our thoughts because a causal explanation involves the
application of those thought structures to reality.

Piaget recognises that this theory is similar to Kant's theory. He says:

> If we keep to the spirit of his pronouncement rather than to the letter, Kant was undoubtedly right in claiming that perception is organised from the outset - and that the same subjective sources which underlie the categories of understanding underlie perceptual organisation. (Piaget, 1969, pp.361-2)

To achieve a causal explanation involves assimilating the observed relationships between material things into the logico-mathematical framework of the subject's thought structures. Reality and the logico-mathematical framework are necessarily isomorphic.

Formal logic is only a 'formalised and highly enriched extension of the logic behind the subject's activities' (Piaget, 1970b, p.43). Psychology studies the way these systems develop into 'systems of implication in the wide sense'. The psychologist, like any other scientist, will use logico-mathematical representations. These will be isomorphic with the actual activities of children for the same reason that there is isomorphism between the formal structures and relations of mathematical physics and the material structures they represent. The explanation of the specific activities of individuals is a result of assimilating them into the logico-mathematical frameworks of the psychologist. There is always isomorphism between the implicatory and causal systems because the latter are 'projections' onto reality of the former (Piaget, 1970b, p.50).

It becomes clear from all this that Piaget's apparently contradictory claims about the nature of his theory of equilibration rest on a philosophical theory about the nature of the human mind and human knowledge which is not in any way an empirical theory.

The next chapter will explore Piaget's concept of knowledge and show its philosophical strengths and weaknesses. The main question will be whether a theory based on the construction of knowledge by the individual could provide an adequate philosophical account of human knowledge.

SUMMARY

In this chapter we criticised the causal explanation of development implicit in the equilibrium model which,

although Piaget does not refer to it as such, is a kind of
learning theory. Apart from suggesting ways in which
cognitive adaptations are engendered, it provides Piaget
with a list of criteria for comparing and contrasting
different stages of development: for example; mobility,
stability, permanence and so on.

The question raised in this chapter is how far Piaget's
explanation in terms of the development of logical structures by an equilibration process between the inner world
of the subject and the outer world of the object could be
counted as a causal explanation at all. Comparisons are
made between the use of concepts like homeorhesis in biology
and Piaget's use of the same concept in epistemology.

We argued that the broad stage-independent model based on
assimilation of reality to mental structures is based on
a priori reasoning about our concepts of rationality,
knowledge and so on. The detailed description of the kinds
of things that children can do at different stages is
empirical.

Chapter 5

Objective knowledge

PREVIEW

Piaget's theory can be seen as an attempt to trace the
increasing objectification of thought. This chapter is
concerned with two major questions. Firstly, what does
Piaget think objective thought consists in? Secondly, is
he correct in this view? The conclusion will be that his
view is not correct since he fails to take proper account
of the social nature of knowledge. This failure leads him
to make misleading statements about the nature of objective
knowledge and the process of objectification of thought.
It also leads him to impute far greater intelligibility
to the child's thought than his observations warrant.

PIAGET'S CONCEPT OF OBJECTIVE KNOWLEDGE

Piaget distinguishes between the objective and the subjective in four distinct ways: (1) Objectivity results when a
balance has been attained between accommodation and assimilation of reality. (2) Thought turns towards reality only
in so far as it becomes structured and begins to reflect
about its own structure. Consequently the objective is
said to depend on the degree of coherence of the subject's
thought. (3) The subjective is closely linked with the
egocentric and consequently the objective with the 'socialised'. (4) Finally Piaget distinguishes between the
subjective thought and action of the psychological subject
which is the individual and the objective thought and
action of the epistemic subject; the supra-individual subject. But Piaget's tests for the objectivity of thought
are concerned exclusively with tests for the internal

116

coherence and consistency of the structures of thought.
Although what is objective is said to correspond to reality
the only way in which it is characterised as being objective
is by participating in one of the two forms of reversibility.
Given that the structure the child is applying is reversible,
the other aspects of objective knowledge are said to follow.
For example, a structure becomes reversible only when it
achieves a state of equilibrium, that is to say, a balance
between accommodation and assimilation. The child only
realises that actions are reversible when he begins to
reflect on the actions themselves rather than thinking about
the objects they are performed on. The more structured the
child's thought becomes the less egocentric it is and consequently the more socialised it becomes. Finally, rivers-
ible structures are the domain of the epistemic subject not
the psychological subject. So although Piaget can be said
to offer several answers to the essential question of what
makes thought objective, they all depend in the end on the
coherence and consistency of the structures of thought.

To take the first criterion, that of the balance to be
achieved between assimilation and accommodation. What can
we make of this?

The concepts of assimilation and accommodation are derived
from biology, the concept of equilibrium, more specifically
from cybernetics. Assimilation refers to the imbibing and
subsequent altering and changing of substances from the
environment in order to contribute to the maintenance and
growth of the organism. Accommodation refers to the changes
that the organism has to make within its own structure or
behaviour in order to be able to assimilate the elements
from the environment. Equilibrium refers to some sort of
state of balance between these two aspects of adaptation
such that the organism succeeds in successfully assimilating
what it needs for maintaining itself.

Piaget does not stress the achievement of a steady state
of equilibrium as some kind of ideal end state of this
process. What he stresses is the continual swings and
checks that such a system undergoes. He is searching for
a model to represent adequately the dynamic, changing,
always moving nature of the 'process' of development.

His model in terms of formal mathematics does not succeed
in capturing this dynamism. He himself (1960) suggests
that the dynamism could be captured by the use of concepts
derived from computer programming analogies, but he does
not himself use such concepts.

The organism itself is rarely in a state of equilibrium
but the structures which it develops do achieve stable
equilibrium. When a person utilises stable structures in
his thinking, Piaget would say that he is thinking
objectively.

A stable structure is one where the assimilatory and
accommodatory functions are in some sort of balance. A
major assumption lurking behind this way of thinking is
that gaining knowledge or understanding is bringing two
things of different natures into relations with each other,
the object and the subject. The subject does the accommodating and the object (or features of it) are assimilated.
Piaget is a dualist. He believes that there are two kinds
of things, subjects which accommodate and objects which
are assimilated and accommodated to.

Epistemology, according to Piaget, starts from the dicho-
tomy of subject and object and is concerned with exploring
the relationship between the two. Objective understanding
results when a balance is achieved between the input from
the environment and the structuring whose source is the
subject himself. His view of knowledge therefore is inter-
actionist. Knowledge results from the interaction of the
subject with objects.

Piaget's second criterion for objective knowledge is that
knowledge is the more objective the more structured it
becomes. Although Piaget has four criteria for objectivity,
all his actual tests for objectivity reduce to tests for
complexity, abstraction and stability of structures. All
the tests concern the coherence of thought, the 'accord of
thought with itself', as Piaget puts it. The way to find
out whether equilibrium has been reached, for example, is
to test the subject's knowledge for coherence. The test
for the level of decentration that has been achieved, that
is, for egocentrism or socialisation in the subject's
thought, is again a test of coherence and the final criterion is that of whether the thoughts should be attributed
to the psychological or the epistemic subject. Actions
are only thought to be attributable to the epistemic subject
if they are structured and coherent.

Apart from the coherence, that is, the 'accord of thought
with itself', Piaget is very concerned to show that he is
a realist in some sense. He believes that our thinking is
constructed by ourselves but that it 'accords with reality'
It is not misleading as to the nature of reality but does
generally reflect its structural features.

This comes about because thought develops through the transformation of one stage into the next. Consequently the
structural properties of the earliest forms of thought in
the subject, endure through multiple transformations of
content and level. The structural properties, then, of
the highest and most abstract forms of thought such as
mathematics are derived from the structural properties of
the sensori-motor period. That period, which involves
action in the environment, is the period when the basic
structural properties of the world are discovered. I say
discovered where Piaget would say constructed but in his
system it amounts to almost the same thing. The structural
properties are those of 'successful actions in the world'.
To be successful, then, actions have to reflect the
structure of the environment. If they did not they could
not succeed.

Consequently the 'accord of thought with things' grows out
of the fact that abstract thought is transformed sensori-
motor 'thought' which to have come about at all must
reflect the structure of the world.

Piaget explains the increasing objectification of thought
in terms of its increasing structural complexity and its
increasing abstraction or freedom from 'the here and now',
freedom from reliance on perception. The subject matter of
concrete operational thought is manipulable, concrete objects. But the subject matter of formal thinking is the
structure of operational thought. The crucial point here
is that we seem to have lost the terms of the relations,
that is, the objects which are to be structured. One of
the most important functions of the biological assimilation/
accommodation model was to show how intelligence could turn
outwards from its initial egocentricity to reality. Objectivity was seen as correspondence with reality. It appears
as if objectivity is being equated with 'consistent structure' and so, by implication, reality is being equated with
consistent structure. But the source of structure according to Piaget is the mind not the external world.

PERCEPTION

This raises the question of the place of perception in
Piaget's theory. Piaget in effect restricts perception to
the functioning of purely sensory systems. His book on
perception (1969) is concerned largely with offering
explanations for perceptual illusions and his explanations
are entirely in terms of sensory mechanisms. They make no

reference to the beliefs or knowledge of the perceiver.
This is not surprising in view of the kinds of illusions
that Piaget chooses to explain. Most of them are concerned
with the over-estimation or under-estimation of the size of
one figure when it is compared to another figure (for
example, p.44, the Müller-Lyer illusion, p.49, the Delboeuf
illusion). The main feature of these illusions is that
they are not in fact affected to any appreciable extent by
the knowledge and beliefs of the perceiver. Even if we
know that the two lines of the Müller-Lyer illusion are
exactly the same length, we still 'see' one of them as
longer than the other. But this is as far as Piaget's concept of perception reaches. He restricts his discussion of
illusions to those which are due to sensory factors, that
is to say, factors involved in the way that the stimulation
of the sense organs takes place and does not consider
illusions which are caused by our own beliefs and values,
for example, the tendency to overestimate the size of a
coin of greater value in comparison with a coin of lesser
value.

Simple Gestalt structures which have their source in the
physiological make up of the subject are what gives rise
to these illusions, and the only way that their effect can
be overcome is by their being incorporated into the system
of operational structures. By talking about their effect
being overcome Piaget does not mean that we no longer
suffer from these illusions. He means that they no longer
affect our judgment. When we can actually measure the
two lines of the Müller-Lyer diagram and see that they
are both the same length then, although we may continue to
see them as of different lengths, we are not misled by
them; we can treat them as if they were of the same length.
We have already discussed several examples in which the
initial beliefs of the child are mistaken because they are
based on perception and are only corrected when he has
developed the appropriate logico-mathematical schemata.
For example, the child might think that a collection of
beads contains more beads when they are spread out than
when they are bunched together.

In view of the distorting effects of perceptual structures
it is not surprising that Piaget denies that the intellectual structures derive from them. The intellectual derives
from the activity of the subject whereas the perceptual
structures derive from his physiology. The link between
perception and intelligence lies in the sensori-motor
period when the child is acting in an intelligent way on
perceptual objects:

The figural structures of perception do not lie at the
source of systems of operational transformations but
prefigure them indirectly (or by collateral kinship) in
so far as they have already been structured by the
operative structures involved in the relevant sensori-
motor activity. (Piaget, 1969, p.359)

Since Piaget restricts perception to these purely sensory
systems and denies that it can be the source of any of the
intellectual structures he is clearly denying the empiricist
thesis that perception is the source of our knowledge. But
he seems to want to claim as Kant did that perception provides the condition for the application of our concepts in
experience. He says:

In other words, while operations elaborate general frameworks and tend to reduce the real to structures of
deducible transformations, perception is of the here
and now and serves the function of fitting each object
or particular event into its available assimilative
frameworks. Perception is not therefore the source of
knowledge because knowledge derives from the operative
schemes of action as a whole. Perceptions function as
connectors which establish constant and local contacts
between actions and operations on the one hand and
objects or events on the other. (1969, p.359)

Kant has managed to make this sort of story much more
plausible by according such an important place to the
'form of sensibility'. The structures which are the result
of the particular form of sensibility that human beings
have are not the same kinds of structure as the formal
structures of the categories, the a priori concepts of the
pure understanding. They show the difference between a
purely formal, consistent 'concept of experience' and a
possible or actual experience. Piaget criticises Kant for
making this distinction so rigidly:

Kant raised an insurmountable problem for the empiricist
position when he pointed out that if space and time are
the a priori forms of 'sensibility' then an organisation
of perceptual forms can originate within the subject
himself. No doubt Kant was referring to a transcend-
ental subject rather than to actual perceptions and
real constructions. No doubt, too, he continued to be
influenced by the traditional, water-tight compartments
of sensibility on the one side and understanding on the
other. But if we keep the spirit of his pronouncement
rather than to the letter Kant was undoubtedly right in
claiming that perception is organised from the outset,
that it does not proceed from an association between

isolated sensations and that the same subjective sources
which underlie the categories of understanding underlie
the perceptual organisation. (Piaget, 1969, p.362)

Piaget is surely wrong here not to stick to the letter of
Kant's pronouncement. The source of the a priori forms of
sensibility is not the same as the source of the categories
of understanding and the difference is very important.   It
allows Kant to make that contact with the world which
Piaget's theory fails to make. Piaget admits that the
initial, physiologically caused structures of perception
can affect what we know and believe but they distort, they
do not add to our knowledge. It is consequently very
difficult to see how perception can provide the link between
the operational structures of intelligence on the one hand
and objects and events on the other hand. Since the features
of perception which make it perception for us are the distorting features overcome by the operations of intelligence,
perception cannot provide any knowledge until it is
'corrected' by the intellectual schemata and concepts so
it cannot serve the function of 'fitting each object or
particular event into its available assimilative framework'.

Piaget refers constantly to his debt to Kant and it is
correct to see Piaget as essentially in the Kantian tradition. His biological theory is expressing essentially the
same points as Kant's epistemology, but they are dressed
up in the misleading biological analogies. However, on
this point Piaget and Kant clearly are in disagreement.

For Kant, what makes a concept objective is the possibility
of the construction of the object in intuition. For Piaget,
a concept is objective if its construction is possible in
'thought'.

Kant is continually emphasising the fundamental difference
between sensibility and understanding while at the same
time he insists on their complementary function. The
minimum organisation that anything which could count as
experience must have is laid down by the categories of
understanding. For any judgment to be objective it must
conform to the categories but in relation to possible
experience. Objectivity is thus relative to sensibility.
The structure of objective judgment thus depends on both
the categories of the understanding and sensibility. It
is not the concept of an intuitive condition that might be
added to a concept or included in its definition that gives
full meaning to the category. It is the actual condition
of sensibility itself, the condition of its actual use in

specific circumstances according to a rule.

Kant saw the importance of the terms of the relations.
What the understanding structures is intuitions and without
those there can be nothing for us to know about. This
explains the importance for Kant of the 'things as they
are themselves' to serve as the source of our intuitions.
For Piaget, content, at the beginning of development, plays
an inescapable part. But even then, Piaget insists, paying
attention to content is what distorts knowledge. However,
by the time mature thought is reached all our knowledge is
characterised by a description of the 'logic of actions'.
The content, the world, seems to have dropped out.

Piaget criticises Kant for making the distinction between
the form of experience and its content an absolute distinction. For Piaget the 'form' is the way that one acts or
thinks and the 'content' is whatever one acts on or thinks
about. The great advances that the child makes from the
concrete operational stage to the stage of hypothetical
thought are brought about through the child's ceasing to
think about the objects he is manipulating and beginning
to think about his own actions and operations themselves
and the 'content' is the dolls, bricks, marbles etc. that
he performs them on and whose presence is necessary for him
to be able to perform these operations at all. At the
level of hypothetical thought, this 'content' is dropped
and the child is able to think about the relations between
the actions that he performed at the previous stage. He
is using as 'content' what was previously 'form'. In
'Structuralism' Piaget says:

> Form and content are correlatives, not absolutes; the
> contents on which logical forms are imposed are not
> formless, they have forms of their own else they could
> not 'potentially be logicised'. And the forms of what
> originally appeared to be 'pure content' in turn them-
> selves 'have content' though less distinctly made out,
> a content with its own form, and so on, indefinitely,
> each element being 'content' relative to some prior
> element and 'form' for some posterior element.
> (1970c, p.29)

The effect of this is to make all knowledge concerned with
formal, structural properties. The structure of a later
stage uses as content what was the structure of a previous
stage. That it is being 'used' as content does not mean
that we cannot recognise it as a structural property. The
child is looking at structural properties in a new way but
it is still structural properties that he is looking at.

This fails to make the point that Kant was trying to make by distinguishing between the form and content of experience; that in experience there are two kinds of things, or properties, structural ones and intuitive ones. Piaget blurs this distinction. His view of the world as we know it at the end of the process of development that he details is that it is a world of possible transformations or operations. It is devoid of content.

So far the argument has been that Kant's distinction between structure and content is a valid and useful one. Piaget denies this and stresses instead that objective thought is concerned only with structural properties which are constructed by the mind. This leaves obscure the question of how perception can do the only job that Piaget assigns it, that of providing the points of application for our concepts.

In fact the whole question of the place of perception in Piaget's theory is obscure. His book on perception (1969) is a mixture of philosophical argument and empirical fact. It is clearly putting forward a certain philosophical viewpoint concerning the nature of perception. This viewpoint is one which restricts perception to the functioning of sensory systems. Any knowledge that might be said to result from perception results in fact from the corrections of the distortions that paying undue attention to perceptual features (what Piaget calls 'centration') of our environment leads us into. The corrections are the result of, in the first place, sensori-motor activities. These lead to 'decentration'. We gradually cease to be unduly influenced by perceptual features of the environment as our activities lead us to discover the structural features.

Perception, then, is initially due to physiological functioning, but is soon affected by our activities. These activities serve as a correcting influence on the distorting effects inherent in the sensory mechanisms that lead to perception. It seems as if the only role for perception is to supply distortions of reality which need to be corrected. Almost all of Piaget's discussion of perception is at the level of what happens on the retina. Clearly perception cannot yield knowledge about the environment. But it is puzzling that we should have a complex sensory system whose sole function is to provide distorted views of reality which require correction by the mechanisms of intellectual functioning.

THE ECOLOGICAL APPROACH TO VISUAL PERCEPTION

Piaget is putting forward a philosophical view of the nature
of perception restricting it to the functioning of sensory
systems. A recently developed and radical theory of perception has been proposed by J.J. Gibson. Gibson would see
himself as diametrically opposed to Piaget not only in his
views of the limited role that perception can play but also
in his general account of what the development of understanding is all about. Gibson (1979) claims that perception
refers to the picking up of information from the environment
and that this process does not involve any mental events
such as beliefs or even schemata.

Piaget sees the development of human understanding as the
construction of abstract structures to be applied to reality,
Gibson sees it as the perceptual exploration of the environment. He defines the environment as : 'the surroundings of
those organisms that perceive and behave, that is to say,
animals' (1979, p.7). In this sense of environment, the
animal and the environment not only interact, they are
mutually dependent and complementary. But this environment
is not the same as the physical world if by that is meant
the world that is described by physics. That world is
structured by the basic concepts of space, time, matter and
energy. These concepts do not lead to a view of the animal
as mutually dependent on a complementary environment. They
lead to the view of an animal as a highly organised part of
the physical world but still a part and still an object.
Every animal is, to some degree, a perceiver of the environment and a behaver in it. But this is not to say that it
perceives the world of physics and behaves in the space and
time of physics.

The size-level, time scale of events, persistence and change
of the environment are all suited to the size, capacities
and needs of animals. The size level is the intermediate
size measured in terms of metres and millimetres. The time
scale of events in the environment is measured in terms of
years and seconds. Some aspects of the environment persist
and others change. Notions such as the conservation of
matter of the physical sciences or the constant flux of
the sense-datum theorist are not applicable to the perceptual
environment.

Information about this environment, including information
about what things can be used for, what they are good for,
is specified in what Gibson calls the 'ambient optic array'.
This is the light which having originally come from one

source of illumination, is reflected from the surfaces of objects in the environment. Since the surfaces differ in their degree of reflectance and in their degree of illumination, the reflected light will be structured in such a way as to reveal the surface texture and shape of the objects. The ways in which surfaces are laid out and their textures and shapes have intrinsic meaning for behaviour, unlike the abstract, formal, intellectual concepts of mathematical space.

Apart from claiming that the environment, as he defines it, has intrinsic meaning for the animal, Gibson points out something which, although obvious and well-known, is overlooked in most theories of perception. This is the fact that a perceiver is usually moving, and is almost always capable of viewing things from different angles and over a period of time. Thus if an object disappears when we turn our head, it will reappear if we just turn our head back and so on. The information gained by a moving observer specifies persistance and change in the environment.

Gibson's theory is complex and fascinating and this brief mention does no justice to it. But it is relevant to a critique of Piaget in that he provides a plausible alternative to Piaget's account of the place of perception and he does it while denying that perception is cognitively mediated. He says:

> The doctrine that we could not perceive the world around us unless we already had the concept of space is nonsense. It is quite the other way around. We could not conceive of empty space unless we could see the ground under our feet and the sky above. Space is a myth, a ghost, a fiction for geometers. All that sounds very strange, no doubt, but I urge the reader to entertain the hypothesis. For if you agree to abandon the dogma that 'percepts without concepts are blind', as Kant put it, a deep theoretical mess, a genuine quadmire, will dry up. (Gibson, 1979, p.3)

Gibson's theory has been criticised largely on the grounds that it fails to discuss the contribution that the perceiver makes to perception. (See, for example, Neisser, 1976, p.9.) But in essence what Gibson is concerned to do is to attempt a new level of description, one that is appropriate to the world of perceiving, knowing subjects rather than one that is couched in terms of physics or mathematics.

Clearly, he is, like Piaget, putting forward a philosophical view about the nature of perception. But it is a view which

accords perception a fundamental role in the development of
an objective view of a common world. It is a view which is,
as Gibson himself says, hardly developed yet. His book,
like Piaget's, is a mixture of philosophical argument and
empirical fact and it is frequently difficult to distinguish
the two. It may, when it is developed into a more consistent form, offer a complement to Piaget's overemphasis of
the development of abstract thought.

OBJECTIVITY AND INTERSUBJECTIVITY

If the child is to be said to have any concepts at all then
he must be able to make objective distinctions. This he
can clearly do, on a small scale, at a very early age. By
the age of two Piaget claims that he has a concept of a
permanent object. However, in describing this concept
Piaget connects objectivity with some intrinsic features
of the conception. For example, it is said to be an objective concept because the child no longer sees the existence
of the object as depending on his own activity. This is
indeed an important part of the meaning of the concept of
an object. But it is not what makes the concept objective.
As Hamlyn has argued (1972), objectivity is connected with
the possession of a common framework of concepts and points
of reference. It is this common framework that the child
must gain entrance to. In the description of the child's
development of the concept of the permanent object in the
sensori-motor period, the child's egocentrism, his failure
to distinguish between aspects of himself and aspects of
the environment is the most important factor in distorting
his understanding. At the beginning of life the child
makes no distinction between the self and the non-self.
Consequently, he interprets things as if they were exten-
sions of himself or his own actions. The child behaves as
if he thought that the object was created by his own act
of perception.

> Through an apparently paradoxical mechanism ... it is
> precisely when the subject is the most self-centred
> that he knows himself the least and it is to the
> extent that he discovers himself that he places him-
> self in the universe and constructs it by virtue of
> that fact. In other words, egocentrism signifies the
> absence of both self-perception and objectivity, whereas
> acquiring possession of the object as such is on a par
> with the acquisition of self-perception. (Piaget,
> 1954, p.xii)

To claim that this is a paradox would seem to be a gross
exaggeration on Piaget's part. It seems fairly obvious
that the child would have to learn about himself and his
own place in the world as a complement to learning about
the world itself. The picture offered by empiricist epistemology is that the person, who is identified with his own
mind and experiences, is opposed to the physical world
which is external to him. He has to make sense of the
external world from the data (including the information
from other people) given to him. If this were possible
then a person would certainly have knowledge of the external world. But the claim made by Kant that we are not
given organised, intelligible experiences would seem to be
essentially correct. Any knowledge that we have is the
result of being supplied with data. However, Kant goes on
to say that we cannot understand anything, cannot represent
anything to ourselves, without first having constructed it
for ourselves. Anything that we might be given we must
organise and make intelligible for ourselves according to
certain synthetic rules. These rules are not given from
outside. They are the product of our own minds: 'We cannot
represent to ourselves anything as combined in the object
which we have not ourselves previously combined ... [such
combination is] an act of the self-activity of the subject'
(Kant, 'Critique of Pure Reason', B 130).

So, if we do know anything at all we not only know something
about the 'external world', but we also know something about
ourselves, something about our own minds. This does not
mean that we are aware of our knowledge as knowledge of our
own minds. What we are aware of is an organised reality.
But since the principles of that organisation derive from
the mind in being aware of an organised reality we are aware
of some of the features of the mind although we are not
aware of them as features of the mind but only as features
of reality.

This seems to be very close to the kind of thing that Piaget
is trying to say. We do have some 'data' from the external
world. It is the 'reality aliments' which nourish the function of assimilation. But we organise it for ourselves
according to the schemata that we have developed. So, in
knowing anything at all we not only know something about
the external world but we also know something about ourselves.
This is similar to Piaget's claim that the child overcomes
his initial egocentrism by becoming conscious of his own
activity as thinking and acting; by developing an understanding of the part played by the mind in structuring experience.
Knowledge of ourselves and knowledge of the world are two

sides of the same Kantian coin. This presents the gaining
of knowledge of the world as having two sides: an objective
side which is derived from external reality and a subjective side which is contributed by our own minds. It is this
sort of view about the nature of knowledge which has led
Piaget to identify having knowledge with achieving a balance
between assimilation (the taking in of 'objective' reality
aliments) and accommodation (the applying of 'subjective'
schemata).

The employment of this biological model suggests that the
balance to be attained is one between something about the
individual which is essentially subjective, that is, the
concept, and something about the world around us which is
objective, that is, the object. Knowledge is thus a blend
of the subjective and the objective. But the relationship
between a concept and the objects which are instances of
that concept is not that between something which is subjective and something which is objective. To have a concept is,
in Kantian terms, to have a rule for synthesising representations. It is to know the principle whereby something is
what it is. So to see something as an instance of a
concept is to see something to which one's knowledge of
the concept is appropriate. This is not a subjective
matter. In fitting something to a concept we are not
imposing on it a subjective point of view for to have a
concept is to know a rule and, as Wittgenstein has shown,
the notion of a subjective rule makes no sense.

Objectivity, as Piaget points out (1932) usually only
results from discussion, the sharing of views, being able
to see another person's point of view. But objectivity is
primarily connected with the achievement of or at least
striving for the attainment of truth. If discussion,
sharing of views and so on did not fairly often lead one to
the truth then these pastimes would not be regarded as
objective. This is not to claim that objectivity and truth
are to be equated. Clearly, adopting the most objective
method will sometimes lead us into error; and it is sometimes the case that a prejudiced, subjective point of view
will succeed in achieving a certain insight into the truth.
However, these are exceptions to the rule that the best way
to find out the truth is to disregard prejudice and subjectivity, vested interest and overwhelming emotion and be as
objective as possible. What this suggests is that objectivity is not a property or characteristic of truth itself or
true propositions but is rather the attitude which it is
appropriate to human beings to adopt in seeking and apprais-
ing the truth. So, to be objective is not to know the truth,

be in possession of the truth: it is to have an appropriate
attitude towards it.   This attitude will be one where
personal interests and grievances are ignored; where arguments are weighed on their merits as arguments regardless
of who advances them; where, in fact, what is of prime
importance is the achievement of truth.

The possibility of having such an attitude will depend on
two things: firstly the existence of agreed, interpersonal
standards for judging when the truth has been reached and
secondly, a commitment to the value of truth.   Because of
Piaget's equation of objectivity with good structure and
(presumably, since he does not discuss it at all) his equation of objective judgment with truth, he does not discuss
how it is possible to achieve 'shared' standards of truth
and a commitment to the value of truth.

In order to arrive at agreement on shared standards of
truth, that is agreement on when the truth has been reached,
there must be common ways of taking things, a common way
of understanding and reacting to things.   This is the kind
of understanding and sharing that Wittgenstein spoke of
when he said 'There must be agreement not only in definitions but in judgements as well.'   What he meant, and it
would seem to be an essential for the possibility of learning, is that in order to communicate with each other people
must not only agree on the definitions of the concepts they
are using but they must also agree on the ways in which
these concepts are applied: they must agree on what counts
as an instance of a particular concept.   This implies that
they must have common ways of perceiving the world, common
sets of values in the sense that they will pay attention
to, find important, roughly the same kinds of things.

Wittgenstein's discussions of how we would go about teaching someone the meaning of a term or something like the
natural number series offer several illustrations of the
necessity for this kind of 'agreement in judgements' since,
after all, in teaching there comes a point when everything
has been said, all the explaining has been done and we rely
on the learner's ability to see things our way, to react as
we do, in order to finally understand.   He gives several
examples of rules of language or rules of procedure being
adhered to and being broken leading up to a discussion of
private languages.   At 'Investigations' ('I') 143 the first
important example is introduced:
    Let us now examine the following kind of language game.
    When A gives an order B has to write down a series of
    signs according to a certain formation rule.   The first

of these series is meant to be that of the natural numbers in decimal notation. - How does he get to understand this notation? - First of all series of numbers
will be written down for him and he will be required to
copy them. - And here already there is a normal and an
abnormal learner's reaction. - At first perhaps we guide
his hand in writing out the series 0 to 9, but then the
possibility of getting him to understand will depend on
his going on to write it down independently. - And
here we can imagine e.g. that he does copy the figures
independently, but not in the right order: he writes
sometimes one, sometimes another at random. And then
communication stops at *that* point. - or again, he makes
'mistakes' in the order. - ... Or he makes a *systematic*
mistake; for example, he copies every other number, or
he copies the series 0,1,2,3,4,5 ... like this: 1,0,3,2,
5,4,... Here we shall almost be tempted to say he has
understood *wrong*.
  Suppose the pupil now writes the series 0 to 9 to our
satisfaction. - ... Now I continue the series and draw
his attention to the recurrence of the first series in
the units; and then to its recurrence in the tens.
- And now at some point he continues the series independently - or he does not.... I only wished to say: the
effect of any further explanation depends on his reaction.

There are several important points being made here. The
first is that there exists a certain rule. When Wittgenstein
is talking about teaching some-one to understand this rule
he is not at all concerned with efficacious teaching methods
or ways in which people learn. He is concerned with showing
the nature of what is there to be learned. 'First of all
the numbers will be written down for him and he will be
required to copy them.' There must be many other ways of
starting someone off in learning the natural number series,
but this way brings out the point, which is reinforced in
the rest of the passage, that there is really not much to
explain. There is a certain way of doing this thing and
that is all there is to it. Once one has been 'shown' one
must understand for oneself; there is very little that one
can be 'told' which will make the number series more
comprehensible.

The second important point that is made is that there is
not only a rule but there is a normal way of interpreting
that rule: 'And here already there is a normal and an abnormal learner's reaction.' The normal learner after
perhaps a few initial mistakes will soon pick up the series
and be able to go on to the next step. This is what Rhees

has called 'consensus of reactions' (1969). The possibility
of there being rules at all depends on the agreement in what
people do. If you teach someone the meaning of red by showing him examples, then he will probably understand and will
go on to use the word in new situations just as you would.
But if he remembered what you had said about the use of the
word 'red' but understood by 'the same' something completely
different from you, then no matter how many colour samples
you showed him he would never learn to use the word 'red'
as you do. Without some sort of agreement over the way in
which words are to be taken we would never be able to understand each other and use words in the same ways. In a sense
this kind of agreement must be prior to language since
language would be impossible without it but clearly it cannot be temporally prior since to talk about a common way of
taking expressions only makes sense when there are expressions to be used. This common way of taking expressions
depends on non-linguistic factors such as a common form of
perception, of social life and so on. Perhaps the abnormal
learner could be illustrated by the example of the dyslexic
child. A child suffering from this kind of abnormality will
have great difficulty in copying the series in the correct
order. Moreover, he will often be unable to appreciate the
difference between his own series and the correct one. The
number series is essentially concerned with order. A child
who cannot appreciate order at all will be unable even to
copy the series. What is missing is a typical way of taking
the example. It could be said to be a form of understanding
since even normal children have to learn to appreciate
order. But it is a form of understanding that is missing
because of some abnormality in perception, not large enough
to suggest a different form of life perhaps but an example
of the sort of abnormality that would leave us non-plussed.
A child that cannot 'see' the order of a series cannot
learn the natural number series. There are no reasons or
explanations that one can go into to convince the child
that he is copying wrong. A part of our normal experience
is missing for him and because of this, as Wittgenstein says,
'communication stops at that point.' When we explain something to someone, when we try to get him to understand, a
great deal depends on his being 'like us', on his reacting
in the way that we do or his making the sorts of mistakes
that we can understand. The possibility of explanation
comes to an end (for example, 'the pupil's capacity to
learn may come to an end', 'I.' 114) when the pupil ceases
to react in the 'normal' way, when he ceases to behave
'like us'.

When reasons run out all we can do is say: 'This is how it
is.' We cannot explain any more and all we can do about
the man who insists that he is continuing the series in the
same way is to say ('I.' 185) 'It comes natural to this
person to understand our order with our explanations as we
should understand the order: Add 2 up to 1000, 4 up to 2000,
6 up to 3000 and so on.' And Wittgenstein adds that:

> Such a case would present similarities with one in which
> a person naturally reacted to the gesture of pointing
> with the hand by looking in the direction of the line
> from finger-tip to wrist, not from wrist to finger-tip.
> ('I.' 185)

This case would present similarities in the sense that there
is no way in which we could explain to someone that when I
point I mean them to look in the direction from the wrist
to the finger tip. If a person naturally reacted to the
gesture of pointing by looking in the direction of the
line from finger-tip to wrist, it would not accomplish anything to point with the right hand and say: 'If I point
this way, I mean you to look this way', and point in the
same direction with the left hand:

> How does one explain to a man how he should carry out
> the order: 'Go this way.' (pointing with an arrow the
> way he should go?) Couldn't this mean going in the
> direction which we should call the opposite of that of
> the arrow? Isn't every explanation of how we should
> follow the arrow in the position of another arrow?
> ('BB', p.97)

Like the example of the number series if someone reacted to
the gesture of pointing in this way we should naturally say
that he did not understand the meaning of the gesture.
But there is no way in which we could explain to him why
the gesture means what it does: nothing 'extra' to which we
could draw his attention. All we can say is that it just
does happen to mean this. And that is to say: that is how
people in general do use it. It is because there exists a
normal use, an established custom which people do normally
observe that we can talk of the 'correct' meaning of the
gesture. We could also say that the gesture gets its meaning in virtue of a human agreement but this is clearly not
a self-conscious agreement in the sense in which a certain
sect or society might agree to imbue a certain gesture with
a secret meaning. It just is a fact that human beings tend
to react to the gesture of pointing in that way. If human
beings did not agree at least in some reactions of this
kind there could be no possibility of human communication.
And if a child did not show at least some of these reactions

it could never be taught the use of language. If necessary,
the meaning of pointing itself could be taught but unless
there were some natural reactions which did not need to be
taught, the teaching process would never get started. And
these natural reactions cannot be rationally 'explained',
nor do they require explanation. They are just facts:

> What we are supplying are really remarks on the natural
> history of man: not curiosities, however, but observa-
> tions on facts which no-one has doubted and which have
> only gone unremarked because they are always before our
> eyes. ('RFM', 141)

But these facts, and the subsequent communication which
they facilitate, are the essential groundwork for the gradual building up of standards of agreement on what is to
count as an example of x; what is to count as rational
argument; what is to count as having reached the truth.

As Toulmin argues:

> The essential task of this notion (forms of life) is to
> direct our attention back to those general patterns of
> human activity within which our collective intellectual
> conceptions come to be given their standard significance.
> (1971, p.58)

Toulmin believes one of Wittgenstein's major virtues was
that he did treat it as a question about the 'natural
history of man' which must be dealt with empirically in
advance of any theorising. This would seem to be a complementary investigation to the conceptual investigation into
the concepts of rationality, maturity and so forth which
are also logically prior to any theorising about development.
To mention again Gibson's ecological theory of perception,
much of what he seems to be doing is setting out some of
these 'remarks on the natural history of man'. They are
neither a priori but nor do they require sophisticated
techniques for their discovery. They are 'facts which no-
one has doubted and which have only gone unremarked
because they are always before our eyes.'

INTELLIGIBILITY AND OBJECTIVITY

One important result of Piaget's neglect of social, interpersonal factors in his account of the growth of understanding is the divorce of intelligibility from objectivity.
Piaget insists that a child has a set of structures which
it applies to reality and thus that it understands reality
in its own terms. The structures that the child has

primarily do derive from the epistemic subject and therefore they are not subjective in the sense that associations
deriving from the psychological subject are subjective.
But they are distorted by the child's own egocentrism and
by their own initial irreversibility. They do not possess
the features definitive of objectivity. Therefore although
Piaget is prepared to say, in fact, insists, that the child
'understands' he is not prepared to say that he has objective knowledge. What is objective is not intelligible to
him, but still, something is intelligible to him although
it is not necessarily intelligible to us. For example: on
studies of the concept of age (1969) Piaget discovered two
related oddities in the child's notion of time. (1) Age
is not distinguished from size (especially height). Bigger
things are older than smaller things, and things which have
stopped growing have stopped getting any older. (2) Age
bears no necessary relation to date of birth. If 'A' is
born after 'B' but outgrows it then it is older. In Piaget's
experiment the child is shown two series of pictures showing
the yearly growth of two trees. One (a pear) was planted
the year after an apple but grew faster and became the
bigger of the two bearing more fruit. The children were
asked which tree was the older.

> Jos (1:6) succeeds in seriating the apple trees by
> saying 'one year, two years, three years, etc.'
> - Look, when the apple tree is two years old we plant
> the pear tree. Which is the oldest? - *The apple tree* -
> And the year after this? - *Still the apple tree* - And
> the year after. Here are photos taken on the same day.
> Which is the oldest? (A4 = P3) - *The pear tree* - How
> old is it? - (Jos counts one by one) *four years old* -
> And the apple tree? - (counts with his fingers) *five
> years old* - Which of the two is the oldest - *the pear
> tree* - Why? - *Because it is four years old* - Are you
> older when you are four or when you are five? - *When
> you are five* - Then which is the oldest? - *I don't
> know ... the pear tree because it has more pears.*
> (Piaget, 1969c, p.229)

At a later stage, older children unhesitatingly connect
age with date of birth and disregard changes in size.
Looking back to Piaget's explanation of what is going on
here one will see that each child is applying a different
structure to reality. With the young child the structure
connects age with size and productivity. The older child
connects age with date of birth. Piaget recognises that
the older child is correct in a way in which the younger
child is not. The older child's structures correspond to
the objective concept of age, the younger child's do not.

So he would deny that the younger child's concept is
objective but he would not deny that the younger child
'has' a concept of some sort. There is some standard to
be reached before a concept can be classed as objective,
but the criterion for objectivity is not the same as the
criterion for intelligibility. The child is said to understand something when it has some sort of structure which it
applies. Something is intelligible to the child if it fits
in with a structure he has already developed, even though
that structure does not have the intrinsic features of
reversibility characteristic of objective structures and
does not correspond very well to external reality. So
Piaget can compare what is intelligible for the child with
what is intelligible for us. He does not want to say that
the understanding of the child is merely a defective, gappy
or mistaken version of the understanding of the adult. He
wants to say that within its own terms, each level of
development is valid; it can be seen to have a constant if
limited structure. He is consequently making the claim that
there are alternative conceptual systems to that of the
mature adult which are complete, within their own limits,
and intelligible to children at different stages of their
development. But he also thinks that from 'our' vantage
point as mature adults we can look at the 'conceptual system'
of children at different stages of development and describe
and understand what they see and how they interpret the
world. The question that arises is how far this is true.
How far can we understand a 'child's eye view' of the world?
To what extent are we distorting their interpretation by
describing it in our own terms? Piaget does not want to
say that children at early stages of development have objective concepts or an objective understanding because he ties
objectivity to reversibility and correspondence with reality.
But he does want to say that they have a concept, that they
have their own understanding. In this sense he is suggesting
a half-hearted kind of conventionalism. Although he has
independent criteria for judging whether the child's structure and concepts are objective, the 'right' ones; he thinks
that they are intelligible and can be 'right' in a restricted
area. Although the child's concept is 'wrong' we can understand it and see its implications. A good example of this
is Piaget's description of the acquisition by the child of
the concept of the conservation of the matter, weight and
volume of an object in the face of changes of shape (Piaget
and Inhelder, 1941).

The experimenter gives the child a lump of clay and asks him
to make another exactly like it - 'just as big and just as
heavy'. After the child has done this the experimenter

keeps one of the balls as the standard of comparison and changes the appearance of the other by stretching it into a sausage, flattening it into a cake, cutting it into several pieces, etc. Then the experimenter tries to find out whether the child thinks that the amount of clay, its weight or its volume have changed or have remained the same throughout these changes in shape.

How the experimenter tries to find out the child's view depends on the type of quantity that is being investigated. For amount, the child is simply asked if the standard ball and the altered ball possess the same amount of stuff - 'La même chose de pâte'. Sometimes this is made more concrete (if the material is appropriate) in terms of 'just as much to eat' or 'just as much to drink'. In the case of weight the child is shown a balance and asked if the two lumps of clay would keep the scale balanced if they were put in opposing pans. In this case of volume the experimenter shows that each piece of clay when put into a glass of water causes the water level to rise to the same height. He then alters the shape of one of the pieces and asks if it would still cause the water to rise to the same height.

The main results of these experiments show that the developmental sequence of the acquisition of each of the three concepts is the same. At first the child denies conservation, then there is a sort of empirically founded concept when the child sometimes maintains conservation and sometimes denies it and finally there is the certain assertion of conservation for the type of quantity being considered. But the concepts of conservation of these different types of quantities are not all achieved at the same time. For Piaget's subjects, conservation of matter seems to become common at the age of eight to ten, of weight at ten to twelve and of volume not until after the age of twelve.

Piaget's interpretation of these facts is complex and brings out to what a great extent the interpretation that he offers of the children's 'reasoning' relies on a sort of conceptual analysis of the objective concepts that they are supposed to be acquiring. In the case of the concept of the conservation of matter, he says that there are two schemata developing together - the first is the capacity to multiply relations. The ability involved is the ability to order things according to two dimensions at once. For example the child could order objects according to their weight and their volume at the same time. In the case where the ball of clay is changed to a sausage shape Piaget says that the child will be more likely to assert conservation of matter if he

notices that both the length and the thickness have changed
and he can compare the two new dimensions. If he just
notices that the length has increased then he will be
likely to assert that the amount has increased: if he just
notices that the thickness has decreased then he will be
likely to say that there is now less than there was before.
The second schema necessary for the understanding of this
concept Piaget calls 'atomism'. The child's belief in conservation becomes more probable if the child can think of
the clay as a whole composed of tiny parts or units which
simply change their position with respect to each other
when the shape of the whole is changed. Conservation of
matter here expresses the idea that the total sum of the
parts remains the same irrespective of their spatial
position.

So, the child's understanding of the concept of matter
depends on his being able to see the relationship between
the length and the width of an object and also on his
having an atomistic view of the nature of matter. These
are all concepts which have some conceptual relation to
'our' concept of matter. We use length and width to work
out volume and common sense notions of the conservation
of matter depend on the belief that it is composed of tiny
atoms which cannot be destroyed (at least not by physical
changes). Piaget appears to have analysed our notion of
matter and read the different stages of the acquisition of
this concept by the child as if each stage represented the
conquering of yet another of the sub-concepts involved in
the 'objective' concept of matter.

One would expect that Piaget would explain the child's
failure to achieve the concept of the conservation of weight
at the same time as the conservation of matter in terms of
there being one or more 'extra' concepts involved in the
notion of weight and this is essentially what he does.
While admitting that the total number of atoms remains the
same through transformation of shape, the subject may
believe that the weight of each atom depends on its spatial
position. The child's concept of weight is still at this
stage egocentric. He defines weight in relation to his own
sensations so, for him, weight is something like 'the
pressure on my hand'. This is the extra hurdle that the
child has to get over.

The concept of the conservation of volume which is the last
to develop requires the development of yet another schema,
the schema of the density of a substance and related concepts concerning compression and decompression. Piaget

suggests that about the time the child becomes capable of
managing problems to do with volume he has the following
conception of matter:

Substances are composed of numerous tiny particles with
spaces between them. They can vary as to how tightly these
elements are packed together. Objects which are heavy for
their size are composed of tightly packed elements; objects
which are light for their size are more loosely packed. It
is through this underlying schema about the nature of matter
that the child finally constructs a consistent notion of
volume which allows him to relate it to weight and to
understand that it remains invariant under certain changes
of shape.

What Piaget appears to be saying is that a concept such as
that of volume can be broken down into several subordinate
concepts or at least can be shown to depend on several subordinate concepts such as an atomistic conception of matter,
and concepts of density and compression. The child must
acquire each of these concepts, must have a full understanding of each of these, before he can understand the concept
of volume. The acquisition of each of the subsidiary concepts implies some sort of stage in the acquisition of the
final concept. Although the child cannot be said to 'have'
an 'objective' concept of volume until he has achieved a
full understanding of all these subsidiary concepts Piaget
thinks that he does have a concept of sorts and that this
can be described and the apparent oddities in the child's
behaviour explained in terms of it. The relatively late
acquisition of the concept of conservation of volume is
explained in terms of the implicit belief, that all the
children are credited with, that each tiny unit of clay
varies in the amount of space it occupies. It compresses
and decompresses, and alters its density, as a function of
its position in space.

Piaget claims, then, that the 'concepts' that the children
have differ in systematic ways from the concepts that
adults have and that these differences can be located and
understood by adults and can be used to explain discrepan-
cies in the child's behaviour. Piaget then is claiming to
be able to understand the concepts that the children have
and to be able to see the consequences that having such
concepts would lead to. However he treats each of these
concepts in relative isolation from each other and does not
undertake any thoroughgoing description of the consequences
that possession of these concepts ought to lead to. For
example if the child really believes that the weight of an

object alters with its position in space he will (if he is
consistent) believe that the ball that he can kick about
in the garden might be too heavy to kick about in the park:
that the boat which floats in the bath might sink in the
pond and so on.

The kind of thing that Piaget might be getting himself into
here can be illustrated by one of Wittgenstein's imaginary
society examples:

Those people - we should say - sell timber by cubic
measure - but are they right in doing so? Wouldn't it
be more correct to sell it by weight - or by the time
that it took to fell the timber - or by the labour of
felling measured by the age and strength of the woods-
man? And why should they not hand it over for a price
which is independent of all this - each buyer pays the
same however much he takes (they have found it possible
to live like that). And is there anything to be said
against simply giving the wood away? ('RFM', I. 147)

So far the alternatives offered to our way of doing things
are comprehensible and by the use of the imagination one
could see that they might provide not only a viable but a
better alternative to our own system. But now:

Very well; but what if they piled the timber in heaps
of arbitrary, varying height and then sold it at a price
proportionate to the area covered by the piles? And
what if they even justified this with the words 'Of
course, if you buy more timber you must pay more'?
('RFM', I. 148)

When first presented with these examples it seems that we
can understand them, and that we can come to know what such
people would be like. We do not happen to do things in
these strange ways but it seems we could. And if these
examples are all perfectly intelligible to us and although
we do not we could have done things in these ways then
surely everything is just a matter of convention, and
learning is learning to do what everyone else does. But,
if we look closely at these examples they are not as intelligible as they seem at first. Barry Stroud (1965)
suggests some problems that might arise for the people
who sell wood at a price proportionate to the area covered
by the pile of wood and who defend their doing so in the
way described, that is, 'You must pay more for more wood'.
They would have to believe that a 1" x 6" board increased
in size or quantity when it was turned from resting on its
1" side to resting on its 6" side. And what would be the
relation between quantity and weight for these people? A

man could buy as much wood as he could possibly lift, only
to find, on dropping it, that he had just lifted more wood
than he could possibly lift. Or is there more wood but
the same weight? Or perhaps these people do not understand
the expressions more or less at all. They must, if they
can say, 'Now it's a lot of wood and costs more.' And do
these people think of themselves as shrinking when they
shift from standing on two feet to standing on one? Also
it would be possible for a house that is twice as large
as another built on exactly the same plan to contain much
less wood. How much wood is bought need have no connection
with how much wood is needed for building the house. And
so on. Problems involved in understanding what it would
be like to sell wood in this way can be multiplied indefinitely. In fact in the end we would have to admit, as
Wittgenstein says, that they are not playing our game.
We do not have the same way of understanding things as
they do and consequently they are unintelligible to us:

> How could I show then that - as I should say, you don't
> really buy more wood if you buy a pile covering a bigger
> area? - I should, for instance, take a pile which was
> small by their ideas and, by laying the logs around,
> change it into a 'big' one. This might convince them
> - but perhaps they would say - 'Yes now it's a lot of
> wood and costs more', and that will be the end of the
> matter. - We should presumably say in this case: they
> simply do not mean the same by 'a lot of wood' and
> 'a little of wood' as we do; and they have a quite
> different system of payment from us. ('RFM', I. , 149)

This is precisely the sort of thing that Piaget does to try
to get the children to understand concepts like that of
conservation and the children react in similar ways to the
wood sellers. The difference is what where Wittgenstein
would say 'they simply do not mean the same as we do'
Piaget tries to show the ways in which the children's concepts differ from ours. But his account of the possibility
of describing the concepts that the children possess derives a great deal of its plausibility from his treating
concepts in isolation from each other. He does not follow
the concepts through and see what their implications are.
For example, in the experiments on the conservation of
volume, Piaget's account is that the children can understand
that the amount of material is invariant through physical
change and that the weight is invariant but they believe
that the density of the substance changes, depending on the
relative spatial position of its constituent atoms. What
could be involved in the concept of density for a child who
believed that the density of an atom varies with its spatial

position? What could be involved in the concept of
spatial position?

In another conservation experiment the child is given two
glasses, one tall and narrow, the other short and wide.
A certain amount of lemonade is poured from one glass into
the other one and the child is asked whether there is still
the same amount of lemonade. The 'pre-conservation child'
will insist that there is either more or less lemonade
depending on which glass it is in. Piaget's explanation
of this is that the child has not yet developed the schema
said to be involved in concepts of conservation which
corresponds to Grouping VII. Although he has the concepts
of height and width he cannot yet compare objects along
two dimensions at once. Consequently, he compares the
glasses either for height or for width and fails to see
that a change in height is accompanied by a complementary
change in width. But again, what could one say was involved
for the child in the concept of height or width if he
believed that a change in height meant a change in amount?
Does he believe that a change in the height of the glass
that contains the lemonade actually, physically causes
there to be 'more or less to drink'? An investigation by
Block (1971) into the beliefs of children who do not seem
to understand conservation of volume asked non-conservers
to suggest a way of increasing the amount of Coca Cola in a
glass. If they suggested adding more from the can they were
asked to find another way, and some taller and narrower
glasses were available nearby. The children did not
suggest pouring the Cola into one of the taller, narrower
glasses and did not agree that this would be an effective
way of increasing the amount when it was suggested to them.
Yet when they saw the liquid poured into a taller and
narrower glass, they said that it was now more. So what
do they really think? Perhaps it is the concepts of 'more'
and 'less' that they do not fully understand. But Piaget
does not ask: 'Would it take longer to drink from the tall
glass?' 'Would it be fair to give the tall glass to John
and the short glass to Mary?' He does not try to find out
what sort of relationship the child sees between the
increase in height and his belief that there is now 'more
to drink'. We cannot see how the child is using the concept. It might be possible to get a better idea of what
is involved for the child in these concepts by asking different questions from the ones that Piaget asks and trying
to see what the implications are for the child of these
'concepts' that he is credited with. But would the result
not be the same as it is in the case of Wittgenstein's wood-
sellers? Would we not find it increasingly difficult to

understand just how the child did interpret the concepts?
Would there not be a progressive decrease in intelligibility?

The point of the many examples that Wittgenstein gives of
alternative systems of concepts (for example, 'RFM' I. 136,
139, 152, 168; II, 76, 81, 84; III, 15, 17; IV, 6, 12, 27,
29, 36, 42, 43, 44) are all supposed to show that the
initial intelligibility of these alternatives diminishes as
we push further into the consequences of the acceptance of
these ways of life. We think we can perfectly well understand the concepts of 'more' and 'less' used by the wood-
sellers until we try to see what its implications are. The
implications jar against more and more of our own accepted
ways of doing things until eventually we are forced to admit
that we do not really understand what is going on here.
These people are not fully intelligible to us:

> And there is even something in saying: he can't *think*
> it. One is trying for example to say: he can't fill
> it with personal content; he can't really *go along with*
> *it* - personally, with his intelligence. It is like
> when one says: this sequence of notes makes no sense,
> I can't sing it with expression. I cannot respond to
> it. Or, what comes to the same thing here: I don't
> respond to it. ('RFM', 116)

The reason why we cannot in the end fill these concepts with
personal content seems to be that in the attempt to get a
clearer understanding of what it would be like to be one
of these people we inevitably have to abandon more and more
of our own concepts, our own ways of seeing things. The
more successful we are in projecting ourselves into their
world the less we will have left in terms of which we can
find it intelligible.

Another example can be given from Piaget's work on space
(1956). The experiment was designed to find out the extent
to which young children 'see' objects as located in a
Euclidean grid of horizontal and vertical co-ordinates.
For the horizontal the child was shown jars with coloured
water in them, and asked to predict the spatial orientation of the water level (by drawings or by gestures), when
the jar was tilted in various ways. Initially the children
appear to be incapable of representing planes at all. For
example, the water in the jar was shown by a scribble with
no apparent level in any orientation. Subsequently, levels
were represented but with reference to the jar not the
external surroundings: that is, the level of water was
always shown as parallel to the bottom of the jar no matter
what the angle of the tilt. The child does realise that
the water moves towards the mouth of the jar when it is

tilted. But he shows this by increasing the amount of
water shown in the jar: that is, the water level is still
drawn parallel to the bottom of the jar but higher up.
Some children do find a certain discrepancy between what
the jar shows and what they draw. But although puzzled
by it they cannot say just what is going wrong. Other
children maintain that their drawing corresponds exactly
to the state of the jar even when it 'obviously' does not:
  Mic 6:7.' Now the jar is going to be tilted the other
  way. Show us with your pencil what the water will do.
  - (His demonstration is more or less correct). Now
  draw it. - (Once again he makes the water parallel
  with the base). - Is it higher on one side than on
  the other in your drawing? - *No, it's the same on both
  sides.* - Now, just let's take a look at that water
  (experiment). Is it right? - *Yes* - Just like you drew
  it? - Yes ... etc.' We are unable to convince him
  otherwise. (Piaget, 1956, p.393)

The child does not admit to a mistake. He insists that
what he has done is the 'same'. Piaget says that he is
'failing to submit to experimental evidence' because the
experimental evidence does not 'fit' into the schema that
he had developed to deal with transformations through
space (that is, objects do not change their shape when
submitted to transformations in space). But how can he say
that this is what is going on? Perhaps it is simply that
the child has a different understanding of what it means
for something to be the 'same' in this case. Piaget can
only repeat the same old examples and explanations. But
he fails to convince the child. Must he not simply say:
'He is not playing our game'?

It is not impossible for Piaget, or any other sympathetic
person, to 'get into the child's world' and understand what
is involved for him in the notions of height, volume, space,
time etc. But it does require one to get into the child's
world. One cannot survey this world from an experimental
perch and hope to understand more than the surface. The
depth of our understanding of an alien world, whether it
be non-human, culturally different or the world of a child,
depends on the extent to which we can put 'ourselves in
their place' and enter into that life to 'fill it with
personal content'. Clearly this will become more and more
difficult the further away from our own everyday world
that it is and it will need a deeper investigation of the
relationships between the child's concepts than Piaget
offers to establish *how* different from our world the world
of a child is. Any investigation of this kind will be

accompanied by the decrease in intelligibility that
Wittgenstein pointed out. We understand things in 'our'
way. The more successful we are in projecting ourselves
into such a world the less we will have left in terms of
which we can find it intelligible.

These arguments suggest that an investigation of the concepts a child does have at any stage and a description of
them with their implications and interconnections might be
impossible for an adult equipped with adult concepts.
Piaget represents the study of the child's mental development as the description of successive, somehow natural and
necessary stages in the child's actual thought. What it
would seem to amount to, rather, is an analysis of the
subsidiary skills and concepts that must be learned before
a certain view of the world characterised as adult, mature,
objective, etc. can be attained. What is involved in
having such a view of the world will not be an empirical
matter but rather a philosophical enquiry such as Kant's
enquiry into the conditions of objective knowledge. This
will be logically prior to any genetic study about how
this knowledge is achieved.

However, given a description of this view of the world the
delineation of the subsidiary abilities and concepts that
must be acquired before the child can achieve this world-
view would seem to be largely a matter of conceptual
analysis. The concept of an object, for example, which
involves the notion of endurance through time, could hardly
develop until the child could remember things for a period
of time. This is not to say that empirical investigation
might not be useful in suggesting or bringing to light
necessary connections like this one. Not all necessary
connections are so obvious as the connection between the
concept of an object and the ability to remember. Any
method, empirical or otherwise, which helps to reveal these
connections, is useful. But the connections themselves are
not contingent. That children do not in fact understand a
certain concept until they have had certain experiences or
can do certain things might suggest that there is a necessary connection to be unearthed. Because it is unearthed
by empirical observations does not make it any the less a
logical, conceptual matter.

SUMMARY

Piaget equates objectivity more or less with structure. His
explanation of how this structured knowledge maintains its

purchase on the real world depends on his view that structures are interiorised actions. The actions which survive
in the sensori-motor period are those which succeed. Since
actions, to succeed in the environment must be structured
in ways compatible with the structure of that environment,
Piaget thinks that the later structures, which are the
descendants of the earlier structures, must also be compatible with the environment. Knowledge, then, is 'realistic' as well as objective through its structures. We
argue that this view fails in the first place to take
proper account of perception as providing the points of
application for the structured knowledge. In the second
place it fails to take proper account of the social nature
of objective knowledge. To have an objective concept is
to know what something is. This is not a matter of
possessing an individual structure which, since it has
its source in the individual mind, must be subjective, to
something which is external to the mind. To have an
objective concept is to know the rules for deciding what
makes something what it is. This is not a subjective
process. Neither can it be a private process. What is to
count as a rule, what is to count as obeying or disobeying
a rule is not a private but a public intersubjective matter.
This makes incoherent any view of the growth of knowledge
as a personal transaction between an individual and his
environment.

Piaget's view that the growth of understanding is such a
transaction leads him to impute far greater intelligibility
to the child's comprehension than is warranted by his data.
It is suggested that Piaget is not actually observing the
structure of children's knowledge. Rather he is doing some
kind of analysis of concepts such as conservation. He is
breaking them down into their logically constituent parts
and then confusing these parts with temporal steps or
stages in the acquisition of these concepts.

Explanations of human development

PREVIEW

Chapter 6 considers the question of what we should expect a developmental theory to look like. It is argued that we should expect a theory of human development to make reference to an ideal end state towards which development aims and that the clarity and consistency of the developmental theory will depend on the clarity and consistency of the conception of this end state.

Piaget's conception of development is of a moving away from egocentricity towards a kind of objectivity involving a conception of the world as a coherent set of transformations. It is argued that even within the general direction suggested by Piaget's theory, that of the move away from egocentricity towards objectivity, there is more than one possible conception of objectivity.

THE CONCEPT OF DEVELOPMENT

Traditionally development has been held to imply the realisation of some latent potentiality. The concept of development current in seventeenth-century zoological studies, relying on preformationist assumptions and crude microscopes, was simply increase in size. The whole animal was thought to be present in miniature in the newly born.

In an article on the concept of development, Nagel (1957) denies that the old preformationist concept will do today. But the criteria that he himself lays down do suggest a certain degree of preformation. He says:

147

> The connotation of development thus involves two
> essential components: the notion of a system possessing
> a definite structure and a definite set of pre-existing
> capacities: and the notion of a sequential set of
> changes in the system yielding relatively permanent but
> novel increments, not only in its structure but in its
> modes of operation as well. (1957, p.17)

Clearly a child, when it is born, has a certain physiological structure, but what of the 'definite set of pre-existing
capacities'? Waddington has argued with respect to physical
development that this set of capacities is limited but not
completely defined by the genotype since the capacities are
realised in interaction with the environment.

In talking about intellectual development, it has been
argued that the understanding that a child has to acquire
is defined by the culture into which he is born. Again one
can see that his intellectual potential might be limited by
his physiology, his brain structure and so forth. But the
particular form in which this potential will manifest itself
will depend on the culture, educational opportunities, needs
and interests of the individual.

Ryle argues that talk of 'potential' and 'capacity' hides
several different distinctions. Ryle distinguishes at least
three senses of 'capacity':
> 'that fish can swim (for it is not disabled although it
> is now inert in the mud); John Doe can swim (for he has
> learned and not forgotten); Richard Roe can swim (if he
> is willing to learn).' (1949, p.122)
Here, the sense in which Richard Roe can be said to swim
(although he has not yet learned) is different from the
sense in which the fish is inert but has the capacity to
swim, Richard Roe has not. Similarly, there are differences
between Richard Roe and John Doe. To accept as true the
statement about John Doe, although we would not require to
see him swimming, we would need to know that he had learned
and that there was no reason why he should have forgotten.
But to accept the statement about Richard Roe's swimming
ability all we seem to need to know is that he is a normal
human being with no important physical handicaps; no mental
abnormalities such as a morbid fear of the water; and with
a willingness to learn. However, what if it were claimed
that a baby had the capacity to swim although he has as yet
neither an adequate physiological structure nor a willingness to learn?

The sense in which a baby can be said to have the capacity
to swim is very different even from that of Richard Roe
although neither of them can actually swim. What we are
assuming is that because it is a human baby he will one day
have the capacity for learning to swim. The only evidence
we have is that he is an apparently normal specimen of a
species that in the past has always developed these capacities. Nagel's condition of 'a definite set of pre-existing
capacities' appears to say no more than that the organism
that we are claiming will develop in a certain way is of
the same kind, shares the same structure, as other organisms
which have developed that way. Bailey (1969) claims that a
'definite set of pre-existing capacities' could be taken as
simply an extended description of what Nagel refers to as a
'definite structure'. So what Nagel is claiming is that
whatever kind of development we are talking about must presuppose as a necessary condition a certain physiological
structure. Which particular physiological structures lead
to which processes of development must be a congintent
matter and one for detailed empirical investigation. But
there are certain very general connections between physiological structures and the development of certain capacities
which are more conceptual than empirical; conceptual rather
than empirical because we could not conceive of something
without a certain degree of complexity, without a certain
degree of structure and organisation having, for example,
purposes, intentions, desires etc. The way that we decide
that a certain physiological structure is a necessary prerequisite for a certain process of development is partly a
conceptual and partly an empirical matter.

Nagel is right to point out that if we are to talk about
development then we must assume as a necessary prerequisite
a certain physiological structure. But this does not imply
preformation in the sense of the innateness of the abilities
and capacities that will develop.

Piaget would agree that mental development is controlled to
some extent by the nature of the initial physiology. He
says: 'It would be out of the question to consider the
organisation of action schemata independently of endogenetic
factors' (Piaget, 1971, p.10). However, the regulation
imposed on development by these innate forms is very general
and amounts to little more than a functional continuity.
It is the continuing regulation brought about by the
establishment of successive states of equilibrium through
the process of equilibration which exerts the most influence
on the direction of development.

This brings us to Nagel's second criterion for a developmental process, that of a sequential set of changes. To
account for the direction of this sequence, Nagel introduces the concept of teleology:

> In addition to this backward reference (i.e. to pre-
> existing structure), the designation of a process as
> developmental also has a prospective one.... No change
> per se is commonly counted as a developmental one,
> although it may be so labelled if it is referred to as
> an explicitly or tacitly assumed consequence of the
> change. The word thus possesses a strong teleological
> flavour ... the imputation signifies that a sequence of
> change is designated as developmental only if it con-
> tributes to the generation of some more or less speci-
> fically characteristic system of things or property of
> things. (1957, p.16)

Philosophers such as J. Mackie (1974) and biologists such
as Beckner (1968) have argued convincingly that animal
development and behaviour cannot be explained satisfactorily
without reference to goals, that is, that explanations concerning living organisms (even explanations making reference
to evolution) are unavoidably teleological. It is possible,
for example, to explain some piece of behaviour on the part
of an animal as food-seeking behaviour. That is, the behaviour is explained with reference to a goal which is in the
future. The sense in which this would constitute an explanation is that we can see if the animal is to achieve the
goal of attaining the food then he is going to have to
engage in certain sorts of behaviour. These sorts of behaviour may vary largely depending on the circumstances, the
type of animal, the type of food, how hungry the animal is
and so on. But we can say that given circumstances x, y,
z an animal, to reach a certain goal, is going to have to
engage in one set, out of perhaps quite a large set, of
behaviours which can all be classified under the description of food-seeking behaviour.

Talking about the teleological explanation of the structural
morphology of an organism, Beckner argues that:

> The morphologist has to find concepts that refer to
> those parts of the organism which, so to speak, represent
> the 'natural' cleavages at a high level of organisation
> - in fact, which represent just those cleavages which
> mark the parts of wide theoretical interest.... In
> practise it turns out that the best policy is to select
> parts that act as a functional unit ... to define
> morphological concepts by reference to structural
> properties is to run the risk of restricting their

applicability so narrowly that it becomes virtually
impossible to formulate laws concerning morphological
parts. (1968, p.117)

If, as Beckner claims, the most useful way for a biologist
to identify the parts of an animal is by referring to their
functions then in talking about the development of those
parts he will be unable to avoid reference to their functions. If one defines an organ by means of its function
then it will be seen to be fully developed when it is
performing this function efficiently.

That biologists frequently do talk in this way is obvious
from any elementary text book. To take as the end point
of development the efficient performance of some function
provides a good reason for choosing that particular point
in the life history of the organ as the end point of
development. But this will be a good reason only if the
organ has a clear function. It is easy to see functions
when we are discussing the development of parts of a whole
as for example the development of the leg muscles of a
child which enable it to walk. One might plausibly claim
that an organism was fully developed physiologically when
it was capable of maintaining and reproducing itself,
this being the function of physiological organisms.

To insist that talk about development involves reference
to functions is not to import into developmental theories
any notion of divine guidance or preformation. It is
merely to claim that knowledge of the eventual function
of the organ determines our description of the developmental process in the same sort of way as the direction
travelled by smoke from a chimney determines the direction
of the wind. To define organs in terms of their functions
and to recognise as the end-state of their development the
efficient performance of their function is to give a good
reason for settling on a certain point as an end-state.
However, this is a good reason only if the organ has some
clear function. Remaining at the biological level one
might claim that the function of an organism as a whole
was to reproduce itself. But once one leaves this level
and begins to think about intellectual, social, emotional
development it no longer makes sense to claim that these
processes are described and explained in terms of some end-
state which is the efficient performance of some function.
To talk about functions implies a wider frame of reference,
a larger aim to which the functions contribute. The heart
functions to maintain the body; the organism reproduces to
maintain the species; but a man does not behave morally in

order to support the society or in order to destroy it.
He does not love poetry so that he can better perform some
function. Learning does not have the functional implications that biological explanations of development inevitably
do have and this shows another way in which biological models
of learning and mental development can be misleading.

Since we cannot characterise knowledge as contributing to
some particular function, it is difficult to be clear about
what would count as a final or end state. We have clear
criteria for when a human being has developed characterist-
ically and we know unambiguously within certain limits how
tall he should be at two if he is to grow to a normal adult
size and so on. But the case of mental development is
entirely different. We can neither say unanimously what
we expect a child to develop towards nor be clear about
what prerequisites are necessary if he is to arrive there.
We know clearly what it is for an adult to be normal height
and weight, to walk normally and so on. But we are not
nearly so clear about what it is to be intelligent, rational,
emotionally mature, make genuinely moral judgments, have
normal relations with other people. It is not simply that
we have not studied enough adults said to be intelligent
and so have not been able to form a clear picture of what
intelligence is. There are fundamental disagreements about
what is to count as intelligence. If intelligence tests
measure learned abilities, is that what we mean by intelligence? Are the Azande less rational than the English because
they believe in magic? Is a person who acts 'because it is
God's will' acting morally? Generally in developmental
theories concerning human behaviour the end product in mind
is not what has been generally observed to be the typical
end product in the past but some kind of ideal. The normal
is not the average but the ideal. A developmental theory
is not simply describing a series of stages through which
most human beings pass on the way to becoming adults as, for
example, all butterflies have been caterpillars. An approved
state of affairs is being taken as the end product and this
approved state of affairs is the yardstick for measuring
and describing progress.

The conclusion that one might draw from this is that to the
extent that our conception of the end state is confused or
incomplete, we will be unable to recognise steps in the process of developing towards that end state. Much in the
description of the developmental sequence will depend on
the clarity of our conception of the end state. We are
successful in talking about physical development because
we do have a clear conception of the ideal or norm which

the organism is developing towards, but in talking about
intellectual development we have concepts like intelligence,
rationality, understanding. We still do not have a clear
conception of what would count as instances of these concepts. As a result, when they are used to characterise
stages in development, the empirical observations can be
quite accurate and detailed but they will be connected by
vaguely understood and ill-defined ideas. Consequently
the developmental theory will be confused, incomplete and
often incoherent.

To summarize, teleological explanations in biology and
anthropology depend on the identification of some end state
that development or behaviour is directed towards. This
end state is usually identified as the requisite state for
the performance of some function seen as essential to the
survival of the organism or the species. In talking about
mental development we do not have any clear and consistent
concepts of the end-state. This is partly because it is
inappropriate to think of these things in functional terms,
at least at the level of the individual. It is also partly
because the end states of intellectual development are
certain ideals about which there is a great deal of disagreement. And partly, it is also because what is to count
as intelligent behaviour depends to a great extent on the
context. Psychology traditionally divides mental development into four distinct strands: intellectual, moral, social
and emotional. This is an attempt to delimit the area
covered by a particular theory rather than a claim that
these distinct strands can be distinguished in behaviour.
Even if we accept this division as heuristically convenient
we do recognise that these divisions are very gross and all
these strands are interconnected. A theory of intellectual
development in general would have as its end state a complex
of inter-related factors all concerned more or less closely
with the way in which we understand the world, having myriad
links with the interconnecting strands of social, moral and
emotional development. It would seem impossible to specify
clearly what this end state must be like in general. What
we accept as intelligent, rational etc. depends very much
on the context. And if this is the case then it would be
unreasonable to expect a general theory of intellectual
development. One might have particular theories about the
pathways that children take to some particular form of
understanding. The acceptability of these particular
theories would depend in some degree on the clarity and
consistency of the view of what that particular form of
understanding consisted in, that is of the particular end
states that they were aimed at. Some attempt at a general

theory might be possible through the integration of all
the particular theories. However, it is unlikely that all
the particular theories could be integrated to form one
general theory of human development since the problem of
the conflict of different ideals of humanity would still
remain.

In Piaget's work there is very little mention of 'learning'
as a way of getting knowledge. His books have such titles
as 'The genesis of the idea of number in the child'; 'The
child's construction of reality'. For Piaget the child
literally constructs reality for himself through the transformation of one structure into the next. This process of
transformation is controlled by the mechanism of the mind.
We have argued that this 'mechanism of mind' contributes
to experience its structure and organisation. It has a
status like that of the pure understanding in Kant's
critical philosophy.

THE NATURE OF MIND

What does talk of the 'mechanism of mind' or 'the nature of
mind' mean? Children develop in a physical dimension quite
naturally. So long as they are not deprived of the essential
nutrients and conditions for growth, they will grow. And
they will grow in specific ways to look like mature human
adults. They do not need to see adult examples to be able
to grow to look like them.

The case with the development of abilities is quite different. Psychologists distinguish between maturation and learning. Maturation refers to the onset of the ability to learn
how to do x. The onset of an ability occurs without training. In fact before the onset of an ability in this sense,
the child cannot be trained, cannot be taught how to do it.
Gesell's study of twins learning to climb stairs illustrates
this clearly. One twin was given intensive training in
climbing stairs, was shown how to do it before he had
evinced any natural ability to do it. The other twin was
given no training. Yet both the twins learned to climb
stairs at virtually the same time (Gesell, 1926).

Maturation refers to the onset of an ability. It occurs
without previous training, but the development of that
ability is another matter. A child may have the ability
to walk in the sense that his muscles have now reached the
required strength; he has a good sense of balance and so
forth. But if he is not faced with an example of walking,

he will not learn to do it. He may have the ability to
learn a language but if he never hears one, he will never
learn one.

The innately programmed behaviour patterns of many animals
are far more complex and specific than the innate behaviour
patterns of human beings. Lorenz, for example, argues that
we have overestimated the extent to which even animals such
as song birds can realise innate behaviour patterns without
mature examples (Lorenz, 1952). But human beings seem
particularly bereft of 'instincts' and the like. This is
compensated for by their enormous powers of learning. But
in order for there to be learning there must be adults or
at least more mature examples to learn from.

The absence of extensive innate behaviour patterns in human
beings is one reason why learning plays such an important
role in human development. Another reason is the overwhelmingly social nature of our behaviour. Human children,
for example, do not just learn to walk. They have to
learn to walk 'properly'. Michael Oakeshott ruefully
remarks: 'Do I not remember being told to "walk properly"
and not shamble along as if I were an ape?' (1972, p.19).
Such things as 'walking properly' have to be learned, and
learned from other people. Even if those people do not
necessarily teach us these things, still their example is
indispensable if we are to pick them up.

When we move to talking of mental development it becomes
even more impossible to see it as a result of some kind of
natural, asocial process. Mental development involves the
development of consciousness and of beliefs. When we
attribute a mind to something we are attributing to it a
certain level of consciousness. When we attribute a human
mind to someone we are attributing to him a consciousness
of a particular character. What this particular character
is will depend on our current culturally determined criteria
for counting something as human. But one of the criteria
that a consciousness which is to be counted as a mature
human mind must meet is that of being able to distinguish
between truth and falsehood. William James has provided
us with a vivid but misleading picture of the child's first
consciousness of the world as being a 'blooming, buzzing
confusion'. Psychologists and philosophers with empiricist
leanings have assumed that the consciousness of the new-
born child must be undifferentiated. What this means is
that he is conscious but of what is not clear. He is incapable of making distinctions or comparisons since, it is
claimed, distinctions and comparisons are things that one

has to learn to make. The reason why James's view of the newborn's world is so misleading is because in order to experience confusion, one must have some conception of order. The newborn has no expectations about what will happen next, no hopes for the future. It is logically impossible for him to be disappointed. The experience of confusion results only when our expectations concerning ways in which experiences can be expected to follow each other are not met. This cannot occur when there are no expectations.

The child, then, has no expectations about the way the world should be, he cannot make distinctions or comparisons. He has to be brought to have expectations; he has to be brought to make distinctions and comparisons. If he is to develop a typically human consciousness, then not just any distinctions and comparisons will do. He has to be brought to make typically human distinctions and comparisons.

Piaget tries to account for this necessity to develop a particularly human consciousness but his account is in terms of the innate possession of a 'specific heredity' which when combined with the general heredity of functioning per se as possessed by all successful biological organisms, gives rise to the typically human consciousness. However, Piaget neglects the historical and cultural dimensions of the development of this consciousness. There is no way in which the specific achievements of human consciousness could be the product of heredity or could be reconstructed anew by each individual. They must be learned by the child through his experience in this culturally and socially constructed world.

As the child moves through the hierarchy of developmental stages his stock of experience is continually increasing. The changes that Piaget claims are brought about by the equilibration mechanism could be accounted for simply by the child's increasing experience of the world. This will not necessarily have the consequence that development can consist only of a piling up of new associations, new experiences, an increase in quantity. It is through new experiences that we come to see old experiences in a new light and to read more into them and understand them more than we did at the time. To achieve qualitatively different kinds of understanding does not require a special kind of non-learning gaining of knowledge through development as opposed to learning. The influence of other adults and other children on the child are crucial to his development. Other adults supply the modes of understanding, the techniques and

categories we use to organise and make sense of the environment and growth in understanding is the result of learning
how to use these techniques and modes of understanding and
applying them in our own experience.

Piaget rejects this view of learning and insists that not
all the concepts that a child possesses can have been
learned either from other adults or from experience. He
argues that: 'Some of the concepts which appear at the
beginning of the stage of concrete operations are such that
I cannot see how they could be drawn from experience'
(Piaget, 1972a, p.40). The example he gives concerns the
concept of substance. He says: consider a child who has
rolled a ball of plasticine into a sausage shape and who is
asked if it now has the same amount of material, the same
weight and the same volume as before. Piaget found that at
about the age of eight the child will say that there is the
same amount of plasticine. Some time later the child
realises that the weight remains the same as well and later
still, that the volume remains the same. So the child is
first of all able to understand the conservation of substance but he has no conception of the conservation of
weight and volume. Both the constancy of weight and that
of volume are prerequisites for any empirical derivation of
the constancy of substance. So Piaget, issuing a Humean
challenge, asks:

> So I would ask you where the idea of the conservation of
> substance can come from? What is a constant and invari-
> ant substance when it doesn't yet have a constant weight
> or a constant volume?... No experiment, no experience,
> can show the child that there is the same amount of sub-
> stance.... He knows that something is conserved but he
> doesn't know what. It is not yet the weight, it is not
> yet the volume; it is simply a logical form - a logical
> necessity. (Piaget, 1972a, p.40)

Again it seems that Piaget's overhasty reliance on his
ability to see into the child's mind has led to an emphasis
on the logic of the situation when what is at issue might
well be some other feature such as the child's method for
judging the amount of plasticine left because, clearly, it
is plasticine that the children are conserving not substance.
Piaget, with adult knowledge, realises that plasticine is
a substance and if a substance is conserved during changes
of shape then both weight and volume will be conserved.
But perhaps the children believe the same amount of plasticine remains because they can see that nobody has taken any
away or added any more. Bruner discusses the apparent
increase in illogicality and self-contradiction shown by

children in these sorts of experiments as they get older.
He carried out a study on children between the ages of four
and eleven (Bruner, 1966). They were given the task of
saying which of a pair of beakers was fuller and which
emptier. Children at all these ages have no difficulty in
giving an appropriate response to pairs of identical beakers,
whether filled to the same level or to different le.els.
Bruner then presented them with a pair of half-filled
beakers of unequal volume. Identifying the glass of larger
volume as A, he found that a child will say that A is fuller
than B and then go on to say that A is emptier than B. Or
he will say that both are equally full, but A is emptier.
The proportion of errors that were contradictory increased
with the age of the child. To account for this increasing
tolerance of contradiction Bruner suggests that the logical
contradiction is not the issue at all. The issue is a by-
product of another psychological process, that is the way
children go about defining fullness and emptiness. All the
children in this age range judge fullness by observation
not by computing. The glass is judged fuller that has the
greatest apparent volume of water; and the favoured indication of greater apparent volume is water level, or, where
water level is the same, then width of the glass, or when
width and water level are the same, then height of the
glass. All these are criteria that can be pointed at. But
the older children have developed a consistency based on
appreciations of the complementary relation of filled and
empty space. For them 'emptier' means the glass that has
the largest volume of unfilled space just as 'fuller' means
the glass that has the largest volume of filled space.
But in consequence, their responses are self-contradictory
because the glass that is 'emptier' in this sense also turns
out to be the glass that is 'fuller', given a large glass
and a small glass. The younger children equate emptiness
with 'liquid littleness'. The glass is emptier which gives
the impression of being smaller in volume of liquid. So
they end up by being consistent in their judgments of
fullness and emptiness.

The point of this illustration is to show that Piaget's
claim that the children have got a concept to which there
corresponds no experience and consequently which cannot
have been learned from experience, is premature. Certainly
the shape of the plasticine has changed, but to a child who
does not define substance in the manner of a logically
sophisticated adult, it may not be significant that some
other features may also have changed. It might be the case
that it is only when children have their attention drawn to
the relationship between conservation of weight and

conservation of substance that they start noticing relationships and experiences which are relevant to their growing
knowledge.

Laurence Kohlberg claims to orientate his work on moral
development on a Piagetian hierarchical stage model and he,
like Piaget, makes a distinction between development and
learning, and claims that learning cannot account for all
the products of development. Kohlberg argues that if a
child passes through several significantly different
intellectual stages, then his development cannot result
directly from adult teaching, for otherwise he should
mirror adult thought patterns from the beginning. This is
similar to Piaget's argument that a child cannot learn from
adults directly since the mental structures they employ are
too alien to his own schemata to be assimilable to them. An
argument that both Kohlberg and Piaget use is that if the
only difference between the child and the adult is the
'quantity' of experience then it would be expected that
the child's intellectual structure would be similar to that
of the adults but incomplete or defective. However, as
the child's intellectual structure seems to be qualitatively
different from that of the adult and as this structure
apparently is the same for all children, then:
> It is extremely difficult to view the child's mental
> structure as a direct learning of the external structure.
> Furthermore, if the adult's mental structure depends
> upon sequential transformations of the child's mental
> structure, it, too, cannot directly reflect the current
> structure of the outer cultural or physical world.
> (Kohlberg, 1972, p.506)

For these arguments of Kohlberg and Piaget to have any force
it would have to be established that adults actually try to
communicate structure, basic logical connections, rules
governing the use of concepts and so on. Unless they do,
it would not be surprising that at first children did not
readily grasp these things. Common experience would suggest
that adults do not usually consciously try to communicate
structure. Adults normally say such things as 'this is a
ball of plasticine'; 'this is a glass of water'; they do
not teach abstract concepts such as substance, mass and
volume. They may point out to their children that plasticine can be rolled from a ball into a sausage, or that Coca
Cola can be poured from a bottle into a cup but they would
rarely try to press home the lesson that the law of conservation of matter holds. For one thing, three and four year
olds do not particularly care about the law of conservation
of matter and for another, they would first of all have to

learn what a 'law' was, what 'conservation' meant, what
'matter' was.

The argument that there is a qualitative difference between
mature adult thought and child thought which could not be
accounted for simply in terms of the increased quantity of
adult experience is a particularly poor argument. Even the
nineteenth-century associationists compared the accumula-
tion of sensory experience with the combining of atoms into
molecules having new, qualitatively different or emergent
properties as for example the combining of hydrogen and
oxygen to form water. This view was able to account (to
some extent) for the emergence of qualitatively new concepts
from combinations of qualitatively similar precursors.
However, the greatest weakness of the argument lies in the
assumption that all experiences are qualitatively alike.
The growth of knowledge facilitates not only qualitative
differences in the concepts and structure of knowledge but
also qualitatively different experiences. Until one has
certain kinds of concepts one cannot have certain kinds of
experiences. The growth of knowledge is like a re-experien-
cing of all the things that one has experienced before but
now seen in a different way, under a different light, and
consequently experienced as quite different things as the
result of the acquisition of new knowledge. Piaget's
rejection of learning from experience and learning from
communication with adults as adequate to account for the
sequence of development is based on an over-narrow conception of experience and learning.

However, if we adopt a more liberal view of the nature of
experience and reject the equation of teaching with telling,
what could one say a priori about the direction in which
intellectual development would proceed?

The picture would likely be very similar to the view that
Piaget gives although clearly the reasons for this direction would be different. If we can think of human intellectual development as the widening and broadening of understanding, then, given the initial state of the human being
as a helpless, ignorant infant, certain very general
principles of human development can be sketched. The
infant has certain basic needs if it is to survive so any
development must start from these essentially concrete
needs and spread from there. Consequently, human development seen as the enlargement of experience will commence
with concrete needs and concerns and only later involve
abstract ones. Given the nature of the child's contact with
the environment and other people (it has not, or does not
usually, for example, possess powers of telepathy or psycho-

kinesis) it can do no other than develop through concrete to later representational and abstract thought. So Piaget's claim that the child develops concrete operations before it can cope with abstract ones is seen to be a consequence of his initial interests and possibilities for action. While not exactly a logical point, it would seem to be a point that could be made on the conceptual grounds that human development is the enlargement of experience and since the infant's experience is concerned with concrete needs he will need to progress from them to abstract matters if his experience is to enlarge at all.

A similar argument can be offered to show Piaget's claim that children's understanding develops from the particular to the general. The initial experience of the infant is of particular events, people, objects. To enlarge this experience he generalises. Again, we have a large amount of observational material collected by Piaget to show this essentially conceptual point. Given the initial condition of the infant and the nature of learning and experience, it could hardly be otherwise.

Given these sorts of considerations about the nature of human knowledge and learning, the main outlines of Piaget's stages, their irreversible sequence and necessary order can be seen to follow. This is not because the mind has such and such a nature and will only permit this sort of development. It is because, given our understanding of what a human being is and given his starting point as an inarticulate, immobile infant, nothing which looked very different from this would count as a process of human development.

We have argued that a general theory of intellectual development inevitably involves two things, judgments based on values, that is, judgments as to what is important in human life rather than what is the case, and also an understanding of what is involved in the possession of these abilities or ways of thinking that human beings value. We cannot, with intellectual development describe and explain the process simply by referring to nature in the sense of what usually happens. Because human intellectual development is the result of education, communication with adults, learning, we are in a position to decide what we want human beings to be, that is, to decide the direction in which we want children to develop. Once we have decided the kinds of achievements, ways of thinking, ways of feeling and so on that we want adults to be capable of we will have to examine these 'end states' carefully and attempt to see what sorts of subordinate skills, abilites, knowledge, understanding and so on they require. So far, the enquiry is entirely philosophical: deciding on the importance of certain values for the achievement of what

we would be prepared to call a mature adult state and then
looking carefully at these achievements to see what kinds
of subordinate achievements they incorporate.

This brings out the point that in describing a process of
development, the end state determines the process and not
vice versa. We must have some criteria for distinguishing
events which form part of the process of development from
all the other events that form part of other processes that
are happening at the same time. And our criteria can only
be derived from our prior knowledge of the end state. Given
this point, the more confused our conception of the end
state is the more difficult will it be to map out a developmental process towards that end state.

Jonathon Bennett in his book 'Rationality' (1964) has
pointed to the kind of preliminary work that is necessary
here. Bennett takes the possession of rationality to be a
defining feature of a human being, a feature that anyone
who claims to be a human being must have. He then attempts
to break the concept down into subordinate classes of behaviours and abilities. The way he does this is to take as
an example a group of animals (in this case honey bees) and
to show what must be true about their behaviour before we
would be prepared to say that they were rational. He gradually adds characteristics to the honey bees' behaviour until
what they do could be described as rational action.

This preliminary analysis is clearly not setting out a
temporal, developmental sequence. It is exhibiting logical
connections between what we would be prepared to call rational behaviour and all the subordinate qualities such as
rule-governed, purposive and so on that Bennett argues for.
Once having achieved an analysis of this sort, a description
of a process of the development of rationality is possible.
It would consist in the gradual achievement of these subordinate abilities. But this description would be a priori
in the sense that nothing else could count as the development of rationality. In criticising developmental theories
with regard to moral development, Bailey (1969) criticises
the developmentalist for considering only situations which
the adult would experience as involving moral decisions;
deciding right from wrong, responding to rules, passing
judgment on actions in stories, considering reasons for
lying and so on. A point brought out by Julius Kovesi
(1967) shows the unreasonableness of this. It is true that
we exercise moral judgments in certain kinds of situations
in response to certain actual problems but it is not just
the material and social circumstances that constitute the

problem but the fact that we view these circumstances in
the light of moral notions which we have learned. Children
make strange responses to Piagetian stories at an early age
not because they have a strange morality but because they
have not acquired certain moral notions which are essential
before what is happening in the story can be seen as a moral
problem. For example such notions as intention, motive,
responsibility, fairness, equity and reciprocity are all
concepts needed to make sense of Piaget's moral tales.
That the children react oddly shows that they have not
acquired these concepts yet. What Piaget is doing here,
rather than tracing the development of these concepts, is
finding out how a child reacts to an adult understanding,
to what constitutes a problem for the adult.

The same sort of point can be made about some of Piaget's
studies of intellectual development. In his conservation
studies, before he can understand what he is being asked
the child needs to have developed concepts concerning
quantity, change, causality and so on. In Piaget's studies
on the development of causality, the child is asked why
things move. When he replies, 'Because they want to' he
is said to have an anthropomorphic concept of causality.
But it may be that the child has no concept of causality
at all. The movements of stars and rivers and people may
all seem to him equally unproblematic. It is very difficult to see just what significance Piaget's stories and
questions have for the young child and difficult to tell,
from what they say and do, just what certain concepts mean
for them. Piaget underestimates these difficulties.

However, a developmental process must, as Piaget realised,
spell out logical steps in the achievement of the end
state. And logical steps do not necessarily coincide
with temporal steps. Unless this is clear, there is the
danger that by basing teaching programmes on knowledge
about the developmental sequence there will be an over
rigid emphasis on logical order. Earlier in this chapter
a distinction was made between maturation and learning.
Maturation was defined as the onset of the ability to learn
something. It is a necessary condition for subsequent
learning. Many of the things that Piaget says about the
child's capacity for assimilation being restricted by the
structures that he has developed sound similar to talk of
maturation. Piaget argues, for example, that a child cannot be trained to comprehend conservation until he has
developed the appropriate structures to assimilate it.
This sounds very like the claim that a child cannot be
trained to climb the stairs until he is 'ready' for it.

But to say these two claims are similar is seriously misleading. The claims concerning 'maturation' are based on
observation of physical maturation and the immunity of a
child to training before a certain point in time. Piaget's
claims are based on logical relations holding between the
subordinate and the superordinate concepts. The child cannot, as a matter of logic, appreciate the relationships
involved in the concept of conservation of volume, for
instance, until he can comprehend the concepts of height,
depth and width. Piaget's explanation of the comprehension
of the conservation of volume depends on the child being
able to compare the relations between these dimensions when
they undergo transformations. Unless the child could
already understand at least something of the dimensions
themselves, he would be unable to compare them. The 'readiness' of a Piagetian child then is not like the 'readiness'
of maturational views. Given Piaget's explanation of how
certain forms of understanding come about, the 'readiness'
is a matter of logical necessity. However, if alternative
explanations of how these forms of understanding come about
were available, the 'readiness' might not be, given those
explanations, a matter of necessity. It may not even be a
matter of fact. If, for example, a child could directly
perceive changing relationships rather than having to
develop a schema based on the separate perception of dimensions, he would not need to be able to identify the dimensions separately before he could notice the changing relations between them. An argument for the direct perception
of relationships and transformations is offered by Gibson
(1979).

The 'readiness' of a child to cope with new concepts depends
on the acceptance of Piaget's explanation of how the child
achieves different forms of understanding. If the general
theory of equilibration is not accepted then the logical
sequence that Piaget's theory lays down, while still remaining acceptable as a description of the logical relations
between different concepts and levels of the form of understanding, will not have any implications for the temporal
order of learning.

THE CONTEXT OF LEARNING

The danger of confusing a developmental process with the
actual learning that a child does before he can use a
certain concept can also be brought out in another way.
Many of the skills and abilities that are essential prerequisites for achieving the final concept may be developed

in contexts very different from the context in which the
concept will eventually be used. This sort of problem has
been hinted at already and brings us back to Piaget's
neglect of the social context of learning and the necessity
for an analysis of the large, overriding concepts like
rationality, intelligence, morality and so on in terms of
subordinate abilities and the prerequisites for achieving
these abilities. Bailey points this out for the development
of moral concepts. He says:

> While some of the characteristics that a person needs
> in order to act morally as an adult may be emerging in
> the child's behaviour in these morality-relevant areas
> at early ages, some other equally necessary character-
> istics are probably emerging more markedly in areas of
> behaviour not normally seen as involving morality. I
> am thinking particularly of certain cognitive character-
> istics involved in moral judgement, like the use of
> language, concepts associated with logical reasoning,
> perception of roles, techniques of discussion and their
> internalization, awareness of the various modes of
> living and feeling, and the sheer bulk and variety of
> knowledge of the world necessary to resist the constant
> temptation to egocentricity and ethnocentricity. (1969)

The relevance of these non-moral abilities to the capacity
for moral judgment is clear. And it is no less clear in
the case of intellectual development that many of the subordinate skills and abilities needed to achieve a structured,
adult understanding will come about not in purely intellectual contexts. The essential prerequisite, for example, that
Bennett points out for rational behaviour, that it should
be rule-governed, is not entirely an intellectual ability.
For my behaviour to be rule-governed I must feel bound by
the rule, I must have some care for it to the extent, perhaps, that I might sacrifice some personal interest in the
interests of rationality. This could not come about without
the development of some feeling such as respect, awe, love
for the products of human history.

We are often misled by our own ability to distinguish and
categorise different strands of human development. We make
these distinctions ostensibly in order to simplify our
study of human development. We traditionally distinguish
cognitive development from social and emotional development.
Sometimes we subdivide cognitive into linguistic and other
kinds of cognitive abilities. We frequently find social
development subdivided into emotional, moral, personality,
interpersonal and so on. From all these distinguished
strands psychologists may choose one to study in depth.

While protesting that they do this only for convenience and acknowledging the interconnectedness of human development they are often, none the less, misled into treating the particular strand that they have chosen to focus on in isolation from all the other strands. The most common result of this is that the particular strand of development chosen is studied by studying behaviour, skills etc. in contexts where that particular strand of behaviour is evident or at least relevant. Cognitive development is often studied in the context of solving intellectual problems, moral development is often studied in the context of novel situations or stories depicting moral situations.

In confining our studies to these 'relevant' contexts we are begging the question of how understanding of these types comes about. It is clear that much learning which is relevant to the ability to recognise moral situations and respond in an appropriate manner to them takes place in non-moral contexts. A person needs a certain level of intellectual and linguistic sophistication, for example, before he can comprehend a moral situation as such. He needs to be able to foresee the consequences of his own actions and realistically assess other people's responses to his actions before he can make a moral decision. He needs all these things in addition to specifically moral notions like 'responsility', 'promises', 'integrity' and so on.

It is perhaps not so obvious that there is an emotional side to cognitive development. But what Hume called the 'calm passions', love of truth, self-esteem, respect and so on are essential to the concern for objectivity and correctness which characterises the growth of objective understanding in human beings. These emotions themselves will not be learned from the solving of problems although they may be developed through learning about the ways in which other people have gone about solving those problems.

There is a great danger then, that in distinguishing the different strands of the development of a person, we underestimate the criss cross of connections with which in real situations the different strands are welded together.

CONCEPT OF MATURITY

We argued earlier in this chapter that the concepts of development and transformation imply a direction which in its turn implies an end state, perhaps an ideal towards which the development is tending.

In Piaget's theory this development is always towards dis-
engagement from immediate experience whether this experience
is in the form of perception or emotion, desires, needs and
so on. The child is initially egocentric and development
involves his moving away from this egocentricity. According to Piaget, one way of overcoming egocentricity is by
gradually distinguishing oneself as a subject and coming to
appreciate that one is only one subject among many, each
with his own particular point of view. The mature intelligence recognises the subjectivity of his own point of view
and one way in which egocentricity is overcome is by co-
ordinating one's own point of view with those of others.
The other way is by placing greater and greater reliance on
the data of reversible intellectual operations rather than
the data of irreversible perceptions. Thought becomes
reversible when the subject realises that an operation can
be performed in compensatory directions. To understand
something properly is to be able to follow the changes it
undergoes or could undergo and to grasp well enough what is
involved in these changes so that one can say what would be
required to return the object to its initial state either
by simply reversing the operation or by some kind of compensatory operation. Irreversible thought is thought which is
not conscious of its own implications. It cannot operate
with the transformations involved nor grasp what they involve
and how they are related to each other. It is a form of
thinking which focusses on the static state of things
without being able to comprehend their relations or the
nature of certain kinds of transformations.

The development away from egocentricity towards objectivity
is a growth towards a certain kind of objectivity. It is
not the kind of objectivity that we have mentioned previously
as being the result of genuine intersubjective agreement.
It is the kind of objectivity which involves a gradual
'standing off' from the subject. It involves a freeing of
thought from the control of the situation as experienced,
from the control by the idiosyncracies of the subject himself, and from control by or overconcentration on certain
static aspects of the situation at the expense of a comprehension of the dynamic transformations. On this view, to
see the world objectively is to see it as a coherent set of
transformations, as something which would ideally be manipulable in a coherent way. The growth of an objective viewpoint
involves a progressive 'standing back', a freeing of self
from reliance on personal experience.

One aspect of intellectual maturity does involve just this
kind of distancing. The disciplines of physics and

mathematics which are clearly the ones that interest Piaget,
require just this kind of standing back from the details of
experience and considering only its structure. However,
this is only part of the story. A mature intelligence is
one which comprehends more than the structural features of
physics and mathematics. Egocentricity as Piaget represents it and as we know it from our own experience, involves
the failure to understand that one's own viewpoint is one
among many. This may be overcome by the gradual co-ordination of viewpoints. But this is only possible where a
co-ordinated viewpoint is a possible goal. A large part
of our coming to understand another's point of view consists
in our coming to understand our own feelings and emotions
as well as those of others. In understanding another's
feelings we often have to face the fact that no agreement
or co-ordination is possible. We have to come to appreciate
that others may have feelings, needs, desires and so on
which are not only different but may be incompatible with
or opposed to our own.

Coming to this kind of understanding also involves some
kind of standing back from being immersed in our own egocentric feelings or fantasies but it is a different kind
of standing back from that involved in Piaget's notion of
reversibility. Taylor argues that:
    Reversibility implies a grasp of things as systems which
    can undergo a coherent set of transformations as ideally
    manipulable entities, and connected with this it implies
    that we abstract from their significance for us in so
    coming to grips with them. (1971, p.412)

To view our own feelings, and emotions, other people's and
our relationships with other people in such a way would be
inappropriate. We regard people who do view others in
this way as at best lacking in sympathy and at worst as
inhuman. To understand one's own reasons for doing things,
for example, is not to grasp oneself as the locus of a set
of coherent transformations; it is to be able to see one's
feelings, desires and situation in a certain perspective.
Nor is there any question of abstracting from the significance for us of what we are examining when we try to
understand our own feelings. It is a question of examining
the significance of things for ourselves. We are trying
to get a balanced view of this significance and of our
own involvement.

Understanding our relationships with others is of course
intimately bound up with an understanding of our own
feelings and motivations. As we come to understand our

own feelings about someone else in a relationship, for
example, our understanding itself alters the relationship
and there is no possibility of a return to a starting point.
We are also trying to understand the relationship from a
shared point of view. To stand back and view it as one
object independent of our own involvement in it is to mis-
construe and distort its nature.

The kind of objectivity involved in coming to understand
one's own failings, someone else's feeling, a personal
relationship and so on is one where one has to understand
one's own involvement, not deny it or abstract from it.

Mature intelligence involves at least two kinds of objectivity and possibly even more. There is the kind appropriate
when we are examining a physical system which is very much
the kind that Piaget identifies with his notion of reversibility. There is also the kind which involves standing
back in another sense, that is, which involves the use of
the imagination to allow us to consider and put into
perspective our feelings and relationships.

The point of presenting this different view of objectivity
is not to deny that Piaget's view may have validity within
the area of the development of mathematical notions and the
notions of natural science. It is to show that even within
the broad outlines of Piaget's theory, the representation
of development as broadly away from egocentricity and towards
objectivity, there are different conceptions of what constitutes moving away from egocentricity and achieving
objective understanding. There may be other concepts than
the two discussed here, different ways of achieving objectivity appropriate to different areas of experience and
understanding. To study the development of objective thought
in each of these diverse areas will lead one to pay attention
to different things in the child's development. Piaget
studies the development of that kind of objectivity which
results in a view of the world as a system of coherent
transformations. He looks at the growth of the child's
understanding of the concepts of physics and mathematics.
If we were concerned to chart the development of that kind
of objectivity which leads to the capacity for balanced,
personal relationships with others then we would be interested in the child's growing capacity to sympathise with
others and assess and comprehend diverse points of view and
values. This might involve the study of the growth of the
imagination in the form of play acting and role playing
among children.

Piaget's theory then concerns one kind of objectivity in
one area of human intellectual development. It could not
be viewed as a general theory of child development. Even
as a theory of intellectual or cognitive development it is
limited to the development of that kind of objective thinking which is involved in seeing the world as a set of
impersonal, reversible transformations.

SUMMARY

In this chapter we try to show what kind of explanation one
would expect to have for human development and argue that a
biological, causal explanation is not only impossible to
achieve but is in any case inappropriate. Piaget is very
eager to show that intellectual adaptation grows out of and
is an extension of biological adaptation.

Clearly, this would be a helpful approach when dealing with
the first appearance of anything that could be regarded as
intelligent action. Unless we are going to accept some kind
of innateness hypothesis then we must be able to show how
learning develops out of biologically innate reflexes and
physiology. But the model soon begins to show signs of
strain if it is extended even to some of the later stages
of the sensori-motor period.

Apart from the importance of identifying the end state of
development before we can characterise the process, we
suggested that to represent the dawning understanding of a
child of, for example, concepts of conservation, as a causal
matter would be misleading. It is only in unusual cases,
perhaps, for example, in cases of so-called 'brain-washing'
that he can be said to have been 'caused' to hold certain
beliefs. More usually we come to have certain beliefs as a
result of reasoning about them and coming to see that there
are good reasons for them.

Finally in this chapter, we criticise Piaget's concept of
intellectual maturity. He offers a picture of the mature
intelligence as one which views the world as a set of objective, coherent transformations. Although this may be an
appropriate way for the mature intelligence to view the
worlds of physics and mathematics there are other worlds to
be viewed. The worlds of the emotions and of interpersonal
relations would not be appropriately viewed as sets of
objective, coherent transformations. But to be said to be
mature, a person must be able to view these worlds
appropriately.

Chapter 7

The beginnings and direction of development

PREVIEW

This chapter tries to show some of the capacities that a child must have if he is to be able to gain access to the world of intersubjective knowledge. Piaget contends that development proceeds from the egocentric to the socialised. Interpreting essentially similar data, Vygotsky from a different philosophical tradition, argues that development proceeds from the socialised to the individualised. Recent psychological studies have shown the abilities of babies to be far greater than had been imagined. Apart from these empirical studies, there are a priori reasons why infants must be credited with far more than mere mechanical responses to environmental stimuli. These views on the social nature of knowledge provide a complement to Piaget's individualism.

EGOCENTRIC TO SOCIALISED

A problem for any theory of development is how the whole process gets started in the first place. In the case of human development the disparity between 'the mewling, puking babe' and the finished product is so wide and the capacities traditionally attributed to infants, so small that the problem appears especially acute.

Piaget attributes to the infant no more than a few maladapted reflexes and a mode of interaction with the environment. This is sufficient according to his theory to lead to the developments typical of the sensori-motor stage which were discussed in Chapter 1. As soon as the infant is born,

contact with the environment leads to the adaption and
refinement of the initial reflexes which are then gradually
transformed into the co-ordinated actions typical of the
sensori-motor stage. These actions gradually become
'operationalised and interiorised' thus giving rise to the
structures typical of objective thought.

Piaget believed that development comes about through the
interiorisation of non-verbal action and that the direction
of development is from the 'autistic', 'illogical' fantasy
of the isolated individual mind to the normalised, logical,
realistic thought of the scientifically objective rational
thinker. Piaget's early books bring out the very great
emphasis that he places on the notion of egocentrism. At
first, he claims, the child's language and thought is
autistic, eventually it becomes socialised and logical but
in the transition between these two extremes it remains for
a long time egocentric. Egocentric talk is characterised
by the child's apparent lack of concern about whether anyone
is listening to him or not. Even if another person is
listening and responds to the child's talk, the child will
either ignore the responses or interpret them in a way
which fits in with his own intentions, taking no account
of the intended meaning of his interlocutor. In an early
work on the language of the child, he says:
>   Directed thought is conscious, i.e. it pursues aims
>   that are present in the mind of the thinker. It is
>   intelligent, i.e. it is adapted to reality and strives
>   to influence it. It is susceptible of truth and error
>   ... and it can be communicated through language.
>   Autistic thought is subconscious, i.e. the goals it
>   pursues and the problems it sets itself are not present
>   in consciousness. It is not adapted to external reality
>   but creates for itself a reality of imagination or
>   dreams. It tends not to establish truths, but to
>   gratify wishes and remains strictly individual and in-
>   communicable as such by means of language, since it
>   operates primarily in images and must, in order to be
>   communicated, resort to roundabout methods, evoking, by
>   means of symbols and of myths, the feelings that guide
>   it. (Piaget, 1926, pp.59-60)

Between these two contrasted ways of thinking:
>   there are many varieties in regard to their degree of
>   communicability. These intermediate varieties must obey
>   a special logic, intermediate between the logic of
>   autism and the logic of intelligence. We propose to
>   give the name of egocentric thought to the principle of
>   these intermediate forms. (Piaget, 1926, p.62)

Egocentrism stands between extreme autism and the logic of
reason chronologically as well as structurally and functionally. He sees the child's thought as originally and naturally autistic. The child's way of thinking becomes logical
and realistic only after a long process of development and
under long and sustained social pressure. But the influences
to which adults subject the child:

> are not imprinted on him as on a photographic plate:
> they are 'assimilated', that is to say, deformed by the
> living being subjected to them and become implanted in
> his own substance. It is this psychological substance
> of the child, or, in other words, the structure and the
> functioning peculiar to child thought that we have
> endeavoured to describe and, in a measure, to explain.
> (Piaget, 1928, p.338)

So, autism is seen as the original and earliest form of
thought: logical thinking appears relatively late as the
culmination of a long process of development and egocentric
thought is the genetic link between them. Piaget states
more than once that the assumption of the intermediate
nature of the child's thought is hypothetical. But he also
says that this hypothesis is so close to common sense that
it does not seem to him to be any more debatable than the
fact of the child's egocentrism. He traces egocentrism to
the practical nature of the child's activities and to the
relatively late development of social attitudes. He says:

> Clearly, from the genetic point of view, one must start
> from the child's activity in order to understand his
> thought; and his activity is unquestionably egocentric
> and egotistic. The social instinct in well-defined
> form develops late. The first critical period in this
> respect occurs toward the age of seven or eight.
> (Piaget, 1928, p.30)

Before this age Piaget sees egocentrism as all-pervading
and all-important. His explanations of the 'mistakes' that
children make all refer to the distorting effect of the
child's egocentrism.

A recent critique of Piaget has castigated commentators
for taking too literally Piaget's pronouncements on egocentricity and failing to take account of work published
more recently than 1926 (Vuyk, 1981). Vuyk says that:
'When Piaget and Inhelder (1956) wrote that the child is
"completely" egocentric, this was never meant to be taken
literally, as Piaget's other writings on egocentricity
clearly show.'

What Piaget's other writings on egocentricity do show is
that he did not intend by the concept to suggest that young
children are completely cut off from all social communication and adult influence. His use of the concept is intended
to emphasise, however, the difficulty that young children
have in seeing anybody's viewpoint but their own. The child
comes to appreciate other viewpoints than his own when he
begins to reflect on the part played in his understanding
by his own activities, when he ceases, that is, to 'centre'
on the objects of his perception and becomes capable of
paying attention to relations between them and to the relations between himself and the objects.

Piaget moves away, in his later work then, from the notion
of social egocentricity to that of cognitive egocentricity.
He calls it centration. He started his work on egocentricity in the context of language studies. There, since the
main purpose of language is communication with others, he
was concerned with socialisation and the apparent social
egocentricity of the child. But later in the 'three moun-
tain experiment' which can be found in Piaget and Inhelder
1956 and which is often used as a test of egocentricity
(see, for example, M. Donaldson, 1978), Piaget was primarily
interested in whether the child can understand a situation
seen from different perspectives, and not whether he can
see from the 'perspectives' of different persons. Similarly,
in the correlation tasks involving the pouring of water
from stout, squat glasses into tall, narrow ones the pre-
operational child centres on the height or width instead
of the relationship. Here no other person enters the picture
at all.

There seem to be two sides to egocentrism then. There is
the social egocentrism which concerns the difficulties that
the child has in freeing himself from his own point of view
and co-ordinating his views and his actions with those of
others. And there is cognitive egocentrism which involves
the increasing ability to 'decentre', that is to fail to be
unduly influenced by one aspect of a situation and to use
the reversible cognitive structure. In the one case the
child is being unduly influenced by his own narrow perspective and in the other case he is being unduly influenced by
what his perception of the environment affords him. The
first kind of distortion resulting from a one-sided view
can be corrected by coming to appreciate others' points of
view. The second kind of distortion can only be corrected
by the construction of complex mechanisms to offset the
distorting effects of perception. Although Piaget uses the
same word for both kinds of distorting influence they are

not really seen to be the same at all. The first is a
commonly recognised problem overcome by procedures, such
as asking another's opinion, which are commonly held to
lead to an increase in objectivity. The second is a problem which can only be comprehended against the background
of Piaget's own views on perception and is overcome by
processes which only have meaning within a Piagetian
theoretical framework.

Egocentrism in this sense of cognitive egocentrism is not
intended to be the iron gate blocking the child off from
all contact with others. It is meant to account for the
difficulty that young children have in understanding operations. Piaget says: 'But I call most behavior (which does)
not manage to understand the difference between two points
of view, unadapted from the point of view of intellectual
cooperation' (1962).

Vuyk argues that Piaget clearly shows that the inability of
the child to cooperate and communicate is not due to a lack
of intention to do so but to his lack of cognitive development. In consequence, the child might well be able to
communicate successfully in tasks and situations that do
not require operations. This is confirmed by observations
of spontaneous talk in different situations where the
percentage of egocentric talk is always smaller than that
of social talk.

Piaget then is not claiming that the child is not a social
creature from the beginning and social interchanges between
child and mother could hardly have escaped his notice when
he made his extended and astute observations of his own
children. What he is claiming is that insofar as intellectual development is concerned, the possibility of understanding operations and eventually developing objective, rational,
scientific ways of thinking, these things depend on the
interiorisation of action, not on verbal instruction or the
interiorisation of language and consequently in these areas,
the child is alone, isolated, building his world for himself
and by himself.

However, although Piaget may deny that he intends the concept of egocentrism to imply that the child is cut off from
all social contact until he is perhaps eight years old, his
theory does imply it. Cognitive egocentrism can also refer
to the total process of assimilation. If we refer back to
the quotation from Piaget, 1926, at the beginning of this
chapter, he says that all new experiences, including adult
influences and social communication, are 'deformed by the

living being subjected to them'. That is, the child tries
to assimilate everything he encounters to what he already
knows and can do. Piaget argues that the child must first
explore his own actions before he can place them in a complex system of images and perspectives. This assimilation
of reality to action is very 'rational' and useful for the
child's cognitive development even if the dominance of
material actions and one's own perspective are irrational
(Piaget, 1968). But it does imply that anything which does
not 'fit' the child's assimilation frameworks, will be
rejected. It is hard to see, on this view, how a child
could ever learn from an adult. The only way in which a
child could be said to learn from an adult would be if what
the adult said, did or showed the child succeeded in upsetting his cognitive equilibrium and so led to an attempt
at accommodation. Adult teaching, then, might accelerate
the process of upsetting and reconstructing equilibrated
structures but it could not replace it or complement it.

LANGUAGE DEVELOPMENT

Whatever is said about the different concepts of egocentrism
that Piaget has emphasised at different times, it cannot be
denied that he seriously underestimates the role played by
language in communication and learning. This is partly
because he was convinced that learning takes place through
the interiorisation of actions, not words. And partly it
was because his theory did not offer a proper account of
language development. Piaget is far more concerned with
the symbolic and representative functions of language than
with communicative functions.

He distinguishes between signs and symbols and insists that
it is the ability to think symbolically, not the ability to
respond to signs, which is the precursor of linguistic
development. Being able to produce or respond to symbols
is quite different from recognising signals or cues. In
recognising a signal or responding to one we might recognise
a whole through one of its parts or recognise a motor schema
through something that accompanied it. This kind of ability
is well within the reach of many animals. Symbols, on the
other hand, initially have private, subjective meanings for
the child. One of Piaget's own children used a handkerchief
as a pretend pillow in pretend-going-to-sleep games and the
handkerchief came to symbolise for her, 'going to sleep'.
The symbolic function in this sense, then, is clearly
representational. One thing stands for another from which
it is clearly distinct.

Another way in which Piaget makes the distinction between
signal and symbol is the context in which they arise.
Signals (and cues) can arise in many different contexts
which are open to humans and animals alike. Thus children
and dogs both learn to operate with signals when they get
ready to eat at the appearance of their feeding dish, or
get ready to go out when mother puts her coat on. But for
Piaget, the symbolic function is tied solely to representational activity. It arises in the first instance out of
the joint activities of imitation and play. With this kind
of background it is easy to see how Piaget's theory in so
far as it is concerned with language development, will view
the initial steps in language learning as the formation of
private symbols, thus the autism of early representational
thought follows. The problem of his theory then is to
explain how these initial private symbols 'become socialised'. How, that is, the child transforms a system of
private symbols into something with which to communicate to
others. Piaget has not studied language extensively. His
solution to the problem of how language becomes socialised
can, however, be discerned. Basically his view is that the
logical, operational structures of thought precede language
and so impart their structures to language. As has been
argued, Piaget believes that logic, since it expresses the
fundamental laws of the co-ordination of actions, is objective and 'socialised'. As the logical structures develop,
and become more objective, so they pass these characteristics on to the linguistic structures which are derived
from them.

SOCIAL CONTEXT OF LANGUAGE DEVELOPMENT

The kinds of objections that were made to Piaget's account
of the objectification of knowledge in terms of the development of individual structures, can be made against
Piaget's account of language development. Recent work in
the area of language development has concentrated on the
social relation between the mother and her child. Hamlyn
has argued that early learning which involves the slow
sorting out of basic categories and distinctions which are
made by human beings in their ways of understanding the
world is not only slow and gradual but relies heavily on
the establishment of personal relationships with other
human beings who not only know what the world is like as
seen through human eyes but who also care that the child
should come to see it that way too. Hamlyn says:
    In humans there have to be some instinctive patterns of
    behaviour, for example, sucking. But so much more

>   depends on such things as expressions of love and
>   affection and on the rapport that is normally set up
>   between parent and child. (Hamlyn, 1973)

The point that Hamlyn is making is the a priori point that
given the nature of human knowledge, human children could
not gain access to it without having some personal relationship with an adult who cared for them and treated them as
human beings. By insisting that a relationship of co-
operation between child and adult is prevented by the
child's egocentricity, Piaget effectively cuts out the
possibility of even a rudimentary personal relationship.
The work of Bruner on the previsions and prerequisites of
verbal communication provides a detailed illustration of
the kind of relationship between mother and child that
Hamlyn argues is indispensable for early learning.

Bruner (1975) claims that two essential prerequisites for
the learning of a verbal language are that the child should
learn the conventions that govern the use of gestures and
utterances within a certain society and that he should
learn to take on the different roles that participants in
verbal communication adopt. That is, he should know the
difference between a communicator and a receiver, a demander
and a complier and so on. As Bruner shows, the child's
learning of the conventional uses of gesture and utterance
is based on both the interpretation of the child's utterances by the mother and the interpretation of the mother's
behaviour by the child. The learning of complementary
roles is brought about by co-operative play between mother
and child.

To illustrate the first point first: to characterise these
conventions Grice (1976) has described assumptions that
participants in a conversation make from which could be
derived some loose-fitting maxims - maxims of relevance, of
quantity, of quality. Speakers in conversation are
expected to stick to the point, to give neither too little
nor too much information about context, to speak the truth
as they see it. Before a child can talk he is likely to be
unaffected by these maxims. But his mother, as an adult
and as his teacher, not only is under the influence of the
maxims but interprets the child's attempts at communication
in accordance with them. Joanna Ryan (1974) points out that:

>   Many young children experience extensive verbal inter-
>   changes with their mothers. During these the mother
>   actively picks up, interprets, comments upon, extends,
>   repeats and sometimes misinterprets what the child has
>   said. (Ryan, 1974, p.199)

Not only do the mothers interpret the child's gestures and
vocalisations in conative terms but also in terms of Grice-
like maxims like 'sincerity' ('He's really faking when he
makes that sound') and 'consistency' ('Won't you please
make up your mind what you want'). The mothers continue
to interpret the child's utterances as if they were grammat-
ically formed and conformed to Grice's maxims, until they
actually do. The mother is treating the child as if it
behaved according to adult conceptions such as intention,
purpose, sincerity, deceit and so on. She is, to some
extent, treating him as an equal. The child, on the other
hand, is given the chance, if his mother is consistent, to
see what she does in response to his utterances and so to
gradually learn both how she interprets his utterances and
how to modify these utterances to get her to behave differently. He is also introduced to concepts like sincerity,
consistency, intention and to appropriate ways of behaving
when these concepts are being applied.

In interpreting what the infant intends to communicate the
mother has a great number of contextual and other cues; and
so does the infant, for if the mother is consistent she
gives forth cues that come increasingly to have a predictable consequence as far as her behaviour is concerned. In
this sense they are both participants in a transactional
situation; their joint behaviour determining its own future
course, that is, it is not necessarily what the infant wants
that determines what it gets but how the mother interprets
its 'request' for what it wants. And how the mother interprets the infant's request for what it wants will affect the
way in which it 'asks' next time.

Ryan (1974) adapts a classification of cues originally
prepared by John Austin (1962) for the analysis of perform-
ative aspects of speech: (1) Aspects of utterance itself
including intonation patterns that suggest insistence,
pleasure, protest, request, etc. As Ryan says: 'What is
important is that adults interpret children's use of intonation in a systematic way, thus allowing children to learn
what is conventional usage' (1974). (2) Accompaniments of
utterance, for example, pointing, searching, playing with a
specific object. (3) Circumstance of the utterance: mothers
typically classify their infant's vocalisations by context;
babbling contentedly in his cot on first waking up, calling
for attention on waking from the afternoon nap, hunger
fretting before feed time, annoyance at not being able to
reach an object etc.

The importance of this interpreting of the infant's cries
and gestures by the parents is that it is through the par-
ent's interpretation and consequent action that the child
learns which sounds and gestures have which consequences,
that is, he learns the conventions. But he only learns them
because he is being treated as a human person from the start.
The mother imputes to him intention, choice, want and so
he can learn to have intentions, choices and wants. It is
by being treated as a human being that he learns how to be
a human being. To quote an example of the mutual modification of the behaviour of mother and child that Bruner
gives:

> Jon A and the development of a signal pattern involving
> reaching outward bimanually while in a sitting position,
> hands prone. It had usually been interpreted by the
> mother as a signal that Jon wanted some familiar hand-
> sized object beyond his reach's terminus, and she gener-
> ally provided him with it, often heightening his antici-
> pation by advancing the object slowly or 'dramatically'
> toward his hand with an accompanying rising voice pitch.
> At eight months, one week, Jon used the signal; M inter-
> preted it as calling for her hand, since there was no
> object close by, and performed her 'walking hand' body-
> game format, with the fingers walking up Jon's front to
> his chin. He tolerated it, though not entering as
> exuberantly as usual. That over, Jon reached out again.
> M interpreted it as a request for repetition. He parti-
> cipated even more reluctantly. M on completion then
> repeated the game though Jon had not signalled. He
> averted his gaze and whimpered a little. She repeated
> again and he was totally turned off. Pause. Then 27
> seconds after Jon first reached out, he reached again,
> this time pulling M's hands to a position where he could
> take hold of the ulnar edges and raise himself to a
> standing position. There was a following sequence of
> 14 episodes extending for slightly over 9 minutes in
> which M and Jon played a game of alternating irregularly
> between the two 'formats' - M's hand either walking on
> fingers to tickle position, or M's hand in stand support-
> ing condition. Under M's control, it was made into a
> 'surprise' evoking alternative format, with her alterna-
> tive interpretations of his reach gestures being rendered
> explicit. (1975, pp.266-7)

In the course of these exchanges as Ryan has already noted
(1974) the child is developing skills that are at least as
essential to speaking and understanding language as the
mastery of grammar or the ability to symbolise. They are
developing an understanding of intention, meaning, purpose

etc. Much of this learning is based on the mother entering
into a personal relationship with the child and interpreting his utterances in the same terms as she would interpret
those of another adult. The child sometimes conforms to
this interpretation and sometimes does not but he learns en
route what interpretations his efforts evoke and how they
can be modified. The relationship between the mother and
child is far more like a personal relationship between
equals than it is like the relationship of constraining
adult on compliant child that Piaget pictures.

The second prerequisite that Bruner discusses, the learning
of reciprocal roles, shows even more clearly the importance
of genuine co-operation between mother and child. Benveniste
(1971, pp.217-8) claims that a grasp of reciprocal roles in
discourse is the essential prerequisite for linguistic
deixis of person, place and time. Again Bruner claims, the
beginnings of this ability to use spatial, temporal and
interpersonal contextual features of situations as aids in
the management of joint reference, has its origin in pre-
linguistic learning of reversible role relationships. He
says:

> Again, the beginnings of a locution-dependent reciprocal
> concept emerges in action well before it is ever used
> in formal language. Established and reversible role
> relationships obviously provide a primitive base for
> later linguistic deixis. The universal prelinguistic
> game of 'Peekaboo' is a striking example (Bruner and
> Sherwood 1980; Greenfield 1972) of such reversible role
> structures, bound as it is by rule constraint with
> respect to who is the recipient and who the agent of
> coverings and uncoverings and how these may be reversed.
> Give-and-take routines early established between mother
> and infant, again with reversibility of roles and often
> marked by distinctive vocalizations for marking the
> giving and receipt of an object (Bruner, 1975) provide
> another example. In such games, once developed, the
> child looks mother directly in the eye for a signal at
> crucial pauses in the play, as if to calibrate his
> intended actions with hers and to check which one is
> playing which role. In the first year of life, then,
> the child is mastering a convention-checking procedure
> not unlike that of adults - indeed, even using eye-to-
> eye contact for determining intent, readiness and whose
> 'turn' it is (Argyle and Ingham, 1972). (Bruner, 1975,
> p.273)

There are many more examples in this work of Bruner and his
associates to show the importance of the relationship

between the mother and child for early learning. But they
make the same points: that this relationship is not one of
constraint and compliance but of co-operation; that the
mother by interpreting the child's utterances in adult
terms, by following the direction of his gaze and interpreting what it is he is looking at, by directing his attention
to things she deems important gives him the chance of learning how she sees the world, and so gives him an entrance to
the common, social world to which she belongs. Without
this relationship, based on the care and interest that the
mother has for the child and the emotional response that a
human baby must make to the person who brings him food,
comfort and love, it is difficult to see how the child
could learn to make typically human distinctions, accept
typically human values and achieve a typically human
understanding of the world.

It might be thought, from all this, that I am suggesting
that the mother deliberately teaches the child, that she
not only cares for the child but consciously cares that the
child should come to see the world through her eyes and
understand it in her terms. This may sometimes be the case.
At some points some mothers do consciously set out to teach
their child to count, or to read, or to name the colours.
But if this was always the case, if the mother deliberately
from the moment of birth set out to teach her child to be
a human being then the relationship between the mother and
child would be that between teacher and pupil not what I
have insisted is the important relationship, a personal
relationship. The emphasis on the personal nature of the
relationship is essential. It is not because the mother
wants the child to develop reasonable wants and emotions,
intentions and purposes and so on that she teaches him what
these are. She just loves him, thinks of him as, to a large
extent, another human being just like herself, and so just
assumes that he has emotions and wants, intentions and
purposes just as she does. Because she cares for him she
responds in an appropriately human way to behaviour that
she interprets as expressing emotion, desire and so on.
So, she gives the child the opportunity to learn how human
beings behave. One can say that she is teaching the child
but she herself would not see what she did as teaching, she
would see it as simply communicating with him, caring for
him, treating him like an individual. It can be seen that
the opportunities that the child has for learning will
depend greatly on the quality of this personal relationship.
The less personal the relationship the less opportunity
will the child be given to learn what it is to be a person.

EMOTIONAL CAPACITIES OF INFANTS

It is the adults, then, in the child's environment who open
the door to the social world of shared standards, values,
concepts and so on to which he must gain access. But the
child, in turn, has to be the kind of creature able to take
advantage of this opportunity and pass through the door.
What characteristics must he have in order to do this?

Piaget and other investigators have documented time and
again the animism of young children and the difficulty that
they have in coming to realise that not all objects in
their environment have feelings, needs, wants, purposes and
so on. MacMurray (1970) argues that the only ability that
the new-born child has is the ability to catch the attention of the adult on whom he is dependent. Arguing from
the nature of human knowledge and the human world he concludes that no creature on its own could learn to cope with
that complex and subtle world. Of necessity, it must be
initiated into that world by other adults. It will then be
uniquely fitted (by evolution) to catch and hold the attention of at least one adult.

It must be true in any culture, that young humans are
dependent for a long time, far longer than any other animal
species, on the care and attention of someone older and
more capable. The child's relationship with this person,
or people, is of major importance to the child for many
years. Hamlyn (1974) argues that such relationships are
not to be construed as mere transactions between the child
and adults nor on any simple-minded stimulus/response
model. It is vital to see how crucial emotional responses
and attitudes are in this. The famous Bowlby's (1965) work
on maternal deprivation while it can be criticised for
insisting that the object of the young child's attachment
must be its mother (Rutter, 1972), drew attention to the
strength and importance of a child's feelings and the
difficulty that it has in growing into a normal human being
if deprived of the opportunity of loving and being loved.

Hamlyn argues that the idea that human beings are rather
more complex than the simple hedonistic picture offered by
mechanistic psychologies does not imply a kind of mysticism.
He says:
> We need only suppose that certain emotional attitudes
> and reactions (by which I mean not simple mechanical
> reactions but complex forms of response to e.g. love
> and concern) are part of our genetic inheritance, thus
> forming the basis of ... the natural reactions of person

> to person (cf. here Bishop Butler's view of man as
> something possessing a set of particular properties
> among which might be benevolence). (1974, p.25)

Darwin followed up his theory of natural selection with its
direct application to humanity and ethologists have always
hoped that one day the relevance of their theories to men
would be appreciated. However, psychologists, sociologists
and philosophers have been slow to respond to the overtures
of ethologists. Psychologists have assumed that all that
is distinctively human rests on the acquisition of behaviour
through learning, anthropologists have stressed the infinite
variability of human culture and the malleability of the
individual and philosophers have insisted on the uniqueness
of men. Mary Midgely (1979) has attempted to bridge the
gulf between the ethological and the philosophical conceptions of man. Her argument is not that man has overestimated his own capabilities in insisting on the difference
that his culture makes between himself and 'the beast' but
that man has underestimated both the 'beasts' themselves
and the genetic inheritance that he has. She shows with
examples taken from Lorenz, Morris and other ethologists
that the capabilities of animals are far greater than we
are accustomed to believe and that in particular, their
capacity for emotion is greater, more complex, and more
subtle than we had given them credit for. All this illustrates persuasively the possibility that human creatures are
born with the capacity for strong, complex emotions, which
are naturally elicited by the adults who care for the child
and so naturally provide the conditions of interest in and
attention to the adult's attempts to initiate the child
into his own world. These natural capacities for emotion,
along with the similar perceptual systems, similar needs
for food, warmth and care, similar vulnerability to suffering, similar physical capabilities and so on, constitute
that shared form of life which Wittgenstein argues is at
the base of our capacity to communicate with one another
and consequently learn from one another.

The traditional view of emotion presents it as a distracting and distorting influence on human rational thought. In
contrast, the view presented here is that a major part of
a person's capacity to come to understand his world depends
on his relationship with other people and that these relationships are based on feelings such as love which are a
part of his natural endowment. To quote from Hamlyn's
treatment of these problems:

> Although it is important that the child has innate
> tendencies and capacities (the programming) and that

its attention is channelled so that it is put in the way of things (the data fed into it), it could never thereby, any more than a computer could, come to an understanding of what it is for things to be so and not so, of what it is to be correct and incorrect. That could come only through relations with others in which feelings, wants and attitudes play a large part. Hence emotion is not simply a distracting and irrational factor; it is an essential component in intellectual development. (Hamlyn, 1978, p.102)

This emotion is rightly directed to other people in the child's environment and through them directed to the things which people consider to be of importance in their lives. The child then is right from the moment of birth, in a social context to which he is fitted to respond appropriately, that is, with complex and powerful emotions.

FROM THE SOCIALISED TO THE INDIVIDUAL

At first, although undeniably powerful and effective in catching the attention of important people in his world, the child's emotional responses are gross and often inappropriate. They are gradually shaped and adapted by the responses that others make to him.

Relying on essentially similar data to that used by Piaget, Vygotsky has argued that the course of development is from this initially socially adapted creature, shaped by others' responses, to a mature independent individual. It is interesting to consider Vygotsky's criticisms of Piaget because his theory is so totally opposed to Piaget's although his observations and the data he relies on are so similar. This shows, once again, the large element of interpretation that is involved in theorising about human development.

Vygotsky sees the interiorisation of speech as a major force in development. Piaget could not award this any importance since he believed that the effective substrata of presocial and logical thinking are non-verbal actions (as we have shown in the previous chapters). Actions, not verbalisations, are for Piaget (Piaget and Inhelder, 1966) the element of early life that develop into the operations of the mind that can act as abstract (not verbal) representations of propositions. While not much interested in the interiorisation of speech he bases his entire theory of intellectual development on the interiorisation of non-verbal action.

This is what makes the discussion between Vygotsky and
Piaget on the notion of egocentric speech of interest.
They are not discussing simply different interpretations
of the same phenomenon. They are disagreeing fundamentally
about the direction of human development and the processes
underlying it.

Vygotsky's main disagreement with Piaget is with his view
that the speech and thought of the child start off as unsocialised. By unsocialised he means (1) uninfluenced by
the adaptive social effects that others' behaviour must
have on the child's behaviour and (2) unable to effect the
necessary adaptations for survival through communication of
need to others. For Vygotsky, whatever communication skills
are present from birth are adaptive for survival. He says:

   The primary function of speech, in both children and
   adults is communication, social contact. The earliest
   speech of the child is therefore essentially social.
   ... Egocentric speech emerges when the child transfers
   social, collaborative forms of behaviour to the sphere
   of inner personal psychic function.... In our conception
   the true direction of the development of thinking is not
   from the individual to the socialised but from the
   social to the individual. (Vygotsky, 1962, p.19)

From birth the use of these communication skills is adapted
and shaped by others' communication and responsiveness.
The process of development is from this socially adapted
little being to a full human intellect whose thoughts may
be quite individualised and unique. Piaget's course of
development is exactly the opposite, from an autistic,
fantasy-bound, isolated mind to an objective, realistic,
socialised one.

There are irreconcilable differences, then, between these
two on the direction that the course of human development
takes. Piaget argues that the developing mind goes from
an autistic-like lack of awareness of the world outside the
infant's own idiosyncratic experience to an adapted or
socialised structure of mind that comprehends the world in
an objective (consensual) way. Vygotsky argues that the
infant starts with socially originating and socially conditioned similar experience of the world and develops towards
greater individuality that arises from using language to
explore experiences, meaning and implications.

Similarly, there are irreconcilable differences concerning
the role that language plays. Piaget argues that language
simply follows and mirrors intellectual structures. Vygotsky

argues that language contributes to intellectual development and, especially in later learning, is the major force for intellectual growth.

Since the data on which these diverse theories are based is essentially similar, the differences between them lie in their different approaches to the data. Their differing interpretations have their roots in fundamental ideological and philosophical differences.

The possibility of objective knowledge rests on the possibility of interpersonal communication and genuine sharing of concepts. This is not something with which Piaget would disagree since he insists at several points that communication, cooperation and the sharing of views are necessary for the achievement of objectivity. But according to Piaget's theory the child's thought is initially asocial and only becomes fully socialised and capable of cooperation when a certain level of cognitive development has been reached. To reach this level the child must work alone with the objective environment that impinges on him.

However, in this connection it has been argued that the child cannot enter the social world of shared concepts and standards alone, but must be brought in by an already knowledgeable adult. He must learn to make the distinctions that actually hold good in the adult world and this involves him in recognising others as sources of knowledge. Hamlyn (1978) argues that the child has to come to accept the existence of others' interests, wants, wishes, feelings and attitudes, sometimes agreeing, but often not, with his own. The child comes to this acceptance through personal relationships with others based on such feelings and attitudes. Gaining access to the social world of shared concepts and standards is far more, then, than a purely cognitive process of learning about the world and other people. It also involves learning what it is to be a person and this, as Hamlyn has argued elsewhere (Hamlyn, 1974), necessarily involves one in personal relationships with others.

The picture of the initial state of the individual presented by Piaget and the story of his subsequent development does not permit the kind of relationships with adults that Hamlyn, following Wittgenstein, would argue is essential for the possibility of a shared understanding and consequently of knowledge. In Piaget's theory, knowledge is constructed at the individual level and later, after a long process of development becomes socialised.

Other philosophers apart from Hamlyn have argued that
Piaget's neglect of the social and the linguistic contribu-
tions to development constitute a fatal flaw in his theory.
Rotman, for example, argues that the problem with Piaget's
views on the nature of mathematics is that it is the individual who constructs mathematics without any influence of the
social language or environment. Piaget writes about the
epistemic subject and admits that decentration of the
individual construction is necessary through the co-operation
of others. But Rotman argues that:

> It is just as reasonable to suppose, in effect, that
> co-ordination of viewpoints is a matter of explicit
> justified agreement about public entities and not, as
> Piaget insists, a question of the inner necessities
> operating within an individual mind. (1977, p.154)

Vygotsky's view, on the other hand, offers just the kind of
picture that is called for by the requirements of interpersonal communication. Vygotsky rejects Piaget's reliance
on biological concepts to explain development and rejects
Piaget's claimed continuity between organic and mental
development. He accepts both evolutionary but also revolutionary changes.

The major revolutionary change in development comes about
with the use of artificial aids to enlarge one's power and
experience. Human beings are active participants in their
own existence and at each stage of their development children
acquire the means by which they can affect their world and
themselves.

A crucial aspect of this mastery beginning in infancy is
the creation and use of artificial stimuli. Through such
stimuli a situation and the reaction linked to it are
altered by human intervention.

These auxiliary stimuli have no natural or inherent links
with the situation and they are highly diverse. They include
the tools of the culture into which the child is born, the
language of those who relate to the child and means invented
by the child himself.

Piaget shares Vygotsky's emphasis on the activity of the
organism. But while Piaget stresses the biologically
supported universal stages of development, Vygotsky emphasises the interaction between the ever-changing social
environment and the biological substrata. Piaget writes as
if the environment remains constant while only the subject
changes. But Vygotsky, because he pays due attention to

the social nature of the environment, emphasises its constant transformations. Consequently, the knowledge and
experience of children will differ since we have a similar
biological system interacting with diverse environmental
systems. He shares Piaget's view that learning alters the
initial individual in the sense that new elements become
assimilated and consequently, as children develop, they
will diverge more and more widely from each other as the
effect of perhaps initially small differences in the environment accumulate.

Because the historical conditions which determine to a
large extent the opportunities for experience are constantly
changing, there can be no universal scheme which adequately
represents the dynamic relation between internal and external
aspects of development. Therefore, a functional learning
system of one child may not be identical with that of
another although there may be similarities at certain
stages of development.

Vygotsky emphasises, then, the social and consequently
changing nature of the environment. But he also emphasises
the role of adults in initiating the child into this environment. He insists that the direction of development is from
the interpersonal, public act to the personal interpretation
and that the personal interpretation comes about only after
a long process of development.

What the child starts off with is a kind of practical,
animal intelligence, physiologically based and showing
itself in outward activity. This activity is observed and
interpreted by adults and it is the shaping of the behaviour
by adults consequent upon their interpretation of it which
initiates the 'meaning' of symbolic activity. An example
that Vygotsky gives is of the establishment of the meaning
of pointing. He says:
> We call the internal reconstruction of an external
> operation internalisation: A good example of this pro-
> cess may be found in the development of pointing.
> Initially, this gesture is nothing more than an un-
> successful attempt to grasp something, a movement aimed
> at a certain object which designates forthcoming acti-
> vity. The child attempts to grasp an object placed
> beyond his reach; his hands stretched toward that object
> remain poised in the air. His fingers make grasping
> movements.... When the mother comes to the child's aid
> and realizes his movement indicates something, the
> situation changes fundamentally. Pointing becomes a
> gesture for others. The child's unsuccessful attempt

engenders a reaction not from the object he seeks but
from another person. Consequently, the primary meaning
of that unsuccessful grasping movement is established
by others. Only later, when the child can link his
unsuccessful grasping movement to the objective system
as a whole does he begin to understand this movement as
pointing. (1978, p.56)

When the child himself realises the meaning of the pointing
gesture, a fundamental change occurs in the function and
orientation of the gesture. It seems to be an unsuccessful
grasping attempt directed at an object out of reach and
becomes instead an act of pointing directed at another
person. It only becomes a true gesture, however, no matter
what the intention of the agent, when it is actually understood by others as such a gesture. Vygotsky says: 'Its
meaning and function are created at first by an objective
situation and then by people who surround the child' (1978,
p.56). Symbolic activity according to Vygotsky thus begins
with a public observable action. This action is transformed
into a public symbol through the recognition of the action
by the people who surround the child. Symbols are thus
public from the very beginning. Vygotsky does not have to
face the problems created by Piaget's theory of the initial
personal, idiosyncratic nature of the child's first symbolic
activity.

The process of internalisation consists of a series of
transformations:
   (1) An operation that initially represents an external
   activity is reconstructed and begins to occur internally.
   (2) An interpersonal process (between people) is transformed into an intrapersonal one (within the child).
   Every function in the child's cultural development appears
   twice: first, on the social level, and later, on the
   individual level; first between people and then inside
   the child. This applies equally to voluntary attention,
   to logical memory, and to the formation of concepts.
   All the higher functions originate as actual relations
   between human beings.

The use of symbols is one of the artificial means by which
humans can transform their initial animal intelligence.
The use of artificial means Vygotsky sees as a revolutionary
change marking an abrupt difference between animal and human
intelligence. These artificial means may be directed to
control of the environment. Such are the tools and machines
that we use to reshape our environment to suit ourselves
better. Some of the artificial means are turned inward and

are used to control internal mental processes. These are
the symbols of linguistic thought. Their function is to
control our thinking. By means of linguistic symbols we
can make plans, form intentions, remember complex things
for long periods of time and so on.

Development is not seen as one of a piece as it is according to Piaget. The higher psychological processes are
based on the use of artificial stimuli and as such have a
different structure and different source from the biologically based practical intelligence.

Some of the forms of behaviour are ones which have developed
socially and historically and do not have any base in the
practical 'animal' intelligence. The internalisation of
cultural forms of behaviour involves the reconstruction of
psychological activity on the basis of sign operation.
Psychological processes as they appear in animals actually
cease to exist; they are incorporated into this system of
behaviour and are culturally reconstructed and developed to
form a new psychological entity. The use of external signs
is also radically reconstructed. The developmental changes
in sign operations are akin to those that occur in language.
Aspects of external and communicative speech as well as
egocentric speech, turn 'inward' to become the basis of
inner speech.

The internalisation of socially rooted and historically
developed activities is the distinguishing feature of human
psychology, the basis of the qualitative leap from animal
to human psychology. The focus on socially mediated learning in Vygotsky's work emerges most clearly in his work on
mediated memory. It is in the course of interaction
between children and adults that young learners identify
effective means for remembering - means made accessible to
them by those with more highly developed memory skills.
For example, he says:
    Natural memory is not the only kind even in the case of
    non-literate men and women. On the contrary, other
    types of memory belonging to a completely different
    developmental line co-exist with natural memory. The
    line of knotched sticks and knots ... even such simple
    operations as tying a knot or marking a stick as a
    reminder change the psychological structure of the
    memory process. They extend the operation of memory
    beyond the biological dimensions of the human nervous
    system and permit it to incorporate artificial or self-
    generated stimuli. (1978, p.39)

These memory skills are not simply passed on to children by
adults, but neither are they discovered independently by
the child working alone. They are the result of a dialect-
ical interchange between the child and the adults surrounding him. The final form that the developed consciousness
will have is the result of an interweaving of two qualitatively distinct lines within the child's development: the
elementary processes which are of biological origin on the
one hand and the higher psychological functions of socio-
cultural origin on the other hand.

This very brief summary of some of the major points of
Vygotsky's theory can hardly do it justice. But perhaps
enough has been said to show that Vygotsky's theory is at
times more philosophically discriminating than Piaget's
whose rationalist background leads him to give undue respect
to the rationality of the individual and to stress the mind
as the source of this rationality. Vygotsky's Marxist
background leads him to stress just those historical,
cultural and social influences that Piaget neglects.
Vygotsky, like Piaget, mixes reasoning from empirical
fact with epistemological arguments about the nature of
knowledge. His argument for the temporal priority of
public speech before private speech is based on an epistemological argument such as one might find in Wittgenstein,
about the logical priority of public speech over private.
As with Piaget's theory, the empirical questions need to
be distinguished from the conceptual ones and the philosophical ones.

Piaget has argued that development follows a single,
irreversible sequence of stages. Vygotsky argues that it
involves two distinguishable but interwoven strands.
These quite different views cite essentially similar
empirical data. Their differences lie in first of all
their interests and secondly the ideological backgrounds
which they both bring to their interpretations. If we
look simply at linguistic development, then from one point
of view, from Piaget's, the child's vocalisations can be
considered as examples of self-expression. He is interested
in linguistic development only in so far as this represents
the development of a symbolic system. The transition, then,
from private significance to objective, communicable concepts can be seen as progress. Vygotsky, on the other
hand, is interested in the multivariate functions of language from its primitive communications to its use to direct
sophisticated thought processes. He sees language initially
as a set of tools governed by the conventions of a particular society. On this view, the move from a conventional

use of language to an individualised use to direct 'inner'
thought processes can be seen as progress.

Piaget has emphasised one and Vygotsky two, strands in human
development. In some places their views are antagonistic,
but in many places they are complementary. They have chosen
three strands from the rope of interwoven strands that make
up human development. That there are many more strands to
be explored is shown by the modern exploration of the mother-
child relationship in language development which was
developed with almost no reference to Piaget; by the
independent theories of J.J. Gibson and his colleagues which
represent as an essential aspect of the development of knowledge, the perceptual exploration of the environment, and
so on.

Human development consists in many interwoven strands. Some
of these strands are essentially biological in origin. Some
of them are essentially socio-cultural. Some of them may be
peculiar to a particular culture whereas others may have
more universal significance. It is essentially that no one
theory of human development should be clung to so dogmatic-
ally as to prevent the proper exploration of all these
different strands.

SUMMARY

A prerequisite for comprehending the points of application
for the public concepts that the child has to learn is a
sharing or an agreement in judgments in the sense of agreeing not on what is true or false but on what is an area of
importance and what is not, what is a human being and what
is an inanimate object; perceptual judgments etc. This
agreement need not be very exact but it must be there in
some measure. Either this agreement must be innate or it
must be learned in some way. Some of this common judgment
must be innate or instinctive if learning is ever to get
started. It is through treating infants as if they were
more mature and more 'human' than they are that they are
given the opportunity to learn how human beings share
other, more subtle, learned values and how they apply the
more abstract, difficult concepts. We used the work of
Bruner and Ryan to illustrate the way in which children
are constantly directed by their parents, constantly
corrected, interpreted and misinterpreted. Because the
mother cares for the child she is constantly trying to
understand him and looking out for possible ways of interpreting his behaviour and utterances. However, her inter-

pretation will, naturally, be in her own terms. So the
infant has the chance, if the mother is consistent, of
finding out what her terms are, how she does see the world.
She will, by what she does, show him things that she might
find impossible to put into words if she were deliberately
setting out to teach him.

Apart from the chance that the mother's propensity for
interpreting the infant's behaviour gives him of learning
how she is going to act it also gives him the beginnings of
an understanding of what is expected of him as a human
being and as a language user.

Essentially, Piaget is convinced that the source of human
knowledge is the interiorised actions of the sensori-motor
period. A different conception of the source and subsequent
development of knowledge is the functionalist view of
Vygotsky. He maintains that there is not continuity but a
radical discontinuity in development. The break comes at
the point when the child ceases to rely on the 'practical
intelligence' with which it has been endowed by its animal
inheritance and begins to use the socially developed tools
of symbolic and finally linguistic thought.

These alternative views,**were** discussed not with a view to
replacing Piaget's theory with any one of them. The point
is rather to show the diversity of views concerning the
origin and development of knowledge. Each of them emphasises a different aspect of human development and it seems
unreasonable to choose one theory to the exclusion of all
others.

The work of Vygotsky, Bruner and many others and lately the
work of Gibson, has shown that the unravelling of this area
is even more complex than Piaget supposed.

Chapter 8

Conclusions

ROLE OF PHILOSOPHY

In his critique of linguistic philosophy Gellner assigns to
philosophy a vital role: 'fundamental thinking aimed at
making explicit our picture of the world, our various modes
of knowing and forms of activity, and introducing new vistas
and at assessing basic alternatives'. This describes the
role that philosophical thinking has played in this book.
Piaget's theory has been subjected to a critical examination
not from the point of view of questioning the empirical
details of his theory from the basis of empirical tests
but from the point of view of making explicit the picture
of the knowing subject at the root of Piaget's theory and
assessing that picture.

PIAGET'S MODEL MADE EXPLICIT

The picture that has emerged is a complex one. The knowing
subject is represented as a totality of abstract structures
shaping and being shaped by the environment in which he
acts. The environment and the subject are reciprocals in
the sense that the limits of the environment are defined
for the subject by the limits of his knowledge and conversely the subject, insofar as he has knowledge, has been
constructed by his interaction with the environment. He
depends on the environment for his identity just as the
environment depends on him for its identity.

In this process the subject is represented as independent
and to a large extent immune from social influence. The
social nature of others does not constitute a feature of

the environment until fairly late in development. Even
then, the nature of other individuals can become an object
of knowledge only by being viewed through the objective
schemata developed by the subject.

The existence of a reality independent of my knowledge of
it presents something of a problem for Piaget. He seems
to view reality most consistently as the result of the
subjects' construction. He says at several points that
reality for a subject is what he understands it to be.
This would seem to leave the way open for talk of different
realities for different subjects. To a certain degree
this must be allowed in Piaget's theory since the mental
structures of the child are so different from those of the
adult that the child must be allowed to experience a
different reality.

The 'reality' of the child, however, is brought into line
as the child develops by two processes that are said to
lead to increasing objectification: the development of
operational structures and the overcoming of egocentricity
by the dialectic between the subject and the environment.
The views and wishes of other people would constitute part
of this environment, insofar as they could be assimilated
to the objective thought structure of the subject. Piaget
does not envisage the possibility that 'increasing objectification' might lead two individuals in different directions. Consequently, he does not admit the possibility
that even people who have developed objective ways of
thinking may inhabit very different realities. 'Objective'
thinking for Piaget has a specific form and a specific
content. It concerns the logical, mathematical and
physical concepts which are used to make sense of the
world of objects.

Sometimes Piaget talks about reality as if there were a
reality existing independently of ourselves. This reality
is sometimes credited with an existence like that of 'things
as they are in themselves' in Kant's philosophy. This
reality provides the occasion for interaction whereas the
capacities of the subject provide the characteristics of
that interaction. However, Piaget is uneasy with the notion
of an independently existing reality, even an unknowable
one, and generally refers to reality as a construction based
on interaction between subject and object.

Finally, there are the biological dimensions to Piaget's
picture. We have argued that the biological model plays a
diminishing role as the individual's development proceeds

and that it also played a diminishing role in Piaget's
theory as it developed. It would, however, be a mistake to
think that Piaget ever abandoned his basic premises that
cognitive activity is to be understood as an extension of
biological activity. This assumption provides the background for Piaget's attempts at a causal explanation of
the emergence of the higher forms of thought, the under-
pinning for his claim that thought and reality are adapted
to each other, mirror each other. A logician might
explain the fact that logic can be used to describe
extremely varied systems as a reflection of the extreme
generality and abstraction of logic. Piaget agrees that
this is one of the reasons for the 'accord of thought with
things'. But in addition, he insists that just as a
biological system that was maladapted to reality would not
survive, so a cognitive system, which is simply an extension of previously successful biological systems, would
not develop if it were not adapted to reality.

ASSESSING PIAGET'S MODEL

I have argued in previous chapters that Piaget's stress on
the active, initiating role that the subject takes in his
own development is one which any philosophy in retreat from
behaviouristic psychologies would applaud. However, most
of the other major claims of the theory would be seen as
more controversial.

At three points in particular a philosopher with a penchant
for realism, some acquaintance with Wittgenstein's philosophy and a distrust of causal models of the mind, would
find Piaget's model unacceptable.

The three points concern first of all Piaget's claim that
in knowing the subject actually alters the object. The
object is what the subject understands it to be. Secondly,
there is Piaget's claim that the individual constructs his
view of the world in isolation from social influences, and
thirdly, there is Piaget's attempt to develop an explanation of why children come to accept the correct answer to
some elementary logical, mathematical and physical problems
in terms of mental mechanisms.

Piaget's view that in coming to understand something about
the world the subject actually alters the world, misrepres-
ents the nature of the relation between the subject and the
object in knowing. While some of my acts alter the object,
if I drop a cup, for instance, it breaks, my knowing some-

thing about it cannot change it since if that were the case
we would never know things as they are but only as I have
constructed them. Reality itself would be unknowable. The
nature of ourselves depends to a large extent on the nature
of the environment that we inhabit, but the nature of that
environment is independent of ourselves. As Gibson would
argue (1979) the environment came first and does not depend
on our experience of it.

The Kantian view which Piaget espouses which represents the
gaining of knowledge as the application of mental structures
to the raw data of perception has been somewhat superseded
by the Wittgensteinian view of the gaining of knowledge as
the learning to view experience through the network of
public, intersubjective concepts that are enshrined in the
language and customs of a culture. Although Wittgenstein's
views are by no means universally accepted in all their
detail, they point out the impossibility of accounting for
human knowledge on any model which views the learner as a
solitary individual discovering, or constructing, the world
for himself.

Consideration of the public nature of the rules and conventions which govern the application of concepts and the
gaining of a 'human' view of reality leads to a rejection
of Piaget's view that the basis of the structures of thought
is the interiorisation of non-verbal, individual action.
It was argued that the initial step in developing a human
view of the world must involve the gaining of access to
the public world of shared concepts and their applications.
This would not be possible without the active cooperation
of already initiated others who ensure that the child
develops the 'correct' way of viewing things.

These considerations led to the questioning not only of
Piaget's interpretation of the initial steps in development, but of his account of its general direction from the
autistic through the egocentric to the socialised.
Vygotsky provides an account of development which relies
on essentially similar empirical data but charts the direction from the initially socially conditioned child, to
the mature, individual adult thinker. While unclear and
open to criticism in many ways, Vygotsky's account of the
direction of development is more philosophically discriminating and sensitive than Piaget's.

The third major point of disagreement with Piaget's model
concerns the apparent attempt to give a causal explanation
of the sequence of progressive changes throughout develop-

ment. Many psychological theories attempt to account for
some fairly restricted set of phenomena often having to do
with error or deviance from the norm. Freud's theory, for
example, although it eventually came to be viewed as an
attempt at a global theory of personality development, was
originally intended as a theory to explain certain fairly
common and typical mistakes that people make: slips of the
tongue, forgetfulness, and so on. It is tempting to
explain these errors in terms of the failure of certain
mechanisms, the undue influence of some aspect of experience over others.

Piaget's theory, however, is not concerned with error. It
claims to offer an explanation of why people get things
right. One is not usually tempted to give an account of
this in terms of the workings of certain mechanisms. And
yet that is what Piaget effectively attempts to do. We
have argued that such an attempt is misguided since it mis-
represents the nature of knowledge and the process of human
development. An account of why people get things right
should make reference to the reasons for why they are right
and to the teaching or other educational processes which
ensure that people come to appreciate these reasons rather
than to any mental mechanisms which cause people to adhere
to what is correct.

Piaget's causal explanation has been criticised on other
grounds than its inappropriateness. Piaget's notion of a
parallelism leads him to claim that the causal explanation
at the level of psychological mechanisms is parallelled by
a deductive explanation at the level of the abstract
representation of the steps of development at the level of
logic. In between these levels is the level of psychological
explanation which concerns implicative rather than causal
relations between mental structures. Piaget insists that
it is appropriate to talk of implicative rather than causal
relations, when the subject of the talk is psychological
structures. And yet his explanation of change from one
structure to the next is in causal terms of the upsetting
of equilibrium, the operation of homeostatic mechanisms and
the return to a state of more stable equilibrium. Psychological structures represent a kind of half way form between
the straightforwardly physical structures with their causal
relations at the level of physiology and the straightforwardly abstract structures of the level of logic with their
implicative relations. Piaget seems to want to claim that
they are related to each other both causally and implicat-
ively. It is difficult to see what this could mean.

It has been argued that Piaget does not make clear the
sense in which concepts like assimilation, accommodation,
equilibration, balance and so on are to be understood in
the context of cognitive development. If we are to understand these concepts as they are used in biology, then
their use in the context of cognition is inappropriate.
And we are not given any other account of how they are to
be interpreted. All the tests that Piaget suggests for
the level of equilibration of a psychological structure
have to do with its logical, formal properties. It is
difficult to believe that Piaget's causal explanation
amounts to more than a misleading way of displaying the
formal properties of the structures.

In summary, if we assess Piaget's theory in terms of more
fairly generally accepted philosophical conclusions about
the nature of human knowledge it is largely unacceptable.
Only the stress that it lays on the active role of the
subject in knowing recommends it.

THE EMPIRICAL AND METAPHYSICAL ASPECTS OF PIAGET'S THEORY

The body of Piaget's work comprises two distinguishable
aspects. On the one hand there are the case histories of
Piaget's own children and the mass of well-attested data
gleaned from the numerous experiments and observations on
local schoolchildren. This data has been augmented in
recent years by researchers working broadly within the
cognitive tradition and engaged in cross-cultural studies
and experiments on large numbers of children from varying
social and educational backgrounds. The interest and
importance of that mass of carefully collected and discriminating data is not being disputed. Piaget is a gifted
observer and chronicler of the details of children's
development. These accounts are valuable for two reasons.
In the first place they made very clearly the point that
children think in surprisingly different ways from adults.
We can never again take for granted that children comprehend
what we are trying to teach them. And this realisation
has had an enormous impact on educational practice and our
assessment of children's understanding. In the second
case, while we might derive principles of human development
from reasoning about the nature of human knowledge, these
are only general principles. They sketch out the grand
design of human development. Detailed empirical observation
of the ways in which individuals fill in the content of
these principles, what people actually do in developing an
objective view of causation, for example, is essential to

our understanding of human development in anything more
than a formal sense. We might, for example, hold the view
that the development of a mature consciousness involves,
among other things, the control of wishful thinking without
the loss of creative imagination. This is the form that
the developed consciousness might take, but the content of
this consciousness cannot be supplied by such abstract
requirements. Only empirical observation can tell us how
different people gain control over their wayward imaginations and learn to use them more productively. And this
kind of empirical investigation is essential if we are to
learn what has gone wrong in the case of individuals who
fail to control their imaginations or who are unable to use
them creatively. Only by these detailed investigations can
we learn practical means for educating individuals in this
area.

The importance and interest of the mass of empirical data
cannot be overestimated. But the other side of the picture
is Piaget's overarching theory. It has been the argument
of this book that Piaget's theory, while it incorporates
some insights concerning the general principles of human
development which are the product of critical thinking about
the nature of human development, gives in general a misleading metaphysical picture of the nature of the person, the
nature of reality and the nature of the relation between the
two. This might not matter too much if the empirical data
and the metaphysical theory could be kept distinct from
each other. But this is not possible. Philosophers such
as Toulmin (1971), and more radically Kuhn (1962) have
clearly demonstrated the interdependence of observation and
theory. They argue convincingly that observations are made
and interpreted within the broad terms supplied by prevail-
ing theory. There is no such thing as a neutral theory-free
description of empirical data. Piaget has never denied the
close connection between his theory and his observations.
He is clearly aware of the amount of interpretation of what
the children do and say. Piaget's interpretative descriptions only make sense within the context of the broad outlines of the theory.

Recently there has been expressed some unease over the
dearth of research aimed at extending and perhaps modifying
Piaget's idiosyncratic theory in an attempt to bring it
more into line with generally accepted practice in psychology. Although Piaget has had numerous collaborators and
co-workers they have, almost without exception, been constrained to work within the framework of genetic epistemology as Piaget interprets it. Shayer (1981), for example,

argues that Piaget's 'fruitful and wide-ranging research
paradigm has been made sterile in any hands but that of its
originator'. Shayer argues that this sterility has been
the result of two prohibitions: the ban on critical replication and the ban on producing standardised tests. Shayer
attributes the failure of Piaget's collaborators to overcome
these prohibitions to the towering personality of Piaget
himself.

There may be something in this argument. But it is more
plausible, given the kinds of considerations that have been
put forward in this book, that the Piagetian system being
what it is, the basic concepts and framework of the theory
have to be accepted before further work aimed at refining
and expanding the theory makes any sense. Piaget's interpretative descriptions only make sense within the context
of the broad outlines of the theory. Consequently, either
one accepts the broad outline of the theory and contents
oneself with exploring particular areas within the existing
guidelines of the theory, or else one attempts to remain
outside the theory and examine it with the critical tools
of more conventional empirical psychology. The first kind
of investigation will lead to some minor, internal modifica-
tions of the details of the theory. The second kind of
investigation leads to the kinds of accusations from Piaget
with which this investigation began, namely that Piaget's
critics do not understand his theory.

The thrust of the argument of this book has been to reveal
the metaphysical nature of Piaget's general account of the
growth of understanding in the child. Piaget takes from
the Kantian tradition certain epistemological points about
the nature of knowledge and understanding, and he constructs
these epistemological points into a metaphysical system concerning the nature of the subject, the nature of reality and
the relations between them. New metaphysical systems often
open up new vistas for the human imagination which allow
new insights and increase our sensitivity to the nature of
reality and our own place in it. Piaget's theory is no
exception to this. Although his epistemological and metaphysical views are not very original, his originality lies
in the use to which he put them. He used them as a framework to connect up all the diverse, often apparently contradictory, puzzling facts about the growth of the child's
intellect. The metaphysical theory gives form to this
diversity and allows us to make sense of what would otherwise appear incomprehensible. The role of the metaphysics
is to connect, organise, impose form on the diversity of
empirical facts. I have argued that sometimes this theory

introduces far more coherence and intelligibility, than is
warranted but nonetheless, in attempting to structure the
facts in this area of child development, Piaget's theory has
opened up new vistas for the imagination. It is no longer
possible to fail to realise that children think differently
from adults and that their thinking differs in systematic
and unexpected ways.

However, Piaget's mistake lies in supposing that the multi-
plicity of interesting, empirical facts that he has observed
about how children actually achieve the steps towards
rational thought which are demanded by the logic, can be
used to support the logic itself. He fails to distinguish
between the framework which is constituted by a certain
notion of what rational thought is, and the details of the
actualisation of that framework in the thought and action
of individuals.

Piaget's accusations that his critics who were not working
within the framework of the genetic epistemology, failed
to give due consideration to his theory, can now be understood. By his theory, Piaget means the metaphysical system
implied by his structuralist-functionalist approach. His
abiding interest is in the explication and maintenance of
that system. His critics, on the other hand, while accepting that the child's development must be viewed within the
context of concepts such as rationality, maturity, creativ-
ity and so forth, are far more interested in the details
of how these abstractions are actualised in the child's
thought and action. Piaget has a great deal that is of
interest to say about the details of this actualisation,
but this is often obscured by his own insistence that it
is the background epistemological claims which are at issue.
They are not. There are good reasons for agreeing that the
child's development of rational thought must proceed along
the general lines laid down by Piaget's theory but these
reasons are epistemological reasons which do not require
the support of empirical facts or the elaborate and misleading metaphysical system of structuralist-functionalism.
In this connection it is worth quoting an elegant passage
from Warnock which expresses the fate of such superfluous
metaphysics:

> Metaphysical systems do not yield, as a rule, to
> frontal attack. Their odd property of being demonst-
> rable, only so to speak, from within, confers on them
> also a high resistance to attack from outside. The
> onslaughts of critics to whom, as likely as not, their
> strange tenets are nearly unintelligible are apt to
> seem to those enshrined inside, misdirected and

> irrelevant. Such systems are more vulnerable to ennui
> than to disproof. They are citadels, much shot at
> perhaps, but never taken by storm, which are quietly
> discovered one day to be no longer inhabited.
> (Warnock, 1958, pp.10-11)

We would argue that Piaget's critics who ignore the theory
and concentrate their critical investigations on the
empirical details of how the steps to rational thinking
are actualised, are wise to do so. The theory is a metaphysical one which is already suffering the fate that
Warnock predicts for such a theory. It has served its
purpose in firing the imagination. It has turned attention
towards the child studies both worthy of interest in its
own right and also helpful in understanding adult forms of
thought. And it has shown that psychological theories of
human intellectual development cannot avoid making epistemological assumptions. The confusions inherent in Piaget's
work also indicate that these epistemological assumptions
should be made explicit and be as open to critical assessment as the more empirical aspects of the theory. But
beyond these useful achievements the metaphysical theory
itself has no more than historical interest. If Piaget's
work is to continue to provide a fruitful source for further
research, the metaphysical theory must be clearly distinguished from the empirical discoveries since they continue
to be of undoubted interest.

Piaget's theory is an immensely imaginative and suggestive
attempt to link a metaphysical theory with empirical fact,
to link child thought to adult thought and to make structured sense out of apparently unconnected events in a child's
developmental history. It is still fruitful for some
purposes to view the child's progress within this developmental perspective. There are many researchers who, while
not being Genevans, are working within the cognitive developmental framework. In particular attempts are being made to
extend Piaget's theory in the direction of Artificial
Intelligence models of cognitive functioning (see Boden,
1979); in education, the stage-sequence model still provides
the theoretical basis for much curriculum construction
particularly at the level of primary schooling, although
whether this should be the case is another matter. A
revived interest in moral education has led to the adoption
by some psychologists and educators of a cognitive-develop-
mental model of moral development (Kohlberg, 1969) and if
structuralism never had much acclaim among Anglo-American
philosophers it is still very much alive in much of Europe.

It is however remarkable how many interesting developments
in child psychology have occurred in the last two decades
which have no connection with the Piagetian tradition.
Some of these developments have already been mentioned,
for example Ryan's work on language development; Bruner's
work on the complex interaction between 'native intelligence'
and social environment.

One of the arguments of this book was that although Piaget's
theory claimed to be a single unified theory of intellectual
development it dealt in fact with only one particular
aspect of intellectual development, the development of
elementary logical, mathematical and physical concepts.
While it cannot be denied that, in Western culture at least,
this is one important strand of intellectual development,
there is more to the whole story. Piaget would not deny
this and his defenders would argue that no one person can
do everything. (See for example Boden, 1979.) However,
the important point is not simply that there may be some
gaps in Piaget's story, it is that a different story may
be necessary to account for other aspects of intellectual
development. The development of a disciplined imagination,
for example, or the kind of understanding that is involved
in knowing other people or understanding works of art, while
they are all aspects of intellectual development, would not
fit into Piaget's picture at all. When it is said, then,
that Piaget's theory has a more restricted application than
he claims, he is not being criticised for a failure to 'do
everything'. It is being claimed that human development is
multi-faceted and that the different facets require different kinds of accounts.

SUMMARY

To summarise, Piaget's metaphysical theory must be distinguished from his empirical discoveries. The metaphysical
theory is based on a priori epistemological considerations.
It has a degree of logical necessity not shared by the
empirical discoveries. It provides the framework within
which the empirical discoveries can be interpreted in a
structured, systematic way. However, having served the
function of suggesting that empirical discoveries about
child development can be interpreted in a systematic way,
the metaphysical system is now being bypassed in favour of
less ambitious, more philosophically sensitive epistemological views on the nature of knowledge and understanding.

The mass of empirical observational material is, however,
another matter. That demonstrates how the general principles
concerning the development of the concepts of logic, mathematics and physics which are derived from epistemological
considerations of the nature of these forms of understanding
are actualised in the day to day actions and thought of the
child.

There is still much scope for research within the broad outlines of the cognitive developmental stage sequence model
but running alongside these researches are other lines of
enquiry concerning different aspects of intellectual
development which require different kinds of accounts.

Piaget's metaphysical theory, then, has no more than historical interest but will continue to engender confusion between
its disciples and those outside the citadel. It is becoming
increasingly clear that Piaget's research concerns only one
strand in the many strands that make up human development.
It may be the case that each of these strands will require a
different kind of account and that the possibility of a unified account of human development is an illusion.

References

ABRAHAMSON, M. (1978), 'Functionalism', Prentice Hall Inc., Englewood Cliffs, NJ.

ARGYLE, M. and INGHAM, R. (1972), Gaze, Mutual Gaze and Proximity, 'Semiotica', vol.4 (1) , 32-49.

AUSTIN, J.L. (1962), 'How To Do Things With Words', Oxford University Press, London.

AYER, A.J. (1956), 'The Problem of Knowledge', Penguin, Harmondsworth.

BAILEY, C. (1969), The Notion of Development and Moral Education, in 'Proceedings of the Annual Conference of the Philosophy of Education Society of Great Britain', vol.III.

BECKNER, N. (1968), 'The Biological Way of Thought', University of California Press.

BENNETT, J. (1964), 'Rationality', Routledge & Kegan Paul, London.

BETH, E. and PIAGET, J. (1966), 'Mathematical Epistemology and Psychology', Reidel, Dordrecht, Holland.

BLOCK. S. (1971), Personal Communication to Halford, G.S. recorded in Halford, G.S., 'The Impact of Piaget on Psychology in the Seventies', printed in Dodwell, P.C., 'New Horizons in Psychology 2', Penguin, Harmondsworth (1972).

BODEN, M. (1979), 'Jean Piaget', Viking Press, New York.

BORING (1952), 'A History of Psychology in Autobiography', vol.IV, Clark University Press, Worcester.

BOWLBY, J. (1965), 'Child Care and the Growth of Love', Penguin, Harmondsworth.

BROWN, G. and DESFORGES, C. (1979), 'Piaget's Theory: A Psychological Critique', Routledge & Kegan Paul, London.

BRUNER, J.S. et al. (1966), 'Studies in Cognitive Growth', John Wiley, New York.

BRUNER, J.S. and SHERWOOD, V. (1980), Early Rule Structure: The Case of Peekaboo, in Bruner, J.S., Jolly, A. and Sylva, K. (eds), 'Play: Its Role in Evolution and Development', Penguin, Harmondsworth.

BRUNER, J.S. (1975), From Communication to Language - A
Psychological Perspective, printed in 'Cognition', vol.3,
255-87.
BURTON, A. and RADFORD, J. (1978), 'Thinking in Perspective:
Critical Essays in the Study of Thought Processes', Methuen,
New York.
BRYANT, P. (1974), 'Perception and Understanding in Young
Children: An Experimental Approach", Methuen, New York.
CARNAP, R. (1966), 'Philosophical Foundations of Physics:
An Introduction to the Philosophy of Science', Basic
Books, New York.
DARWIN, C. (1859), 'The Origin of Species', London.
DONALDSON, M. (1978), 'The Child's Mind', Fontana, Glasgow.
FELDMAN, C.F. and TOULMIN, S. (1976), Logic and the Theory
of Mind, printed in Arnold, S.J. (eds.), 'Nebraska Symposium
on Motivation', University of Nebraska Press.
FLAVELL, J.H. (1963), 'The Developmental Psychology of Jean
Piaget', Van Nostrand, New York.
FLAVELL, J.H. and WOHLHILL, J.F. (1969), Formal and Functional
Aspects of Cognitive Development, in Elkind, D. and Flavell,
J.H. (eds.), 'Studies in Cognitive Development', Oxford
University Press.
FREUDENTHAL, H. (1973), 'Mathematics as an Educational Task',
Reidel, Dordrecht, Holland.
GELLNER, E. (1979), 'Words and Things', Routledge & Kegan
Paul, London.
GESELL, A. (1926), Maturation and Infant Behaviour Patterns,
'Psychological Review', vol.36, 307-19.
GIBSON, J.J. (1979), 'The Ecological Approach to Visual
Perception', Houghton Mifflin, Boston.
GOODMAN, N. (1955), 'Fact, Fiction and Forecast', Harvard
University Press, Cambridge, Mass.
GREENFIELD, P.M. (1966), On Culture and Conservation, in
Bruner, J.S., Oliver, R.R. and Greenfield, P.M. (eds.),
'Studies in Cognitive Growth', John Wiley, New York.
GREENFIELD, P.M. (1972), Playing Peekaboo with a Four Month
Old: A Study of the Role of Speech and Non-speech Sounds
in the Formulation of Visual Schema, 'Journal of Psychology',
82, 287-98.
GRICE (1976), Logic and Conversation, printed in Cole, P.
and Morgan, J. (eds.), 'Syntax and Semantics, Vol.3,
Speech Acts', London.
HAECKEL, Ernst (1866), 'Generelle Morphologie der Organismen',
2 vols, Berlin.
HAMLYN, D.W. (1970), 'The Theory of Knowledge', Macmillan,
London.
HAMLYN, D.W. (1971), Epistemology and Conceptual Development,
in Mischel, T. (ed.), 'Cognitive Development and Epistemology', Academic Press, New York.

HAMLYN, D.W. (1973), Human Learning, in Brown, S.C. (ed.),
'The Philosophy of Psychology', Macmillan, London.
HAMLYN, D.W. (1974), Person Perception and Understanding
Others, in Mischel, T. (ed.), 'Understanding Other
Persons', Blackwell, Oxford.
HAMLYN, D.W. (1978), 'Experience and the Growth of Under-
standing', Routledge & Kegan Paul, London.
HARRE, R. (1960), 'An Introduction to the Logic of the
Sciences', Macmillan, London.
HEMPEL, C.G. (1966), 'Philosophy of Natural Science',
Prentice Hall, Englewood Cliffs, NJ.
HUME, D. (1888), 'A Treatise of Human Nature', edited by
L.A. Selby-Bigge, Oxford.
INHELDER, B. and PIAGET, J. (1979), Procedures and
Structures, 'Arch de Psychol', vol.47, 165-76.
JORDAN, N. (1972), Is There an Achilles Heel in Piaget's
Theorising? 'Human Development', vol.15, 379-82.
KANT, I. (1929), 'Critique of Pure Reason', tr. N.K. Smith,
Macmillan, London.
KANT, I. (1953), 'Prolegomena to Any Future Metaphysic',
tr. P.G. Lucas, Manchester University Press.
KNEALE, W. (1952), Review of Piaget's 'Traite de Logique',
in 'Philosophical Quarterly', vol.3.
KOHLBERG, L. (1969), Stage and Sequence: The Cognitive-
Developmental Approach to Socialisation, in Goslin, D.
(ed.), 'Handbook of Socialisation Theory and Research',
Rand McNally, New York.
KOHLBERG, L. (1971), From Is to Ought, in Mischel, T. (ed.),
'Cognitive Development and Epistemology', Academic Press,
New York.
KOHLBERG, L. (1972), Early Education: A Cognitive Develop-
mental View, in Lavatelli, C. and Stendler, K. (eds.),
'Readings in Child Behaviour and Development', 3rd edition,
Harcourt, Brace, Jovanovich, New York.
KOVESI, J. (1967), 'Moral Notions', Routledge & Kegan Paul,
London.
KUHN, T. (1962), 'The Structure of Scientific Revolutions',
University of Chicago Press.
LANKESTER, E.R. (1900), 'Treatise on Zoology', London.
LORENZ, K. (1952), 'King Solomon's Ring', tr. M.K. Wilson.
Methuen, London.
MACMURRAY, J. (1970), 'Persons in Relation', Faber & Faber,
London.
MACKIE, J.L. (1974), 'Cause, the Cement of the Universe',
Clarendon Press, Oxford.
MIDGELEY, M. (1979), 'Beast and Man', Harvester Press,
Sussex.
MISCHEL, T. (1971), Piaget: Cognitive Development and the
Motivation of Thought, in Mischel, T. (ed.), 'Cognitive
Development and Epistemology', Academic Press, New York.

MISCHEL, T. (1979), Piaget and the Nature of Psychological Explanation, in Murray, F.B. (ed.), 'The Impact of Piagetian Theory', University Park Press, Baltimore.

MODGIL and MODGIL (1976), 'Piagetian Research: Compilation and Commentary, Vols 1-8', NFER, Windsor.

NAGEL, E. (1957), Determinism and Development, in Harris, D.B. (ed.), 'The Concept of Development', University of Minneapolis Press.

NAGEL, E. (1961), 'The Structure of Science', Harcourt Brace, New York.

NEISSER, U. (1976), 'Cognition and Reality', W.H. Freeman, San Francisco.

OAKESHOTT, M. (1972), Education, the Engagement and its Frustration, in Dearden, R.F., Hirst, P.H. and Peters, R.S. (eds.), 'Education and the Development of Reason', Routledge & Kegan Paul, London.

PIAGET, J. (1928), 'Judgement and Reasoning in the Child', Routledge & Kegan Paul, London.

PIAGET, J. (1932), 'The Moral Judgement of the Child', Routledge & Kegan Paul, London.

PIAGET, J. (1937), La problème de l'intelligence et de l'habitude réflexe conditionné, 'Gestalt' ou assimilation? in 'Proceedings of the 11th International Psychological Congress', 433-4.

PIAGET, J. (1949), 'Traité de Logique, Essai de Logistique Opératoire', Armand Colin, Paris.

PIAGET, J. (1950), 'Introduction à l'Epistémologie Génétique' vol.III, Presses Universitaires de France, Paris.

PIAGET, J. (1951), 'Play, Dreams and Imitation in Childhood', Norton, New York.

PIAGET, J. (1952), 'The Origins of Intelligence in Children', New York, International University Press.

PIAGET, J. (1957), Logique et équilibre dans les comportements du sujet, in Apostel, L., Mandelbrot, B. and Piaget, J., 'Logique et équilibre; Etudes d'épistémologie genetique', vol. III, Presses Universitaires de France, Paris, 27-117.

PIAGET, J. (1959), Apprentissage et connaissance, in Grew, P. and Piaget, J. (eds.), 'Apprentissage et Connaissance, Etudes d'Lpistémologie Génétique', vol. 7, Presses Universitaires de France, Paris.

PIAGET, J. (1960), Reply to J.S. Bruner, Individual and Collective Problems in the Study of Thinking, 'Annals of the New York Academy of Science', vol. 91, 22-37.

PIAGET, J. (1962), Comments on Vygotsky's critical remarks in Parsons, A. (trans.), Hanymann, E. and Vakar, G. (eds.), MIT Press, Cambridge, Mass. (Pamphlet published in conjunction with Vygotsky's 'Thought and Language').

PIAGET, J. (1967a), 'Six Psychological Studies', Random House, New York.

PIAGET, J. (1967b), Logique et connaissance scientifique, 'Encyclopédie de la Pléiade', Gallimard, Paris.

PIAGET, J. (1968), Explanation in Psychology and Psychophysiological Parallelism, in Fraisse, P. and Piaget, J. (eds.), 'Experimental Psychology, Its Scope and Method', Basic Books, New York.

PIAGET, J. (1969), 'The Mechanisms of Perception', Basic Books, New York.

PIAGET, J. (1969), 'The Child's Conception of Time', Routledge & Kegan Paul, London.

PIAGET, J. (1970a), 'Genetic Epistemology', Columbia University Press, New York.

PIAGET, J. (1970b), The Place of the Science of Man in the System of Sciences, in 'Main Trends of Research in the Social and Human Sciences', Morton, UNESCO, Paris and the Hague.

PIAGET, J. (1970c), 'Structuralism', Basic Books, New York.

PIAGET, J. (1971), 'Biology and Knowledge', Edinburgh University Press.

PIAGET, J. (1972a), 'Psychology and Epistemology', Penguin, Harmondsworth.

PIAGET, J. (1972b), Development and Learning, in Laviatelli, C.S. and Stendler, K. (eds.), 'Readings in Child Behaviour and Development', Harcourt, Brace, Jovanovich, New York.

PIAGET, J. (1975), 'The Development of Thought: Equilibrium of Cognitive Structures', (trans. 1977), Viking Press, New York.

PIAGET, J. (1976), 'The Grasp of Consciousness', Harvard University Press, Cambridge, Mass.

PIAGET, J. (1977), in Inhelder, B., Garcia, R. and Voneche, J.J. (eds.), 'Epistémologie génétique et équilibration' (Colloque de Juillet 1976), Neuchatel/Paris.

PIAGET, J. (1978), 'Success and Understanding', Routledge & Kegan Paul, London.

PIAGET, J. (1979), Relations between Psychology and other Sciences, in 'American Review of Psychology', 301-9.

PIAGET, J. and INHELDER, B. (1941), 'Le Développement de quantités physiques chez l'enfant', Delachaux & Niestle, Neuchatel.

PIAGET, J. and INHELDER, B. (1956), 'The Child's Conception of Space', Routledge & Kegan Paul, London.

PIAGET, J. and INHELDER, B. (1969), 'The Psychology of the Child', Routledge & Kegan Paul, London.

POPPER, K. (1959), 'The Logic of Scientific Discovery', Hutchinson, London.

PUTNAM, H. (1962), The Analytic and the Synthetic, in 'Minnesota Studies in the Philosophy of Science', vol.3, 358-97, ed. by Feigl, H., Maxwell, G., University of Minnesota Press, Minneapolis.

QUINE, V.W. (1953), Two Dogmas of Empiricism, in 'From a
Logical Point of View', Harvard University Press, Cambridge,
Mass.
RHEES, R. (1954), Can There be a Private Language? in
'Proceedings of the Aristotelian Society, Supplementary
Volume XXVIII', 77-94.
ROMANES, George (1882), 'Animal Intelligence', London.
ROMANES, George (1888), 'Mental Evolution in Man', London.
ROTMAN, B. (1977), 'Jean Piaget, Psychologist of the Real',
Cornell University Press, Ithaca, New York.
RUTTER, M. (1972), 'Maternal Deprivation Reassessed',
Penguin, Harmondsworth.
RYAN,   (1974), Early Language Development, in Richards,
M.P.M. (ed.), 'The Integration of the Child into a Social
World', Cambridge University Press.
RYLE, G. (1949), 'The Concept of Mind', Hutchinson, London.
SIEGEL and BRAINERD (1978), 'Alternatives to Piaget:
Critical Essays on the Theory', Academic Press, New York.
SHAYER, M. (1981), BERA September Conference.
STROUD, B. (1965), Wittgenstein and Logical Necessity,
Philosophical Review, vol.74.
TAYLOR, C. (1971), What is Involved in a Genetic Psychology?
in Mischel, R. (ed.), 'Cognitive Development and Epistemo-
logy', Academic Press, New York and London.
TOULMIN, S. (1971), The concept of 'stages' in Psychological
Development, in Mischel, T. (ed.), 'Cognitive Development
and Epistemology', Academic Press, New York and London.
VYGOTSKY, L. (1962), 'Thought and Language', trans. Haufman
and Vakar, MIT Press, Cambridge, Mass.
VYGOTSKY, L. (1978), 'Mind in Society', Harvard University
Press, Cambridge, Mass.
VUYK, R. (1981), 'Overview and Critique of Piaget's Genetic
Epistemology 1965-1980', Academic Press, London.
WADDINGTON, C.H. (1957), 'The Strategy of the Genes', George
Allen & Unwin, London.
WADDINGTON, C.H. (1973), The Development of the Mind', in
'The Development of Mind, The Gifford Lectures, 1973',
Edinburgh University Press.
WARNOCK, G.J. (1958), 'English Philosophy Since 1900',
Oxford University Press, London.
WASON, P.C. (1977), The theory of formal operations: a
critique, in Geber, B.A. (Ed.), 'Piaget and Knowing: Studies
in Genetic Epistemology', Routledge & Kegan Paul, London,
119-35.
YATES, F.E. et al. (1972), Integration of the Whole Organism,
in Behnke, J.A. (ed.), 'Challenging Biological Problems',
Oxford University Press, New York.

Index